THE WORKING CLASS AND POLITICS
in Europe and America

The Working Class and Politics in Europe and America, 1929–1945

Edited by Stephen Salter and John Stevenson

LONGMAN
London and New York

323.3223
WOR

Longman Group UK Limited,
Longman House, Burnt Mill, Harlow,
Essex CM20 2JE, England
and Associated Companies throughout the world.

Published in the United States of America
by Longman Inc., New York

First published 1990

British Library Cataloguing in Publication Data
The Working Class and Politics in Europe and America, 1929–1945.
  1. Western world. Politics. Role of working classes, 1929–1945
  I. Salter, Stephen   II. Stevenson, John   323.3'2

ISBN 0-582-05285-8 CSD
ISBN 0-582-00622-8 PPR

Library of Congress Cataloging-in-Publication Data

The Working class and politics in Europe and America, 1929–1945/
  edited by Stephen Salter and John Stevenson.
    p. cm.
    Bibliography: p.
    Includes index.
    Contents: Introduction/Stephen Salter and John Stevenson
  —Austria/Tim Kirk—Finland/David Kirby—France/Roger Magraw—
  Germany/Stephen Salter—Great Britain/John Stevenson—Italy/
  Paul Corner—Poland/John Coutouvidis, A. Garlicki, Jaime Reynolds
  —Spain/Martin Blinkhorn—The Soviet Union/Hiroaki Kuromiya—
  United States of America/Patrick Renshaw.
    ISBN 0–582–05285–8.—ISBN 0–582–00622–8 (pbk.)
    1. Labor and laboring classes—Europe—Political activity—History—
  20th century. 2. Labor and laboring classes—United States—
  Political activity—History—20th century. I. Salter. Stephen, 1957– .
  II. Stevenson, John, 1946– .
  HD8378.W67 1990   322'.2'094—dc19   89–2395
                                                          CIP

Set in 10/12pt Baskerville Linotron 202

Produced by Longman Singapore Publishers (Pte) Ltd.
Printed in Singapore

26/10/90

Contents

Preface

The aim of this volume is to examine the experience of the working class in Europe and North America from the onset of the Depression to the end of the Second World War. Its rationale lies in an attempt to document workers' experience of depression, dictatorship and war across national boundaries, both highlighting common experiences and responses and noting national particularities. A decision was taken at an early stage not to extend the scope of the study beyond Europe and North America both in order to avoid an excessively encyclopaedic approach and to retain the possibility of meaningful comparison between societies with a degree of common background in terms of culture and development. In addition to its presentation of a range of national studies this volume seeks to move away from the equation of the history of the working class with the history of those economic and political organizations which claimed to speak on behalf of this class; attempting to summarize for the non-specialist the now vast literature on workers' political attitudes and behaviour viewed 'from below'. Each of the essays has been written by a specialist actively engaged in research in his area.

We would like to offer our special thanks to those people who helped to make this book possible; Dr Martin Clark (University of Edinburgh), Professor R. W. Davies (University of Birmingham), Dr Rod Kedward (University of Sussex), and Dr David Levy (formerly of the University of Salford) for their suggestions of possible contributors; Mrs Pat Holland, Mrs Susan Sharman and Mrs Maveen Smallman of the Department of History at Sheffield, who typed much of the manuscript and most of the correspondence connected with the volume; and Longman for patience and flexibility in overseeing the preparation of the essay collection for publication.

Stephen Salter
John Stevenson

CHAPTER ONE
Introduction

Stephen Salter and John Stevenson

Between 1850 and 1914, industrialization transformed the economic and social structures of much of continental Europe. Accelerated economic growth, the extension of the factory system, major occupational and locational redistributions of the labour force saw the creation of a large class of wage workers, often concentrated in the rapidly growing industrial conurbations. In many states, new organizations emerged to represent the economic interests of this new class and this period also saw the widespread development of political parties claiming to represent the interests of workers at the political level, parties which generally subscribed to socialist ideas, in most cases of at least nominally Marxist variety. Yet only in France, Germany and the United Kingdom were these parties major political forces by 1914; seldom, most notably in France, did the rare combination of universal adult (male) suffrage with constitutional arrangements ensuring that government was genuinely accountable to representative parliamentary institutions permit the full expression of the political weight of parties claiming to represent the interests of the working class.

The First World War was to change this situation dramatically, leading as it did not only to a major expansion of trade-union membership throughout Europe but also to the collapse of the three imperial semi-autocracies of Austria-Hungary, Germany and Russia and their replacement by a range of new states informed by both the nationalist concept of self-determination and, usually, democratic principles. By 1920, democratic republics had been established in Austria, the Baltic States, Czechoslovakia, Germany and Poland, which now joined those democratic states which had remained monarchies – Italy, Norway and Sweden,

1

Denmark, Belgium and the Netherlands, and the United Kingdom – along with Europe's major democratic republic of pre-1914 vintage (France). All of these states witnessed either the confirmation or extension or introduction of a democratic adult suffrage which, significantly, in some instances was now extended to women (in Germany, Austria, Czechoslovakia, the Soviet Union, Luxembourg, the Netherlands, Poland, Bulgaria and Sweden: female suffrage – of varying degrees of comprehensiveness – was a feature of Finland and Denmark before 1918 and was introduced in the United Kingdom in that year).

The working class in Europe was the major beneficiary of these political developments and in most European states the bulk of the labour movement was to see the preservation (or extension) of multi-party representative parliamentary government based on a democratic franchise as amongst its principal political objectives. Much of the European middle classes, by contrast, viewed these developments with feelings ranging from vague disquiet through consternation to reactionary panic, as those institutions which, through excluding the majority of the population from effective political action, had seemed to offer a guarantee of property rights and security for the middle class, now collapsed. Lenin in the newly established Bolshevik dictatorship of the Soviet Union, confidently predicted the further political radicalization of the working classes of Europe and the imminent replacement of bourgeois democracies through proletarian revolutionary activity by communist states on the Soviet model. The anxieties of European élites met such revolutionary optimism in their shared expectation that the political future belonged to the masses, that further political change might be expected to be in the direction of an extension of proletarian power rather than of the restoration of middle-class and élite social and political hegemony.

Yet, seen from the perspective of 1939, both middle-class and élite anxieties and revolutionary optimism seemed to have been seriously misplaced. Not only had a further extension of the political and economic power of the working classes of Europe failed to materialize but also such shifts in the balance of social and political power as had taken place in the immediate aftermath of the First World War had in many, if not most, cases been reversed. On the eve of the Second World War, democratic parliamentary government survived only in Scandinavia, the Low Countries, Switzerland, the United Kingdom, Eire and France. In most European states, the institutions of liberal democracy – freedom of the press, freedom from arbitrary arrest and an impartial judicial system, open peaceful competition between rival political parties, free and secret elections based on a wide suffrage, the accountability of governments to representative parliamentary institutions – had disappeared. In some polities, such institutions had barely got off the ground. In Hungary, for example, the prospects for liberal democracy had effectively been destroyed by the civil war of 1919 and, from March 1920, the country was subjected to the authoritarian rule of the royal regent, Admiral Horthy. In the Soviet Union, the Communist dissolution of the January 1918 constituent assembly and the suppression of oppositional parties during and after the civil war (1918–20) marked the final demise of any possibility of establishing liberal parliamentary institutions. In other states, such institutions were short-lived. In Italy, liberal democracy had been under severe pressure from its inception in 1919 and Mussolini's appointment as Prime Minister in October 1922 was to lead to the establishment of a one-party state by November 1926. In Poland, Marshal Piłsudski, ostensibly a socialist, exercised scarcely concealed control from May 1926 onwards, acting to bypass the *Sejm* (parliament) when it seemed as though a Centre-Right coalition would be returned to power. In Yugoslavia and Romania, parliamentary democracy gave way to royal dictatorship in 1928 and 1930 respectively. In Germany, the appointment of Hitler as *Reich* Chancellor in January 1933 led within six months to the total destruction of the model Weimar republic; whilst in Austria, the brief civil war of February 1934 led to the replacement of parliamentary democracy by a conservative–clerical authoritarian régime, itself to fall prey in March 1938 to the expansionism of Nazi Germany. In Spain, the democratic Second Republic, which succeeded the dictatorship of Primo de Rivera (1923–30), was faced with military insurrection in 1936 after only five years and was finally to perish in 1939 after a bloody and protracted civil war. Spain's Iberian neighbour, Portugal, having endured massive political instability after the 1910 revolution, was to be subjected to the rule of its most enduring dictator, Salazar, in 1928. Czechoslovakia, potentially the most stable of the new democracies which had emerged from the collapse of the Austro-Hungarian, German and Russian empires at the end of the First World War, was to suffer dismemberment between September 1938 and March 1939 as a consequence of German expansionism, huge internal tensions between its component nationalities and the acquiescence of the British and French governments. The establishment of dictatorships in Lithuania in 1926, in Latvia and Estonia in 1934, in Greece in 1936 and in Bulgaria in 1934–36, saw the disappearance of democracy in eastern and south-eastern Europe. Of the successor states to the pre-1914 empires of central and eastern Europe, only Finland – having endured a civil war in 1919–20 – remained a democracy by 1939; and this state was soon to be confronted by a bitter struggle to retain its independence from the Soviet Union and a war which was to force it into an uncomfortable informal alliance with Nazi Germany.

The overthrow – either from within or from without – of liberal democratic institutions in the bulk of European states in the inter-war period was generally accompanied by a reversal of the economic gains made by the working classes in the aftermath of the First World War and often by the destruction of working-class economic organizations, the suppression of independent trade unions being a hallmark of authoritarian régimes in the inter-war years.

Even where liberal parliamentary democracies survived – in northern and western Europe – by 1939 workers had generally witnessed a significant erosion of the gains they had made in the aftermath of the First World War and during the early 1920s. In the United Kingdom, not only had the Depression had a debilitating effect on the organized labour movement but also the divisions within the political wing of the movement over how best to handle the consequences of the Depression led to a major split in the Labour Party, whose parliamentary representation was decimated in the 1931 general election and which was condemned to marginal impotence for the remainder of the decade. In France, the apparent triumph of the parties of organized labour (in co-operation with the liberal Radical Party) signalled by the May–June 1936 elections to the Chamber of Deputies was soon to be revealed as illusory: the economic gains made by the trade unions, through the Matignon agreements of June 1936, were to be rapidly eroded; whilst foreign policy difficulties, a series of exchange-rate crises and the consequent adoption by the Popular Front governments of progressively more conservative domestic expenditure policies, undermined their support amongst their erstwhile supporters against a background of growing political polarization. Perhaps only in Norway, Sweden and Denmark, were the 1930s much short of a disaster for the working classes and their economic and political representatives: by 1939 socialists participated in the governments of all of these states.

Whilst the political history of inter-war Europe is fairly familiar, that of the political attitudes and behaviour of workers is much less so. Long generally the preserve of historians with close links with contemporary labour movements, the history of the working classes in Europe has until comparatively recently tended to be written largely in terms of the history of these economic and political organizations – i.e. trade unions and socialist, social democratic or communist political parties – which claimed to speak for, and represent the interests of, workers. This has been particularly the case where attention has been concentrated on the political behaviour of workers. Yet, properly speaking, 'class' is a category of socio-economic rather than political analysis: social classes as such do not engage in political action and the relationship between membership of a social class and political affiliation or action is often a complicated and indirect one. Only relatively recently have historians turned their attention from workers' economic organizations and political parties to the broader study of a whole range of features of workers' lives which might elucidate those forces shaping workers' political values and behaviour. Often the focus of such research has been regional or local, or has concentrated on the workforces of individual industries. The role of workers' lives *outside* the workplace has come to be accorded a major place in the shaping of political and economic behaviour and, at long last, historians have begun to pay something like adequate attention to changing patterns of working-class family life and gender relations. In the history of the relationship between 'everyday life' and workers' political behaviour, the politically and economically unorganized and unmobilized are assuming a role as significant as that of the mobilized and organized; quiescence and apathy as significant a role as militancy and action; conformity and deference perhaps as significant a role as non-conformity and protest.

The historical literature on European workers' political behaviour has now assumed proportions which make it difficult even for the specialist to keep up to date with the latest research, even within his own area of expertise. This essay collection seeks to offer a range of national accounts which attempt to summarize the findings of recent research and to present these in a form accessible to the non-specialist. Whilst the format (discussion of workers' political behaviour within individual national frameworks) may suggest uniformity, each author has his own emphases and peculiarities of approach. Thus, to take an obvious example, contributing authors differ in their definition of what constitutes 'the working class'. Many adopt a fairly prosaic definition: the working class as manual wage-earners in industry and handicrafts (and, sometimes, transport) and their dependants, as revealed by the census statistics. Others choose to place greater emphasis on common values and attitudes, stemming from common experience, as important elements in the constitution of class.

These differences of emphasis notwithstanding, the individual essays making up this collection are broadly informed by common concerns. One such common concern – the need to break away from consideration of workers and politics solely from the perspective of ostensibly 'working-class' organizations – has already been mentioned. Yet other, perhaps more substantive, themes unite the individual contributions. The first of these common concerns is with the impact on the working class in Europe of the most severe economic recession in the history of the industrialized world. Qualifications must, of course, be made even here. The onset of the Depression, its duration and severity varied from economy to economy; and workers' experience and understanding of the Depression was generally shaped by their national economy's place in the world market, the position of their industry or sector within the national economy, and by their personal fortunes. Yet the Depression affected, directly or indirectly, all workers in the industrialized world and had important consequences both for workers' political behaviour and for the political environment within which they had lived. Even in the Soviet Union, isolated to a greater extent than any other industrialized or industrializing economy from the fortunes of the world market, the political ramifications of the apparent realization of the collapse of the capitalist world order long-heralded by official ideology, were not without significance for workers. How did workers respond to the experience of the Depression? How far did the experience of unemployment or the threat of this produce political radicalization, how far promote apathy and disengagement? Did common behavioural patterns emerge across national boundaries? If so, how far did national particularities – political, social and cultural, as well as economic – serve to modify such common patterns?

A second common theme uniting many of the contributions is the experience of workers subject to, and workers' reactions to, dictatorship. On the eve of the Second World War, only a minority of the individual working classes surveyed in this volume were not subject to dictatorship of one kind or another; whether of a traditional, militaristic, oligarchic kind (Spain, Poland, Austria to 1938) or of a new type characterized by mass mobilization and pretensions to totalitarian control of all aspects of life in civil as well as political society, dictatorships which claimed indeed to have transcended this distinction, (as in Germany, Italy and the Soviet Union). How far were workers won over to positive support for such régimes, how far economically and politically neutralized, how far capable of sustaining resistance or opposition to such régimes? What factors determined the degree of political integration which characterized the working classes subject to such régimes?

A third common theme – that of the experience of war – is of even more general concern. By 1945, all of the working classes examined in this collection had experienced war or civil war, and six of the ten had experienced defeat and occupation of their national states. What mechanisms did the democratic and authoritarian states use to seek to mobilize workers for the war effort? How successful were these mechanisms? Confronted by the experience of war, how far did affective solidarity prevail over awareness of class differences to integrate individual working classes into their belligerent societies? How far were workers willing to subordinate their own material interests to the objectives their governments pursued and the policies these necessitated? Did the centrality of labour in the war effort of all belligerent states result in any significant long-term changes in the position of workers within their individual societies, or in the composition of working classes or workers' political behaviour? Is it possible to identify class-specific consequences of the experience of defeat and occupation? Was resistance to occupation in any way shaped by class concerns?

Some or all of these themes are explored by the contributors to the essay collection. It would perhaps be unhelpful to attempt to summarize the conclusions reached by the contributors in their individual studies, but a number of general points might be seen to emerge from the essay collection as a whole.

The first of these concerns the relationship between the organized labour movement and the state, the most important locus of power in modern societies. Despite the optimistic expectations of the communist wing of the European labour movements, nowhere in Europe were established state apparatuses overthrown by action undertaken by industrial workers even where these were in alliance with members of other social classes. In every instance in which workers confronted state power directly – usually in an attempt to defend the organizations of the labour movement (Austria in 1934, Italy in 1921–22) – it was the state rather than the labour movement which emerged triumphant. Even where the labour movement confronted the state indirectly, deploying the strike weapon – as in the United Kingdom in 1926 – or the threat of this – as in Germany in 1932 – the limited nature of workers' power became apparent: large-scale political strikes proved remarkably difficult to organize and sustain, even during periods of relatively full employment, and were invariably defeated. In possession of almost unlimited coercive powers, it might seem, the modern state breaks down only in the most exceptional circumstances – usually defeat in wartime. By and large, workers achieved significant gains only in co-operation *with* the state, not in opposition to it; which may serve as a retrospective vindication of the social-democratic path adopted by much of the organized labour movement and its political representatives during the period from 1918 to 1945.

Similar points may be made about the relationships between the working class and other social classes; and between these and the state. The essays in this collection generally document the relative immunity of workers to appeals from fascist and right-wing authoritarian movements. Yet, in no instance, were workers and their organizations able to prevent the capture of state power by determined authoritarian movements with mass support drawn from outside the ranks of organized labour. Which may suggest that the defence of liberal democratic institutions cannot be guaranteed by workers' political action alone; and that an essential bulwark of democracy is a strong conservative party, both capable of defending middle-class interests and articulating middle-class grievances and, at the same time, committed to the parliamentary process. In the twentieth century the challenge to the inheritance of nineteenth-century constitutionalism was to come in practice not, as many had feared, from the working class but rather from the middle class. In a sense, then, it was they who proved to be the 'dangerous class' of the twentieth century. As a consequence, any consideration of the working class and politics, in isolation from the political behaviour of other classes, cannot be entirely satisfactory.

Likewise, both the presence of a strong economy *and* the ability of a liberal democratic *state* to mediate effectively between conflicting claims at the national economic level, seem to have been necessary prerequisites of the survival of liberal democratic politics and the organized expression of workers' economic and political interests there sheltered. The long boom of the pre-1914 European economy had generated sufficient growth to provide for improvement in the real living standards for many sections of the working class, including redistributive welfare payments via the state, without causing irreconcilable conflict with middle-class interests. The First World War served to raise the expectations of workers to new levels, but its effects in the longer term were to make such expectations less easy to satisfy without the erosion of middle-class living standards. After 1918 in the context of the Depression and the disruption of the post-war economic order, conflicts of interest were generally much more likely to occur, and in some countries were to prove insoluble within the confines of liberal democracy. The only successful, forcible arbitration in favour of the working class was in the Soviet Union; elsewhere it was more common for the state to be called in to defend middle-class and propertied interests against a real or perceived threat from the working class. These strains were felt most acutely in the underdeveloped countries of southern and eastern Europe where a relatively poor agricultural base and restricted industrial development left little scope to satisfy the interests of workers and peasants and to preserve those of the propertied middle class. As a result it was, broadly speaking, in the Mediterranean, the Balkans and eastern Europe that liberal democracy proved most fragile. Difficult as the Depression years were, the ability of the more advanced economies of Europe to generate sufficient economic growth to deliver improved standards of living and of welfare to the working classes while maintaining those of the middle classes goes a considerable way to explaining the ability of Scandinavia, the United Kingdom, France and the Low Countries to survive as liberal democracies. Here, the United States of America is relevant, as an example of an economy buoyant enough to satisfy the demands of organized labour without encroaching on the well-being of 'middle America'. Germany was, of course, an exception, but an exception that proves the rule, in being the single economy most severely disrupted by the post-1918 settlement and witnessing first in the Great Inflation and then in the Great Crash profoundly unsettling economic conditions. Even if the German economy did ultimately possess the potential to satisfy the interests of both workers and middle class, the apparent impossibility of doing so from the perspective of 1929–33 produced the flight of middle-class voters to the only strong available party of 'order'.

A final point relating to the state concerns its essentially territorial and national character in modern societies. By 1914 the forces of national education and the metropolitanization of national cultures had already gone a long way towards dividing the workers of one nation state from those of others. They were soon to be equally characteristic of the successor states which were set up after the First World War. Against this tide of national homogenization, attempts by socialists, acting supra-nationally, to prevent the slide into war in 1914 proved fruitless. Similarly, the ostensibly internationalist policies pursued by the constituent parties of the Comintern and examples of workers' solidarity across national boundaries such as the International Brigades notwithstanding, this period seems to suggest that the national unit is the most general at which effective political action can be undertaken. More salient was the conflict of workers' interests at the economic level across national boundaries – as exemplified by the boom of the Polish and German mining industries during the British coal-miners' strike of 1926.

If workers' political action across national boundaries was exceptional and usually ineffective, concerted economic or political action at the national level was scarcely less so. Indeed, perhaps the most striking feature of the history of the European working classes and politics in the period covered by the contributions to this volume is the limited usefulness of class as an instrument of political analysis. Not only were members of the working class divided from one another along sectoral and skill lines (i.e. by intra-class differences) but also by cultural and social factors which fit awkwardly into any reductionist explanatory model. Regional, religious and gender divisions might perhaps be reduced *ultimately* to class factors but seem to have enjoyed an autonomous existence and to have resulted in patterns of political behaviour and action only distantly related to class.

Whilst much has undoubtedly been learned from the study of workers' lives independent of the history of those economic and political organizations which claimed to speak for workers, these reflections may prompt the thought that it is only at the level of organization that the divisions which plagued working classes during this period could be overcome, thus permitting workers to exercise through their representatives a political weight commensurate with their economic and social significance. In other words, if the history of workers and politics cannot be adequately studied through the history of 'working-class' economic and political organizations alone, nor can it be adequately studied if the two are divorced.

CHAPTER TWO
Austria

Tim Kirk

INTRODUCTION

In October 1919 the Treaty of St Germain reduced Austria from the third-largest country in Europe, with a multi-national population of some fifty million, to a German-speaking 'rump' state, slightly larger than Scotland, and with a population of less than seven million. A quarter of these were concentrated in Vienna, which enjoyed the status of an autonomous federal province with considerable freedom to pursue policies independent of, and to a great extent opposed to, those of the federal government. The rest of the population was heavily concentrated in the eastern, relatively industrialized provinces.

Austrian industry, and with it the industrial working class, was concentrated in a belt stretching south-west from Vienna, Wiener Neustadt, and St Pölten in Lower Austria to the heavy-industrial towns of Styria. Here, the concentration of industrial workers was high, but the towns themselves were small, and situated in a predominantly rural province. In contrast with the relative economic diversity of the capital, the iron and steel (and related) industries were dominant almost to the exclusion of other economic activity, and the area was particularly dependent on the *Alpine-Montangesellschaft*, German-owned since the 1920s. The third major industrial area important during this period was Upper Austria, where massive expansion was undertaken with the establishment of the *Hermann-Göring-Werke* at Linz after the Nazi occupation. Industry here, in the tradition of the long-established *Steyr-Werke*, was predominantly armaments-related.

It is difficult to define who were the industrial working class.

11

The working class and politics

I have taken those people in the census category 'Industry and Crafts' designated as workers, and their dependants.[1] In 1939 this sub-category accounted for 27 per cent of the population of Greater Vienna and 22.6 per cent of the population of the rest of Austria. (The average for the Greater German *Reich* was about 31 per cent.) Vienna, Austria's only major city, was less industrial than most of the largest cities of Germany, and both the industrial and commercial, and the trade and transportation sectors of its economy were declining.[2]

Nevertheless Vienna was the bastion of politically organized labour. At its peak in 1929 nearly 60 per cent of the membership of the *Sozialdemokratische Arbeiterpartei* (SDAP) was concentrated there. Over a third of the *entire* Viennese electorate – 418,055 people – were card-carrying Social Democrats.[3] In the general election of 1930 the party commanded the support of 59 per cent of the same electorate (67 per cent in the eastern suburbs).[4]

The capital was also the bastion of the (Social Democratic) Free Trades Unions. Fifty-five per cent of their members in 1929 were Viennese. Right-wing unions had a predominantly non-metropolitan membership: just over a third of Christian trades unionists and less than a third of German National trades unionists were Viennese. The latter were in any case much smaller than the Free Trades Unions.

Trades Union Membership in Austria, 1929

	Austria	Vienna
Free Trades Unions	737,277	410,197
Christian Trades Unions	107,657	39,223
German Trades Union League	47,250	15,555

Source: Adapted from *Statistisches Handbuch für die Republik Österreich, XII,* (Vienna, 1931) p. 162.

The experience of the Austrian working class between the onset of the world depression in 1929 and the end of the Second World War was characterized by long-term material impoverishment and political repression. In contrast with the years before the end of the First World War, which had culminated in the revolution of 1918, workers' responses to the erosion of their civil rights and living standards were largely defensive, and constrained first by economic insecurity and later by political terror.

A decade before the depression the working class had seemed to be in a relatively strong position. The SDAP had emerged from the revolution as the dominant force in the land, and the stronger partner in the coalition government of Karl Renner. More radical than other Social Democratic parties in Europe, it had avoided the damaging rift suffered by organized labour in Germany, France and Italy. The Communist Party of Austria (KPÖ), founded in November 1918, attracted little support, and was of negligible importance before 1934. SDAP participation in government from 1918 to 1920 ensured the passage of important social-welfare and industrial-relations legislation, implementing long-standing Social Democratic policies[5] and under Austria's federal constitution Vienna, with a third of the country's population, was guaranteed the status of an autonomous state. This enabled the SDAP, relying on a solid electoral majority in the city, to implement the radical social policies which made Vienna famous throughout Europe as a model of municipal socialism and the biggest thorn in the side of government and bourgeoisie alike.[6]

Nationally, the political tide had already begun to turn by 1920. The shift to the right was part of a wider tendency throughout Central Europe. Conservatives were encouraged by the fall of the Councils' Republic (*Räterrepublik*) in Bavaria and, more importantly in Hungary. Hopes of an *Anschluß* with a Social Democratic Germany were dashed by the conditions of the Treaty of St Germain, and the drift to the right in Germany itself.

In January 1920 Otto Bauer, Foreign Minister and intellectual leader of the SDAP, complained (in a letter to Karl Kautsky) that the Christian Social Party (CSP), which represented Conservative and clerical interests, was sabotaging all the coalition's work, and that the *Länder* simply refused to obey Vienna.[7] In July of that year, following tensions within the coalition on the question of the formation of a new army, the Social Democrats withdrew from the government. A new cabinet was then formed on a proportionate basis (containing all political parties), pending the general election in October. At this election the CSP overtook the Social Democrats and became the largest party in parliament, albeit without an absolute majority. The Social Democrats did not take part in government again until 1945.

In 1923 Bauer described the political situation in Austria between the revolution and the Geneva protocols of 1922 as a political equilibrium.[8] He argued that a balance of class forces existed between the organized industrial working classes concentrated for the most part in the east of the country – in 'Red Vienna', Upper Styria and Lower Austria – and the Conservative forces of the capital's bourgeoisie and the overwhelming majority of the rural population. Many of the latter were not only hostile to socialism, but also unsympathetic towards both the Republic and parliamentary democracy. In truth Social Democracy had been unable to extend its support beyond its most natural constituency: not simply industrial workers but, on the whole, industrial workers living in relatively homogeneous communities and working in large factories. The social and political divisions of Bauer's description remained fixed and deepened considerably over the following ten years.

Although the SDAP recovered from its electoral low of 1920 to constitute an increasingly real threat with every subsequent general election, the political initiative continued to lie with the ruling Christian Social Party (CSP). Since neither party was able to win an absolute majority of votes there was no possibility, under Austria's system of proportional representation, of single-party government, but the CSP was the largest party and could rely on the support of the German Nationalists in anti-Socialist coalitions. Employers took advantage of the new Conservative hegemony in the state to undermine or circumvent the Republic's industrial relations legislation, and the extreme right could rely on the indulgent partisanship of the authorities in its increasingly provocative and anti-democratic activity.

Proportion of the vote gained by three major political groupings 1919–30

	Labour*	National	Catholic–Conservative
1919	41	18	36
1920	36	17	42
1923	40	13	45
1927	42	7	48
1930	41	16	42†

Source: Adapted from Sully, *Continuity and Change*, p.19.
*includes Communists.
†includes *Heimatblock*.

In the political history of the First Republic the events of 1927 are widely regarded as a watershed. In January of that year right-wing *Frontkämpfer* shot and killed a war veteran and a child in a violent clash between rival left-wing and right-wing demonstrations at Schattendorf in the Burgenland. When those responsible were acquitted by a Vienna court in the same year, workers in the capital responded with spontaneous strikes and demonstrations outside Parliament. The crowd became unruly and in the ensuing battle the Palace of Justice was burned down and ninety demonstrators were killed.

The SDAP leadership was taken by surprise by events, not for the first or last time, and responded in a conciliatory manner, deploying the *Republikanischer Schutzbund*, the party's paramilitary organization, only in an attempt to contain the situation, which it failed to do.[9] A strike declared by the socialist Free Trades Unions the same evening lasted barely three days, and the incident served only to underline the waning strength of the labour movement as a political force. In the years that followed it faced an increasingly self-confident challenge both on the streets and in parliament, while the material position of the working class was being undermined by the depression.

THE WORKING CLASS ON THE DEFENSIVE: ECONOMIC AND POLITICAL CRISIS 1929–33

The Austrian economy had never achieved lasting stability between the wars. The creation of the state itself had been unwelcome to most Austrian politicians, who considered it unviable, and favoured union with Germany.[10] The early years of the Republic had seen high inflation and high unemployment, and even in the relatively buoyant years of the mid–1920s Austrian unemployment had never fallen below 8 per cent.[11]

The effects of the world depression of 1929 were exacerbated in Austria by the collapse of the *Creditanstalt*, the country's leading bank in 1931, which triggered off further economic crises. Austrian governments responded to the slump with a continuation of their deflationary economic policies, punctuated by appeals to the League of Nations for assistance and, especially later in the 1930s, attempts to come to some sort of accommodation with Germany which would allow closer economic co-operation.[12]

The effects of the government's policies were to be seen in continued stagnation of the Austrian economy right up to the German invasion of 1938. By 1932 industrial production had fallen to 61 per cent of its 1929 output, and unemployment had reached 21.7 per cent of the workforce. It remained at this level throughout the mid-1930s and still stood at 20.4 per cent in 1937 when – in so far as it is possible to make valid international comparisons – the proportion out of work had fallen to 4.5 per cent in Germany and stood at 9.4 per cent in Britain.[13]

The standard of living for those in work declined as wages fell further and faster than prices. Unemployment benefits were meagre and lasted for only one year, so that the long-term unemployed – perhaps half as many again as the number of claimants – had no means of support.[14] The effects of the depression on an ordinary working-class community in Austria have been described in the famous sociological study of the village of Marienthal.[15] Three-quarters of the families in this community were dependent on unemployment benefits; those still at work were mainly shopkeepers and local state officials. For most families meat virtually disappeared from the diet, and such meat that was eaten was now more often rabbit, horsemeat and even cats and dogs.[16]

Rising unemployment strengthened the hand of the employers in the labour market and they attempted to dismantle what was left of the Republic's labour legislation. In 1931, for example, all 1,300 miners at a Styrian pit were made redundant and then offered re-employment on the basis of individual contracts which excluded the possibility of collective bargaining.[17]

The impact of unemployment on working-class militancy is difficult to assess. There was a noticeable effect on the incidence of industrial action. The number of disputes fell from 242 in 1928 to 30 in 1932, and over the same period the total number engaged in strikes declined from 32,948 to 5,429 and the number of days lost from 562,992 to 79,942.[18] This decline almost certainly reflected a climate of greater economic insecurity.

The impact on political activity was more complex. Membership of the SDAP, arguably the strongest and most united party in Europe, peaked at 718,056 in 1929, when party membership accounted for over a tenth of the entire Austrian population. By 1932 it had lost 60,000 members nationally. Some of these went to the KPO, but the numbers involved were modest. Communist Party membership doubled in the first half of 1931, but only from 3,508 to 6,813.[19] On the other hand the loss was perhaps not as great as it might have been. In Styria, where both party and unions had suffered dramatic losses in the mid 1920s, SDAP membership remained 10 per cent higher in 1932 than in 1925.[20] Electoral evidence is also ambiguous. Between the general elections of 1927 and 1930 the Communists made some gains; the SDAP share of the overall vote

Industrial disputes in Austria 1927–32

Year	1927	1928	1929	1930	1931	1932
Strikes	195	242	202	83	56	30
Factories	440	687	535	169	253	150
Strikers ('000s)	28.8	32.9	23.8	6.2	8.5	5.4
Workers ('000s)	37.5	44.0	37.5	10.7	11.7	6.6
Days lost ('000s)	476.7	563.0	286.5	40.9	100.4	79.9

Source: Adapted from *Statistisches Handbuch für die Republik Österreich.*

declined slightly, not only nationally, but also in Vienna and Styria, while the party improved its performance – again only slightly – in Lower Austria and Carinthia. The overall impression gained from the electoral statistics is one of remarkable stability in the labour camp. The inroads made by the German Nationalists and the extreme right into the Christian Social vote were far greater: it fell from 48 per cent of the total in 1927 to 36 per cent in 1930. If there was political radicalization in Austria during the depression it took place on the right.

The relationship of the working class to fascism was similar to that in Germany. Neither the Austro-fascism of the *Heimwehr* nor the Austrian branch of the NSDAP achieved a mass following under democratic conditions, and the absolute numbers used in statistical analyses of membership have been small and restricted to sections of the party such as leaders or militants. With these qualifications in mind it seems that industrial workers remained relatively immune to the attractions of both varieties of right-wing extremism, with the degree of immunity dependent on certain identifiable characteristics: Viennese workers were more immune than those in the provinces; politically conscious Social Democrats or trades unionists more so than the politically or economically unorganized; workers in large heavy-industrial concerns more so than those in small workshops.

As in Germany, workers often emerge as the largest social group in a fascist organization, but are under-represented in relation to their numerical strength in society as a whole. For example, in an analysis of new NSDAP members in Austria between 1926 and 1942 workers account for between 21 per cent (1926–31) and 39 per cent (1942–44), but constitute just over half the total working population in Austria over the same period. It is worth noting, in order to keep a sense of perspective, that total NSDAP membership in Austria was still only 164,300 in March 1938.[21] Nazis were a small, if active and vocal, political group in the First Republic.

The *Heimwehr* remained an overwhelmingly rural movement. 'Independent' unions, founded by the fascist *Heimwehr* and supported by employers claimed great success in Upper Styria where they claimed to have recruited between 15,000 and 20,000 workers. However, this was largely a result of the labour-recruitment policy of the German-owned *Alpine Montangesellschaft*, a heavy-industrial complex with a virtual monopoly in the local labour market. After July 1927 members of independent unions were employed in preference to members of Socialist unions as a matter of policy, and as unemployment increased workers were forced to respond to this pressure. Significantly, little headway was made by the same *Heimwehr* unions in Vienna.[22]

Later, in the 1930s, as the successful penetration of Austrian industry by German interests accelerated, employers increasingly applied similar policies in favour of Nazi party members, a policy directed as much against the government as against the left.[23] By then the Social Democratic monopoly of working-class loyalties had been broken by the brief civil war of 1934 and the collapse of the party itself.

The evidence from the Marienthal study suggests that the depression led to resignation and political apathy among the working class, but that there was a difference between the unemployed, who rapidly lost interest not only in politics, but also in other social and cultural activities, and those still in work, who continued to participate.[24] Basing his conclusions on a statistical analysis of political violence, Gerhard Botz suggests that whereas the unemployed were depoliticized, those still in work were 'politically mobilized and more inclined to the use of violence'.[25] He also adds that workers prevented from pursuing their aims within the framework of industrial relations were radicalized to the extent that frustrated economic conflicts became political ones. The picture which emerges is more complex than one of demoralization and apathy: many workers were indeed radicalized by the frustrations of poverty and by political repression and provocation.

CIVIL WAR, DICTATORSHIP AND OPPOSITION 1933–38

The parliamentary majority of one achieved by the *Bürgerblock* coalition of anti-Marxist parties in the 1930 election prompted the Christian Social Party to question its continuing commitment to parliamentary democracy[26]. The ground it had lost had been to the breakaway radical right (*Heimatblock*) in its own Catholic-Conservative camp, on whose support it now depended to remain in government.

As early as 1932 the government began to rely on emergency decrees under the War Economy Enabling Law of 1917. Outside parliament, in conflict after conflict with workers and labour organizations, the *Heimwehr* could be confident that government and security forces would generally be indulgent, if not encouraging, while the *Schutzbund* was held back by its leaders' insistence on legality, and the authorities' partisanship.

Following the suspension of parliamentary government by Dollfuβ in 1933 the labour movement was driven further onto the defensive in a concerted government effort to break the power of organized labour. Government policy was deliberately confrontational and it is difficult to draw a line between government provocation through the state security services and provocation by the paramilitary organization of the government party. Police had been used to intimidate workers and their leaders while ostensibly enforcing the law during the railwaymen's strike of March 1933.

The response of the hesitant SDAP leadership, caught between its own fears of a civil war which the workers would inevitably lose and the demands of the rank and file for decisive action, was to name four possible government measures to which the party would respond with an immediate general strike: the dissolution of the party itself; dissolution of the Free Trades Unions; interference with the autonomy of Vienna; or the promulgation of a Fascist constitution. The government was now conveniently able to proceed with its 'salami' tactics of undermining the movement little by little and provoking conflict while avoiding the specific measures which might give rise to united working-class resistance.

One such tactic was the carrying out of provocative searches for *Schutzbund* weaponry, instituted under Public Security Minister and *Heimwehr* leader Emil Fey. The successful discovery of weapons caches would serve as a justification for the arrest and imprisonment of Social Democratic and *Schutzbund* leaders: the party would be dissolved piecemeal and with a superficial legality which would deflect concerted opposition.

National leaders of the labour movement still counselled caution. Many in the rank and file of the party saw it as the last chance to act. On 12 February 1934, after duly warning the national leaders of the party (Otto Bauer), *Schutzbund* (Theodor Körner) and the Free Trades Unions (Johnann Schorsch), *Schutzbund* men in Linz, led by Richard Bernaschek, carried out their threat of meeting any further provocation – weapons search or the arrest of any party or *Schutzbund* official – with armed resistance.

Fighting broke out in Linz and the Vienna *Schutzbund* demonstrated support by attacking the police station in Simmering. Power workers cut off the electricity supply and the trams came to a standstill. A general strike was belatedly and reluctantly called, but it was incomplete and ineffective. The British press reported that even in Vienna many people continued to go to work and that essential services were maintained, and a British foreign correspondent recorded that workers were confused, ill-informed and uncertain what to do.[27]

In the capital there was not so much a major conflict between workers and security forces as a series of isolated armed clashes in working-class suburbs, with police attacking *Schutzbund* positions, often with military support. Resistance was probably stronger than the government side expected. Much of the working-class district of Simmering was still under *Schutzbund* control by 14 February and order could only be restored in Floridsdorf by the sixteenth.[28]

The conflict was by no means restricted to Vienna. Fighting was particularly intense in Styria, but there was little hope of success against the overwhelming forces of the government without a national general strike. There was some limited response to the strike call in the province but the failure of most railway workers in particular to come out hastened the defeat of the *Schutzbund*. The conflict was particularly intense in the provincial capital, Graz, and at Bruck an der Mur, an industrial town in Upper Styria, where *Schutzbund* men led by Kolomann Wallisch opened fire on police breaking a strike. The workers were only dislodged from their positions and dispersed with the deployment of artillery and mortars, and the fighting in this part of Styria was perhaps among the fiercest in the civil war.[29]

The Workers' Club in Linz, where the conflict had started, was taken over by security forces within hours, and the fighting was over within a day, except in the Urfahr district outside the city centre on the left bank of the Danube, where the *Schutzbund* held out until the following morning.[30] There was also fighting in Steyr, a nearby industrial town noted for the strong Social Democratic sympathies of its working class. Workers at the *Steyr-Werke* went on strike, cleared the factory and occupied the telephone exchange. The bitterest fighting concentrated around the barracks and the Ennsleithen housing blocks, and the *Schutzbund* was defeated in the end only by the use of heavy artillery.[31]

Outside the urban centres of Upper Austria preparations were made for resistance but they came to little: railway stations and post offices were occupied, the gendarmerie was disarmed and workers issued arms instead. In some cases the workers held out for up to a week.[32]

Essential services were maintained in Linz and, again, the trains ran. The very arrival of the first trains in the provinces was an indication in itself, in the absence of other reliable information, of the failure of the nationwide general strike. The (almost) punctual arrival of the 11.00 a.m. train from Vienna in the small railway town of Attnang-Puchheim alerted striking railwaymen to the failure of the strike in a number of key towns along its route, including Vienna, St. Pölten and Linz.[33]

There was little fighting in the other provinces, and almost none outside industrial towns. There were skirmishes in Lower Austria and at Hallein near Salzburg, and strikes in Carinthia. Apart from isolated incidents at Wörgl the alpine provinces of Tyrol and Vorarlberg were unaffected, as was the Burgenland.[34]

By the 17 February the fighting was over. In Vienna alone 131 civilians were killed including 25 women and children, and a further 358 were wounded. On the government side there were 55 dead and 251 wounded.[35] The combined forces of military, police and *Heimwehr* broke all resistance within days by simple superiority in numbers and sheer firepower. The determination of the government to break the back of the opposition is perhaps best demonstrated by its use of artillery to bombard Viennese workers' council flats. (Popular bourgeois demonology had always claimed these to be purpose-built fortifications sited adjacent to communications lines in preparation for just such a civil war.) It is difficult to say whether a successful general strike would have altered the outcome much. In any case it did not happen; most workers were reluctant to take risks. The depression had undermined their individual and collective security and the government had made it clear that politically unreliable workers would lose their jobs. They were not encouraged by the lack of confidence of the hesitant leadership, and were ill-prepared for a fight, unable even to locate or obtain the weapons hidden by the *Schutzbund* for such an eventuality.[36]

The SDAP was dissolved on 12 February 1934, and within a fortnight over 2,000 of its members had been arrested. Summary courts were set up and nine death sentences were carried out almost immediately in the capital. Kolomann Wallisch was arrested and hanged on the same day in Styria. Others fled abroad, where the *Auslandsorganisation Österreichischer Sozialisten* (ALÖS) was formed.

Government persecution continued long after the immediate aftermath of the fighting. Steps were taken to exclude any potential Social Democratic sympathizers from the legal processes, including defence lawyers and jurors, and the deterrent nature of the justice meted out was made clear. The assassination of Dollfuβ by the Nazis in July prompted an escalation of the repression. When the summary courts had finished their business, the ordinary courts settled down to deal with cases which had been referred to them, and these were followed by proceedings against the party and *Schutzbund* leaders, which went on into 1935.[37]

It seems certain that for the most part workers remained loyal in their commitment to the principles of Social Democracy, but were unable to engage in any political activity. If the possibility of industrial workers' participation in the conflict of February 1934 had been limited by their economic insecurity, their industrial relations position now deteriorated further. There was no doubt that employers no longer felt any qualms about taking the offensive. By July a hundred collective wage agreements had been broken by employers in Vienna alone, and wages fell on average between 4 and 8 per cent.[38] For most industrial workers active resistance or any illegal political activity remained out of the question, and their response to the repression of labour organizations was one familiar in the history of central European Social Democracy: simply to maintain contacts and meet informally in the course of working-class social life.

Those activists remaining in Austria who had not been arrested were forced underground and illegal socialist and trades-union movements were established. However, the labour movement was now severely fragmented. The survivors of the civil war and government persecution became the Revolutionary Socialists (RS). Despite their more radical political position the RS faced considerable difficulties in maintaining rank-and-file loyalty from the start. Radicalized *Schutzbund* members went over to the KPÖ, which flourised as it never had as a legal party. The Communist paper *Rote Fahne* claimed in March 1934 that KPÖ membership in Vienna had more than doubled, and that of the Communist Youth

League had increased tenfold, while in nine districts of Vienna the Social Democratic *Rote Falken* formations had gone over collectively. In Wiener Neustadt flysheets were distributed by local Socialist functionaries enjoining loyalty to the party, whose immediate reconstruction was promised, and warning against defections to the Communists or the Nazis.[39]

While it is not disputed that a considerable number of Socialists joined the KPÖ, the question of defections to the Nazis is more controversial.[40] Willibald Holzer refers to short-term co-operation between illegal *Schutzbund* units and Nazi party members 'here and there', a desperate measure prompted by defeat and the solidarity of shared persecution.[41] Gerhard Botz has estimated that in western Austria and Carinthia up to a third of *Schutzbund* members switched their support to the Nazis, while a much smaller proportion of Viennese members did so.[42] It is difficult to establish with accuracy the number of such conversions, the motives behind them or their durability.

It is clear that there was no general upsurge in working-class membership of the NSDAP in Austria in 1934. The number of workers as a proportion of total Nazi-party membership had increased during 1933 from about a fifth to about a quarter. Total Nazi-party membership rose from 43,100 to 68,400, about a tenth of SDAP membership.[43]

A further threat was the attempt by the government to integrate workers in the new order. However, there were few converts to Christian Socialism from the Social Democratic industrial workforce after 1934, and the *Heimwehr* remained very much a rural organization. Participation in the government's own industrial organization, the so-called 'Unity Union' (*Einheitsgewerkschaft*) held some appeal to those trades unionists and activists who thought that a degree of autonomy in the organization of labour might be regained through such an accommodation with the government. These hopes were disappointed when Dollfuβ and his Minister for Social Affairs, Neustädter-Stürmer, rejected Socialist proposals for internal democracy within the union. Illegal trades unionists, supported by the Revolutionary Socialists, now called for a boycott of the government union, which was then extended to other government organizations and institutions in the summer of 1934, when workers' leaders did not expect the new Austro-fascist 'corporate state' to last.

After the assassination of Dollfuβ in July and a wave of arrests in January 1935, it became increasingly clear that a swift end to the dictatorship was not to be expected. Committed activists both in the Revolutionary Socialists and the KPÖ undertook such resistance as they could, sometimes working together, as in the latter half of 1934. Their activity consisted largely of conspiratorial organization in small groups; the distribution of propaganda and the collection of donations for the wives and families of imprisoned comrades by the relief organizations, *Sozialistische Arbeiterhilfe* and *Rote Hilfe*.[44]

Illegal trades unionists engaged in similar activities on the shop floor, and the government union clearly had difficulties in industry. The Revolutionary Socialists concentrated increasingly on industrial agitation and a strike in two Vienna car factories (Fiat and Saurer in Floridsdorf) early in 1936, in support of a claim for a 15 per cent wage increase was an indication that workers were once again prepared to take the initiative in industrial relations. The strike was quickly put down by the authorities, but the tactic of a short strike came to be increasingly exploited by workers in support of wage claims, as a modest upturn in the economy became apparent. The Revolutionary Socialists saw in such industrial disputes a means towards weakening the political system; shop stewards on the other hand were often more interested in winning realistic concessions within the system, and were only prepared to co-operate with activists to a limited extent.[45]

Ultimately, no concessions were made by the government towards organized labour, and this remained the case when Austria was threatened with imminent invasion by Nazi Germany. Last-minute secret negotiations between the chancellor, Dr Kurt von Schuschnigg, and representatives of the underground movement in March 1938 came too late. Shop stewards demanded the lifting of restrictions before they could guarantee working-class support for Schuschnigg, and this was confirmed at the meeting of illegal trades unionists which the government allowed to be held in the Vienna suburb of Floridsdorf on 7 March: although they recognized that Nazism was a greater evil than the Schuschnigg régime, they could not persuade the people they represented to throw their support behind the chancellor without a radical change of policy.[46] Schuschnigg reluctantly agreed to the demands put before him, but less than a week later, on 11 March, German troops occupied Austria.

The German occupation was met with no military resistance, and very little popular opposition. The attitude of workers was one of indifference to the fate of the government and its party – a feeling that one kind of fascism was as bad as any other – tempered by hopes that a Nazi government would bring the economic expansion and return to full employment that Germany had experienced.

ECONOMIC RECOVERY 1938–39: APPEARANCE AND REALITY

There was no attempt by the Austrian government to reflate the economy during the mid-1930s.[47] In fact federal expenditure on industrial investment fell from 248.4 million Schillings in 1930 to 98.4 million in 1931 and 12.5 million in 1932. Government investment fell from a tenth to less than one per cent of total federal expenditure.[48] Attempted work-creation projects were largely unsuccessful, and the only stimulus to the economy came as a spill-over from the German armaments boom and was restricted to heavy industry and the armaments-related sector, foreshadowing the structural economic change that was to follow the German occupation.

Nazi leaders were well aware of the potential appeal of economic recovery for the working class in particular, and propaganda aimed at workers in the first weeks after the *Anschluß* was dominated by two themes: the shared persecution of Nazis and Socialists in the Corporate State, and the promise of a return to full employment.[49] The measures that were taken in the short term were largely cosmetic. The price of gas was reduced by a few *Groschen*; benefit payments for the long-term unemployed, abolished by the Corporate State, were now restored; and one-off bonuses were paid to a number of workers. Many of the Viennese workers who found jobs in the first month of National Socialist rule did so in the course of a 'special programme' and many were Socialists and Communists dismissed for political reasons by the old regime.[50]

The economic integration of Austria into the *Reich* was not without problems. The fall in unemployment though spectacular compared with previous years, was neither as rapid nor as uninterrupted as expected.[51] The Austrian unemployed were largely inexperienced or de-skilled and Austrian plant and machinery was old and outdated. Economic recovery was to come through structural change to gear the country for a war economy, and in particular through the expansion of heavy industry and other branches essential to the production of arms. So while a massive new heavy-industrial complex was planned at Linz in

Upper Austria, the textile industry underwent a crisis with serious consequences for many individual communities in Lower Austria and Vorarlberg. Many small towns and villages suffered problems similar to those of Groβ-Sieghardt in the Lower Austrian *Waldviertel* where the impact of 450 redundancies following a factory closure was disastrous in a community with 2,331 inhabitants.[52]

Nor did the living standards of those finding work immediately live up to the promises of the régime. It had proved difficult to effect a smooth adjustment of Austrian wages and prices to German levels, and while prices rose quickly enough, wages were often 30 to 40 per cent lower in Austria than in the '*Altreich*', and the problem persisted despite a wages-and-prices freeze in May 1938. Wages were relatively high in mining, the chemical industry and construction, which was attracting workers from low-paid jobs in quarrying, and particularly low in the textile and clothing industries where employers did not benefit from lucrative government contracts. The wages of agricultural workers were still often below the level of unemployment benefit.[53] The situation was further aggravated by the increase in deductions from pay packets since the German occupation, and the introduction of German income tax in February 1939.

Nevertheless, as in Germany in the mid-1930s the problem of unemployment eventually gave way to one of labour shortage, especially after the outbreak of war. In 1939 and 1940 the number of people employed in Austrian industry declined by over 10,000 (2.1 per cent) largely as a result of recruitment to the armed forces. In Austria the problem was exacerbated by the continuing drain of workers to Germany; the Austrian labour market never recovered from the first few weeks after the German occupation, when workers left for Germany in droves before the imposition of controls. In March 1940 the Austrian branch of the department of labour supply reported a seasonal increase in demand from agriculture and construction and further demands from the expanding armaments industry, while the supply of labour had been 'substantially reduced by the further loss of workers, and in particular of highly skilled workers in shortage trades, to the *Altreich*'.

Little could be done to relieve the shortages. Various *ad hoc* measures were introduced but were largely unsuccessful.[54] There was a small rise in the number of women, who comprised 27.7 per cent of the industrial workforce in 1939 and 31.1 per cent in 1944,[55] and this reluctance to mobilize women for industrial work reflected the situation throughout the *Reich*.

Much of the shortfall in labour was covered by the recruitment
of foreign workers. By April 1941 the proportion of the total
workforce made up by foreigners ranged from 5.3 per cent
in Vienna and Lower Danube to 11.5 per cent in Styria and
Carinthia.[56] In the new munitions factories of Upper Austria 38.8
per cent of all workers were foreigners or prisoners of war by the
end of 1942.[57] In some important arms factories the proportion of
foreigners continued to rise. By February 1943 69.7 per cent of all
workers in the Linz nitrogen works were foreign, as were 64.7 per
cent in the aluminium works at Ranshofen near Branau, and 60.7
per cent at the important *Eisenwerke Oberdonau*. Here foreigners
were employed on the jobs with the most unpleasant working
conditions, and in some parts of the works accounted for over
90 per cent of the workforce.[58]

The difficulties associated with this situation, familiar from
Germany, [59] were now repeated in Austria, and it is significant
that the authorities were to be far more concerned with problems
of labour (and raw materials) supply than with political dissent or
industrial indiscipline.

Despite the disappointments the increase in employment alone
effected a general rise in working-class living standards, and this
is indicated by the rise in the general level of consumption of
food and consumer goods. By December 1938 consumption of
groceries had risen by 23 per cent, and the consumption of luxury
and consumer goods by even more: beer by 74 per cent, household
goods by 160 per cent, and women's clothing by 211 per cent.[60] The
boom continued in 1939, and despite the fact that on the whole
wages were lower and prices higher than in Germany, the rise in
the standard of living was sustained.

POLITICAL RESISTANCE AND POPULAR
OPPOSITION 1938–45

Anxious as the Nazis apparently were to get across to the workers
their message of reconciliation, they distinguished clearly between
the 'good German worker' and the Marxist agitators who had led
him astray. The occupation was followed immediately by yet another
wave of arrests and repression, and again, those lucky enough to
escape went into emigration.[61]

The responses of the two principal political groups within the labour movement differed considerably. The Revolutionary Socialists, recognizing the qualitative difference between the methods of the Schuschnigg régime and the brutality of the Gestapo abandoned all activity, provisionally for three months, but effectively for an indefinite period.[62]

The KPÖ on the other hand was uncompromising in continuing its resistance activity, and gained more recruits from the ranks of like-minded Socialists with no organization of their own. There were other differences between Socialists and Communists, notably the propagation by the latter since the Seventh Comintern Congress of 1935, which advocated the popular front strategy, of the idea of the Austrian nation. Socialists continued until 1943 to adhere to the goal of national re-unification within a democratic Greater Germany.[63] The intention behind the policy was to secure the co-operation of other anti-Nazi groups in a popular front, which the party failed to get. The effect was to expose party members to charges of high treason.

The basis of the Communist resistance network was the party itself. A centralized, disciplined organization which concentrated on recruitment and the dissemination of propaganda, it retained these characteristics in its underground work. Effectively the party came to consist of a network of small local cells arranged in a vertical communications-and-command structure: cells were not to contact each other and individuals were not even to know the identity of other members outside the group.

Despite these precautions, the nature of much of the KPÖ's work, and particularly the dissemination of propaganda, exposed successive 'generations' of party activists to detection, arrest and execution or imprisonment. Nevertheless, the party seemed to be able to replenish itself after each Gestapo crackdown, and Communists accounted for the vast majority of all those involved in resistance in Austria.[64] However, although usually led by Communists, many nominally 'Communist' cells consisted entirely of Socialists, who had gone over to the KPÖ in the absence of an organization of their own. Such groups often preferred not to mix with Communists, and preserved a Socialist identity.[65]

Direct involvement in an underground organization was limited to a very small minority, and the clandestine nature of much Communist resistance activity – in particular the infiltration of National Socialist industrial and political organizations and the production and distribution of propaganda – meant that it operated largely outside the working-class community. Both Communists and Socialists established resistance cells in industry but agitation was more difficult under the Nazis than in the Corporate state.[66] There was no possibility of mass participation by the workers, but the work of the relief organizations widened involvement and served to mobilize the support of larger numbers. Indeed the Socialist relief organization *Sozialistische Arbeiterhilfe* (SAH) was something of a substitute for a resistance organization proper, and the first trial at the 'People's Court' in April 1939 was directed against its leadership.[67]

Rote Hilfe, which like its Socialist counterpart had been established under the Dollfuβ-Schuschnigg dictatorship, was also an important part of the Communist resistance. Apart from providing financial help to the families of those persecuted by the régime, the contributions were used to finance the entire organization, and were the party's only source of income. The authorities seized on this more readily than many of the – otherwise politically uncommitted – contributors themselves and regarded such contributions as membership subscriptions. The consequences of a small donation, generally of two or three Marks a month, could be disproportionately serious; the KPÖ's stated aim of regaining Austrian independence laid open its members to charges of high treason, which could carry the death penalty.[68]

The activities of *Rote Hilfe* illustrate aspects of the relationship between the KPÖ and its potential mass base in industry which have received little attention in organizational histories of the Communist resistance. Any appeal to the workers to engage in collective direct action against the régime on a large scale, in the form of a general strike or uprising, was bound to fail. This was recognized by the party itself, which concentrated its efforts on conspiratorial work. On the other hand the exercise of raising money through the relief fund was relatively successful in its own terms. It paid for the organization, assisted the wives and families of imprisoned workmates, broadened the constituency of opposition to the régime, and alerted more passive workers to the persecution of activists. It also demonstrated a degree of common solidarity among workers which the authorities were clearly not prepared to tolerate.

A further instance of wider participation in the resistance movement was the partisan campaign along the borders of Styria and Carinthia and in Lower Styria and Carniola, areas of Yugoslav Slovenia annexed in 1941. The partisans were a mixture of Slovenes from Austria and the annexed areas (an estimated 80 per cent), Austrian Germans, Carniolans and others. Most of the Austrians were Socialists and Communists from Styria and Carinthia, and although national resentment was probably the most important motivation for Slovene partisans, a great many of them were Communists too. Activity was chiefly restricted to the annexed areas, but spilled over into Austria proper, and particularly the linguistically mixed part of Carinthia south of the River Drau (Drava).[69]

Partisans were primarily interested in disrupting the war machine and the apparatus of occupation, and the pattern of their activity established itself fairly rapidly. Most attacks were on the security forces and communications, for example, ambush of a post bus, derailment, cutting a telephone line.

Little impact was made by the partisans until 1943 when reports of attacks on industry became more frequent and the attacks themselves more serious. They were accompanied by an increase in the practice of 'compulsory recruitment' (*Zwangsrekrutierung*), the press-ganging of local workers into the partisan ranks. This was less direct than material sabotage, but in the long term more disruptive through its impact on the stretched labour-supply situation. Towards the end of the war the local security forces began to lose their grip on the situation. A security report from August 1944 speaks of partisans operating 'in groups of up to three thousand' and 'effectively unhindered' by the inadequate security forces.[70] Armed clashes between partisans and security forces also became more frequent until, in the spring of 1945 these gave way to regular military operations in the area as the German army retreated.

DEVELOPMENTS IN INDUSTRIAL RELATIONS AND LABOUR DISCIPLINE 1938–45

Outside the organized resistance movement the response of workers was determined by factors other than political commitment. The attitude of industrial workers to the Nazi régime was more complicated than straightforward opposition or approval. Expressions of opposition were often restricted to particular aspects of policy or government actions and limited in their objectives and duration. Oppositional behaviour was often an individual matter, and such collective action as took place rarely went beyond one shop or department and even more rarely beyond the factory itself. Finally, certain types of workers were more likely to express opposition than others: notably women, young people, and above all foreigners. In this respect the situation in Austria reflected that in the *Reich* as a whole.[71]

Outright strikes were almost out of the question in the Third Reich, although there are instances recorded by the Nazi authorities of short, limited stoppages, described in more euphemistic terms as 'interruption of work' (*Arbeitsunterbrechung*), 'downing tools' (*Arbeitsniederlegung*) or 'refusal to work' (*Arbeitsverweigerung*).[72]

More common were less confrontational responses such as absenteeism, go-slows (*Langsamarbeiten*) and changing jobs in breach of employment contract. Such behaviour, which has been interpreted as a continuation of class conflict by other means,[73] increased at times of crisis or in response to particularly unpopular policies.

The first such wave of industrial unrest in Austria came in the autumn of 1938, coinciding with the international tension of the Munich crisis. In Vienna there had been increasing activity on the part of the Revolutionary Socialists, and the illegal Free Trades Unions had intensified their activity in many larger concerns, particularly in Floridsdorf, where membership fees and donations had been collected.[74] Outside the capital there had been strikes and serious breaches of discipline at the *Steyrwerke* in Upper Austria and the *Alpine-Montan* in Upper Styria.[75] Foreign political successes, first at Munich and later the annexation as a protectorate of Bohemia and Moravia, probably did as much to take the wind out of the sails of the opposition as the arrest of leading Austrian Socialist and Communist functionaries ordered by Himmler in September.[76]

A year later the War Economy Decree of 4 September 1939 elicited a similar wave of disaffection on a much larger scale. Under the provisions of the decree bonuses for overtime, shift work, Sundays and statutory holidays were abolished. In addition wages, and working hours were to be 'adjusted' in accordance with the new circumstances, and there was to be more civil conscription.[77] The response of Austrian workers reflected that of others throughout the *Reich*. There were discipline problems in industry. The Vienna Gestapo reported a number of cases, particularly on construction sites, where workers had downed tools and walked away from the job, and in one instance refused to pay contributions to the government labour organization, the *Deutsche Arbeitsfront* (DAF).[78]

The working class and politics

Also typical was a steep increase in sickness rates, which had reached 20 per cent of the workforce in Floridsdorf.[79] Problems of labour discipline caused such disruption in the *Reich* as a whole that the War Economy Decree was effectively revoked. Although the war economy measures provoked particularly strong reactions, similar labour-discipline problems surfaced again and again throughout the rest of the war. On the whole, however, the morale and discipline of the 'German' (i.e. native Austrian) members of the workforce was good. It was among newly employed workers and conscripts that absenteeism and refusal to work were particular problems. Some firms complained that workers allocated to them had simply refused to take the job; five such cases were reported from Vienna factories in March 1940.[80]

Evidence of collective or politically motivated action for absenteeism, and for the large number of cases of breach of employment contract is difficult to find. Offenders themselves most frequently excused their behaviour by claiming illness or pressing domestic circumstances. Although, of course, the statements of workers brought before court for such offences cannot always be taken at face value, and there are often indications of concealed or secondary motives, it is difficult to interpret such behaviour as evidence of widespread disaffection or opposition to the régime.

Stefan Karner, in his study of breach of contract in Lower Styria during 1944 found a correlation between absenteeism among former peasants at seed-time and harvest, so that in addition to the cycle of higher absenteeism on Saturdays and Mondays, there is also a long-term cycle which corresponds to periods of peak demand for agricultural labour.[81] It is clear that similar problems existed in other parts of Austria, and in particular in areas undergoing industrial expansion, such as Upper Austria, and especially among new recruits to the industrial workforce, such as women, young people and former agricultural workers.

Many large concerns established relatively efficient internal procedures for dealing with internal discipline problems before it became necessary to go to court. One such firm was the *Eisenwerke Oberdonau* in Linz. As elsewhere the motives of offenders were obscured by claims of illness and domestic circumstances, but it is striking that by 1944 the majority of offenders had already been penalized for similar offences, some of them several times. Between April and November 1943, 188 offenders of 18 different nationalities were dealt with. Of these 33.5 per cent were French and 16 per cent were Czech. Germans (9 per cent) constituted

32

the third-largest national group. As with other statistics relating to such offences, the most notable feature is the predominance of foreigners. It is also worth noting that the problem of absenteeism was a relatively minor one, involving a very small proportion of the workforce.[82]

Such structural resistance as there was in industry never posed a serious direct threat to the régime's stability or authority. Absenteeism, for example, never involved more than a small proportion of workers at any given time and, along with other forms of disruption, was dealt with as quickly and efficiently as could be expected. The picture which emerges is one of marginal industrial-relations problems reflecting a latent opposition which was potentially widespread but never put to the test.

DEMORALIZATION AND DEFEAT

During the early years of the war the Austrian working class, as citizens of the *Reich*, had been spared many of the privations suffered by those in other parts of Europe. In the latter years of the war the increasing shortages and deteriorating quality of food and consumer goods sharpened attitudes towards the régime.

The beginning of 1942 marked a turning point in the food situation. The local difficulties which had so far arisen now gave way to a general shortage of food, so that a great many people, though not starving, were consciously hungry. The availability of food was often less than the ration allowed. From western Austria, for example, there were frequent complaints about the shortage and poor quality of eggs.[83] The shortages were of course most acutely felt in large cities and other industrial areas, where – as early as 1942 – doubts were expressed about the *Reich's* capability for economic survival, and (perhaps rather hasty) comparisons drawn with 1918. Rumours of forthcoming reductions in bread, meat and fat rations had a direct effect on working-class opinion, and there was particular concern among those with long walks to work or no access to canteens, such as transport workers and shift workers. Working wives also pointed out that their households in particular used more bread since lunch hours were not long enough to prepare a warm meal.[84]

The régime's aim of avoiding the widespread hunger and disaffection of the First World War[85] became more difficult to fulfil as the tide of war turned. Occupied Europe had borne the brunt of keeping the *Reich* well-fed and, the régime hoped, relatively happy. As the occupied territories were lost it became more and more difficult to maintain adequate food supplies.

In September 1942 Ernst Kaltenbrunner, a leading Austrian Nazi – he had replaced Heydrich as head of the *Reichssicherheitshauptamt* – gave an unsolicited assessment of the mood in Austria. The mood in Vienna, among all classes, was one of dejection and confusion and the city was rife with rumour from the Eastern Front. Austrian nationalism was on the increase, creating fertile ground for the Communist Party, and the mood in the working-class districts of the outer suburbs, particularly before work or at the change of shifts, was decidedly unpleasant.[86] Successive situation reports from Austria in the last winter of war confirm this impression. They describe morale deteriorating rapidly in the face of food shortages, lack of heating fuel, resignation in the face of defeat and fear of the advancing Red Army. Severe food shortages occurred in the winter of 1944–45, and in the first week of March 1945 the SD in Vienna reported unrest among the working class as a result of the cuts in fat and bread rations.

A week later the SD were reporting a situation in Vienna's working-class districts which was so alarming that Berlin asked for independent confirmation. For the most part these districts were no-go areas for Nazis who were regularly cursed, threatened and even stoned. Women played a leading role in the disturbances, protecting rioters and organizing protests and demonstrations. Confirmation of the reports came from Nazi district leaders in Vienna on 2 April, by which time the Soviets were already at the outskirts of the city.[87]

The Soviet presence in eastern Austria damaged rather than enhanced the popularity of the KPÖ, and the party attracted the support of only 5 per cent of the electorate in the election of that year. Social Democrats on the other hand re-emerged as a significant force in the Second Republic, and the healing of any rift between left and right within the party was reflected in the decision to drop both 'democratic' and 'revolutionary' from the new party's title: *Sozialistische Partei Österreichs* (SPÖ). Such influence as the Communists retained in 1945 declined rapidly; like its predecessor in the First Republic the SPÖ of the Second Republic has been able to count on the loyalty of the majority of working-class voters, while both the membership and electoral support of the Communist Party have become statistically negligible.

CONCLUSION

Between 1929 and 1945 the working class faced a political offensive from the right whose origins lay in the resentment provoked by the achievements of the coalition government of 1918–20, and afterwards by the municipality of Vienna. The ability of workers to respond was restricted on all sides. The hesitant political leadership of the labour movement avoided open conflict for fear of losing what had been gained; the economic position of workers themselves was undermined by the depression, and when a conflict eventually came, few of them felt certain enough of the outcome to put their livelihoods on the line.

By the time the economy began to improve workers were leaderless and faced a system of surveillance and terror which defied collective action. Industrial action was rare, limited in its objectives and often unsuccessful. The organized resistance operated outside the working-class community, and those who did participate were quickly detected and arrested. The combined effects of repression and domestic distractions prompted people from all sections of society to withdraw from any sort of public life into the domestic sphere.

Consequently, despite all the unrest there was no repetition in 1945 of the revolutionary upheavals of 1918. The overwhelming impression of workers' behaviour during the years of 'total war' is one of individual preoccupations, and distractions increased as aerial bombardment intensified and the front line drew nearer to Austrian territory.

Yet resistance was not held at bay by repression alone. In the early years of occupation and war the régime had managed to neutralize much working-class opposition, first by providing employment and then in attempts to maintain living standards well into the war. Many of the problems which occurred in these years might arguably be accounted for by the return to a full-employment economy. If workers were never integrated into a 'people's community' of the type which Nazi propaganda idealized, and their querulousness at work and at home indicates they were never really won over, potential dissent was muted. When, later the régime failed to deliver the goods, the popular mood soured noticeably, and underlying resentments resurfaced.

The working class and politics

NOTES AND REFERENCES

1. Of course, this category does not correspond exactly to the industrial working class as the term is normally understood. It includes artisans and excludes transport workers. However, it does give some indication of the geographical distribution of the working class.
2. 'Wien im großdeutschen Reich. Eine statistisch Untersuchung über die Lage Wiens nach der Wiedervereinigung der Ostmark in das deutsche Reich' in Gerhard Botz, *Wien vom Anschluß zum Krieg. Nationalsozialistische Machtübernahme und politisch-soziale Umgestaltung am Beispiel der Stadt Wien, 1938–1939* (Vienna, 1978) pp. 589–637. Original in Bestand des Statistischen Amts der Stadt Wien. (Original at the Vienna Statistical Office Magistraturabteilung 66).
3. Melanie Sully, *Continuity and Change in Austrian Social Democracy. The Eternal Quest for a Third Way* (Boulder, Colorado 1982) p. 109.
4. *Statistisches Handbuch für die Republik Österreich*, vol. XII (Vienna, 1931) pp. 207–10.
5. Norbert Leser, *Zwischen Reformismus und Bolschewismus. Der Austromarxismus als Theorie und Praxis* (Vienna, 1968) p. 320. See also Charles A. Gulick, *Austria from Habsburg to Hitler* (Berkeley and Los Angeles, 1948), Vol. 1 ('Labour's Workshop of Democracy') pp. 190–255, for a detailed account of this legislation.
6. See Jill Lewis, 'Red Vienna: Socialism in One City', *European Studies Review*, Vol. 13 (1983).
7. Francis L. Carsten, *Revolution in Central Europe 1918–1919* (London, 1972) p. 302.
8. See Gulick, *Habsburg to Hitler*, (Vol. 2) pp. 1374–80.
9. Francis L. Carsten, *The First Austrian Republic 1918–1938*, (Aldershot 1986) p. 122.
10. See Bruce F. Pauley, 'The Social and Economic Background of Austria's *Lebensunfähigkeit*' in Anson Rabinbach (ed.), *The Austrian Socialist Experiment. Social Democracy and Austromarxism, 1918–1934*, Boulder and London, 1985, pp. 21–37.
11. *Statistical Year Book of the League of Nations 1937–1938* (Geneva, 1938) p. 65.
12. Cf. Hans Kernbauer and Fritz Weber 'Von der Inflation zur Depression. Österreichs Wirtschaft 1818–1934' in E. Tálos and W. Neugebauer (eds.) *'Austrofaschismus'. Beiträge über Politik, Ökonomie and Kultur 1934–1938* (Vienna, 1984) pp. 1–30.
13. *Statistical Year Book of the League of Nations 1937–1938* (Geneva, 1938) p. 65.
14. School-leavers were also excluded from claiming benefit. Karl Stadler, *Austria* (London, 1971) p. 124.
15. Marie Jahoda, Paul F. Lazarsfeld, Hans Zeisel, *Marienthal. The Sociography of an Unemployed Community* (London, 1974), originally *Die Arbeitslosen von Marienthal*, (Leipzig, 1933).
16. Ibid., p. 19, p. 26.
17. Jill Lewis, *The Failure of Styrian Labour in the First Austrian Republic*, Ph.D dissertation (Lancaster, 1984) p. 246.

18. *Statistisches Handbuch für die Republik Österreich*, vol XII (Vienna, 1931), p. 181; vol. XIV, (Vienna, 1933) p. 170.
19. Melanie Sully, *Political Parties and Elections in Austria* (London, 1981), p. 123.
20. Lewis, *Styrian Labour*, p. 236.
21. Gerhard Botz, 'Strukturwandlungen des österreichischen National-sozialismus' in Isabella Ackerl *et al.*, *Politik im alten und neuen Österreich Festschrift für Rudolf Neck zum 60 Geburtstag* (Vienna, 1981) p. 185; p. 176.
22. Robert Hinteregger, 'Die steirische Arbeiterschaft zwischen Monarchie und Faschismus' in Gerhard Botz, H. Hautmann, H. Konrad and J. Weidenholzer (eds.) *Bewegung und Klasse. Studien zur österreichischen Arbeitergeschichte*, (Vienna, 1978) pp. 269–96. Here p. 281f. F.L. Carsten, *Fascist Movements in Austria From Schönerer to Hitler* (London, 1977), pp. 122–3.
23. Everhard Holtmann, *Zwischen Unterdrückung und Befriedung. Sozialistische Arbeiterbewegung und autoritäres Regime in Österreich 1933–1938*, (Vienna, 1978) p. 26.
24. Jahoda *et al.*, pp. 39–42.
25. Gerhard Botz, 'Strategies of Political Violence: Chance Events and Structural Effects as Causal Factors in the February Rising of the Austrian Social Democrats.' in Rabinbach (ed.) *The Austrian Socialist Experiment*, pp. 99–118, here p. 110.
26. Cf. Emmerich Tálos and Walter Manoschek, 'Zum Konstituierungsprozeβ des Austrofaschismus' in Tálos and Neugebauer, '*Austrofaschismus*', pp. 31–52.
27. Carsten, *First Republic*, p. 189; G.E.R. Gedye, *Fallen Bastions. The Central European Tragedy*, (London, 1939) pp. 101ff.
28. Kurt Peball, 'Februar 1934: Die Kämpfe' in *Das Jahr 1934: 12 Februar. Protokoll des Symposiums in Wien am 5 Februar 1974* (Vienna, 1975) pp. 25–33; Ilona Duczynska, *Workers in Arms, the Austrian Schutzbund and the Civil War of 1934*, (London, 1978) pp. 167–71.
29. Peball, 'Die Kämpfe' p. 30; Lewis, *Styrian Labour* pp. 282–4.
30. Duczynska, *Workers in Arms*, p. 172.
31. Brigitte Perfahl, 'Linz und Steyre: Zentren der Kämpfe' in Josef Weidenholzer, Brigitte Perfahl and Hubert Hummer '*Es Wird nicht mehr verhandelt . . .*' *Der 12. Februar in Oberösterreich* (Linz, 1984) pp. 25–56; here pp. 49–56.
32. Duczynska, *Workers in Arms*, p. 173.
33. Hubert Hummer, 'Der Widerstand auf dem Land' in Weidenholzer *et al.*, op. cit. pp. 57–81.
34. Peball, 'Die Kämpfe' p. 30.
35. Holtmann, op. cit., p. 95.
36. Ibid., p. 177.
37. Ibid., pp. 95–143.
38. Ibid., pp. 27–8.
39. Ibid., p. 180. Radomir Luza, quoting *Komunistcá Internacionála* (Prague, 1972), a publication of the Czech Communist Party, puts the increase in party membership at over 500 per cent (rising from 3,000 to 16,000) within 'a few months'. Radomir Luza, *The Resistance in Austria*

1938–1945, (Minneapolis, 1984), p. 22. Richard Bernaschek, leader of the Linz *Schutzbund* and instigator of the fighting in February, was one such tactical convert.

40. See, for example, the discussion of Kurt Peball's paper '*Diskussion zum Beitrag Peball in Das Jahr 1934: 12 Februar. Protokoll des Symposiums in Wien am 5 Februar 1974*' (Vienna 1975). Compare the debate between Conan Fischer and Dick Geary concerning Nazi penetration of the working class in Germany, *European History Quarterly*, 1985, Nos 3 and 4.

41. Willibald I. Holzer, *Im Schatten des Faschismus. Der österreichische Widerstand gegen den Nationalsozialismus 1938–1945* (Vienna, 1981).

42. Gerhard Botz, 'Changing Patterns of Support for Austrian National Socialism 1918–1945' in Stein Larsen, *et al. Who Were the Fascists?* (Oslo, 1979) pp. 202–226, p. 216.

43. Botz, 'Strukturwandlungen', p. 186.

44. See the publications in the series *Widerstand und Verfolgung in Österreich* prepared and published by the *Dokumentationsarchiv des Österreichischen Widerstands* (DÖW) under the general editorship of Wolfgang Neugebauer.

45. Holtman, op. cit., pp. 279–81.

46. Gedye, op. cit., pp. 262–8.

47. See Siegrfied Mattl, 'Die Finanzdiktatur. Wirtschaftspolitik in Österreich 1933–1938' in Tálos and Neugebauer, "*Austrofaschismus*", pp. 133–60.

48. Dietmar Stanzel, 'Die Arbeitslosigkeit in der Ersten republik in problemorientierter Sicht' *Zeitgeschichte*, November 1985, pp. 52–65, here pp. 61–2.

49. Cf. Robert Schwarz, '*Sozialismus*' der Propaganda. *Das Werben des 'Völkischen Beobachters' um die österreichische Arbeiterschaft 1938–1939* (Vienna, 1975).

50. Gerhard Botz, *Wien vom Anschluβ zum Krieg*, pp. 129–38.

51. Unemployment fell by 40.5 per cent from 21.7 per cent of the workforce in 1937 to 12.9 per cent in 1938. Felix Butschek, *Die österreichische Kriegswirtschaft 1938–1945* (Stuttgart, 1978), p. 60.

52. USNA Captured German Records Microfilmed at Alexandria T84 R14 41106. (SD situation reports from Vienna). 18 September 1939.

53. Österreichisches Staatsarchiv: Abt. Allgemeines Verwaltungsarchiv. Reichskommissar für die Wiedervereinigung Österreichs mit dem deutschen Reich (Bürckel-Akten) 72/1907.

54. Stephen Salter, *The Mobilisation of German Labour 1939–1945. A Contribution to the History of the German Working Class*, D.Phil. dissertation, Oxford 1983, pp. 17–37.

55. Butschek, op. cit., p. 124.

56. Hans Pfahlmann, *Fremdarbeiter und Kriegsgefangene in der deutschen Kriegswirtschaft 1939–1945* (Darmstadt, 1968).

57. BA/MA (German Federal Military Archives, Freiburg) RW 21–38 K I R, RII-KAA I IH7, I I

58. Harry Slapnicka, *Oberösterreich als es Oberdonau hieβ (1938–1945)*, Linz, (1978) p. 172; Helmut Fiereder, *Reichswerke Hermann Göring in Österreich (1938–1945)*, (Vienna/Salzburg, 1983) p. 217.

Austria

59. See T.W. Mason, *Arbeiterklasse und Volksgemeinschaft. Dokumente und Materialien zur deutschen Arbeiterpolitik 1933–1939*, (Opladen, 1975) and Stephen Salter, *The Mobilisation of German Labour 1939–1945*.
60. Butschek, op. cit., p. 67.
61. See Karl Stadler, *Österreich 1938–1945 im Spiegal der NS-Akten* (Vienna, 1966).
62. This position was made clear by the exiled leadership in Paris. See *Der Sozialistische Kampf* No. 3, 2 July 1938, p. 53f., cited in DÖW, *Widerstand und Verfolgung in Wien 1934–1945 Eine Dokumentation*, (Vienna, 1975) Vol. 2, pp. 42–3 (Doc. 54). This position did not prevent the continuation of Socialist resistance on the ground in Austria (see Luza, op. cit. Chapter 9), but the Communist resistance was numerically overwhelmingly more important.
63. See Karl Stadler, *Austria* (London, 1971) p. 146f; Luza, op. cit., pp. 81–3.
64. DÖW, *Widerstand und Verfolgung in Wien 1934–1945. Eine Dokumentation*, Vol. 2, p. 79. In a quantitative analysis of a resistance élite based on a sample of 2,307, Luza categories 887 (51.06 per cent) as skilled or unskilled workers, about 80 per cent of whom belonged to the KPÖ. Luza, op. cit., p. 305.
65. DÖW 5120 SD Wien, Außenstelle 3 28.6.1938.
66. DÖW, *Wien*, Vol. 2, pp. 309–400; *Widerstand und Verfolgung in Oberösterreich 1934–1945. Eine Dokumentation* (Vienna, 1982), Vol. 1, pp. 164–79 and pp. 305–35.
67. DÖW, *Wien*, Vol. 2. p. 8 and pp. 46–50 (Doc. 62).
68. Instances are recorded in the DÖW series, for example, *Wien II*, p. 393 Doc. 158a; p. 399, Doc. 168.
69. Thomas M. Barker, *The Slovene Minority of Carinthia*, (New York, 1972) p.199/ Ch. 6. There was often an exchange of fire, and a number of dead and wounded, and in such cases firearms and ammunition were also taken, where possible. Other attacks were mainly to gain supplies of food, clothes and medicine. The Nazis responded with reprisals.
70. BA/MA RW 21–24/22.
71. See Stephen Salter, 'Structures of Consensus and Coercion: Workers' Morale and the Maintenance of Work-Discipline 1939–1945' in David Welch (ed.) *Nazi Propaganda. The Power and the Limitations* (London, 1983) pp. 88–116.
72. DÖW, *Wien I*, p. 407ff.
73. Notably by T.W. Mason; see 'The Workers' Opposition in Nazi Germany', *History Workshop Journal 11*, 1981, pp. 120–37.
74. BAK R58/446 Vienna, September 1938.
75. BAK R58.723. *Stimmungsbericht von Steyr und Umgebung* (August 1938); Fiereder, *Reichswerke*, pp. 103–4.
76. DÖW 1576.
77. Mason, *Arbeiterklasse*, Chapter XX.
78. DOW Film 78 (BAK R58 1210) Gestapo TR 5 12–15.9.1939.
79. SD Wien 25.10.1939 40965.
80. BA/MA RW 20–17/12 28.3.1940.
81. Stefan Karner, 'Arbeitsvertragsbrüche als Verletzung der Arbeitpflicht im Dritten Reich. Darstellung und EDV-Analyse am Beispiel der

The working class and politics

untersteirischen UDM-Luftfahrwerkes Marburg/Maribor' in *Archiv für Sozialgeschichte*, XXI, 1982, pp. 269–328.
82. DÖW 13.288. Some distortion arises out of the different treatment of Germans and foreigners.
83. Heinz Boberach (ed.) *Meldungen aus dem Reich. Die geheimen Lageberichte des Sicherheitsdienstes der SS 1938–1945* (Herrsching, 1984) Vol. 9, p. 3189, 19.1.1942.
84. Ibid., p. 3448 12.3.1942.
85. T. W. Mason, *Sozialpolitik im Dritten Reich. Arbeiterklasse und Volksgemeinschaft* (Opladen, 1977) Chapter 1.
86. 'Ein unbekannter bericht Kaltenbrunners über die Lage in Osterreich im September 1944' in Ludwig Jedlicka, *Der 20. Juli 1944*, (Vienna, 1965) pp. 92–5. Cited in Stadler, *Austria*, p. 248 DÖW 5120.
87. Karl Stadler, *Austria*, pp. 248–50.

CHAPTER THREE
Finland

David Kirby

THE WORKING CLASS: CONDITIONS

The classic working class of urbanized industrialized western Europe has never featured prominently in Finnish life. In 1940, almost three-quarters of Finland's population of 3.7 m. lived in the countryside. The industrial workforce had risen above the 200,000 mark in the late 1930s, but only 18 per cent of the economically active population in 1940 was engaged in manufacturing, mining and construction, in comparison with 37 per cent in neighbouring Sweden.

The rural, agrarian character of inter-war Finland invites ready comparison with the other new states of eastern Europe. It would however be misleading to equate Finland with Romania or even Poland, for the economic infrastructure of the northern republic was somewhat different from that of the more fertile southern countries. There was no wealthy landowning aristocracy, for instance, nor were there huge latifundia of the kind found in parts of eastern or southern Europe. In 1929, three-quarters of the landholdings in Finland were smaller than ten hectares, an even greater proportion than in 1901. The development of producers' co-operatives and the relatively high levels of agriculture expertise and training helped ease some of the burdens of farming; but the smallholder, trying to earn a living in an inhospitable climate and on stony, poor soil, was essentially farming to feed his family. Many thousands had to seek work in the forests during the long winter months in order to make ends meet.

The huge increase in demand for pit-props, deals, boards and battens in western Europe during the last quarter of the nineteenth century effectively saved Finland from agricultural and social crisis. The 'green gold' gave a welcome injection of capital into agriculture, stimulated the land market, and also provided work for thousands of the rural proletariat during the winter months. A survey of working conditions amongst lumberjacks and loggers carried out in 1921 estimated that over 80,000 workers were thus employed, whilst a meeting of unemployed workers in Rovaniemi at the end of 1929 claimed that there was normally work for 20,000 men in the forests of Lapland during the winter months. In 1946, admittedly an exceptional year in view of the massive demand for timber on world markets, over 250,000 were employed in the forests.[1] Between them, the timber and paper industries accounted for over 80 per cent of the total value of Finnish exports between the wars, and provided employment for between one-quarter and one-third of the industrial workforce. In sum, Finnish society, as the sociologist Heikki Waris noted in 1948, was composed largely of people with meagre resources: workers – mostly on the land or in the forests – and small farmers.[2]

SOCIETY AND GOVERNMENT

The demand for timber had far-reaching effects upon the rural economy and society. The influx of capital helped break up the patriarchal society of rank. Those who prospered distanced themselves from their farmhands, whom they had once lodged and fed under their own roof. The living conditions of the farmworkers were often poor. A survey conducted in 1919–20 found that a large proportion of the wages of skilled farm workers such as dairymen and bailiffs was paid in kind, especially in remote districts. Single-roomed dwellings were common, and the survey revealed that 69.5 per cent of these single rooms were occupied by at least four persons. For the farm worker with a family 'living conditions in Finland are in large measure unsatisfactory', the report concluded.[3] Many of the small farmers, especially in the north and east, lived in equally depressing circumstances, and overcrowding was also a serious problem in working-class quarters of the large towns.

The economic resurgence in the last decades of the nineteenth century was accompanied by a flurry of organizational activity inspired by Finnish nationalism. The labour movement which began to emerge in the 1880s was very much a part of this development. Lacking a middle class sufficiently numerous, articulate and self-confident to pursue the struggle against the Swedish-speaking élite, the Finnish-language nationalists had to turn to the common people. The youth clubs and temperance societies, and the workers' associations, were part of this drive to mobilize the people. Social reformists from the nationalist camp continued to play an active role in the provincial labour movement even after the workers' party formed in 1899 adopted a Marxist programme in 1903. After 1905, however, the situation changed. During the patriotic national strike which was Finland's contribution to the 1905 revolution within the Russian Empire, organized labour gained a degree of self-confidence which it had hitherto lacked. Thousands flocked to join the party; by 1906, it could claim over 85,000 members, a fivefold increase within two years. Most of these new recruits lived and worked in the countryside, and it was the rural poor who voted for the social democratic party in large numbers in the elections to the reformed parliament after 1907. The party's rough-and-ready touring agitators offered a new kind of evangelism to a people for whom religious faith had earlier offered a more certain solace and identity than the romantic notions of the élitist nationalists, and the party also proved more adept than the two Finnish nationalist parties at organizing key groups such as the leasehold farmers. In short, the labour movement was able to offer a means of cultural identity, as well as acting as the articulator of the aspirations of the proletariat.[4]

The whole-hearted identification of the rural and industrial working class with the social-democratic labour movement endured even the tragedy of civil war, which erupted during the early days of independence in 1918. The collapse of tsarism led to a crisis of political authority in Finland as well as in the rest of the empire. Growing economic and social distress further aggravated tensions, which an abortive general strike in November 1917 did little to dispel. The non-socialist government which took office after this strike preferred coercion to compromise in endeavouring to establish its authority, and in so doing effectively extinguished the faint possibility of a peaceful accord with the labour movement. Under pressure from the radical Red Guards, bombarded with pleas from the rank and file for some sort of action to alleviate distress, the SDP leadership reluctantly took the decision to seize power at the end of January 1918.

The three months during which a Red government exercised power in southern Finland were distinguished by the fact that the Finnish People's Commissariat showed little inclination to imitate the example set by Lenin: the Finnish revolution, such as it was, followed a strictly democratic path. Unlike other labour movements which became caught up in the turmoils of civil strife, the Finnish social democrats remained united. Those who disapproved of the seizure of power either withdrew into private life, or swallowed their qualms and took office in the service of the People's Commissariat. Furthermore, large numbers volunteered to fight on the Red side in a full-blooded war, fought along a front stretching from the Gulf of Bothnia to the Karelian isthmus. Over 80,000 Reds were placed in prison camps at the end of the war and up to one-quarter of these prisoners perished of hunger and disease. Thousands more were shot out of hand or executed after trial.[5]

The social democratic party was revived in the autumn of 1918 by moderates who had remained on the sidelines during the civil war, and within a year had registered over 67,000 members. The victorious Allies insisted on the full restitution of democracy in a country which had closely tied itself to Germany during the last months of the war, and in the March 1919 elections, 356,046 voters (38 per cent of the total) returned eighty social democrats to the 200-member parliament. This massive show of solidarity was not to last. The party leadership came under fire from the rank and file for failing to press vigorously for an amnesty for those imprisoned for their part in the civil war, and in 1920, dissident elements formed the Finnish socialist workers' party (*Suomen sosialistinen työväenpuolue* – SSTP). In the 1922 elections, the SSTP took over one-third of the votes cast for the left. One year later, the government struck. The entire parliamentary group and leading officials of the SSTP were arrested, the party was disbanded and its assets sequestrated.

The dissolution of the SSTP effectively brought to a close an era in which the rural poor had rallied enthusiastically to a movement which offered the prospect of self-improvement and promised a new world. During its period of maximum membership growth, the SDP had recruited strongly amongst the leaseholders and landless labourers of the southern and south-western provinces, and this 'Red' area remained loyal to the party after the civil war. The SSTP failed to build up an effective organization in the farming regions of Satakunta, Häme and Mikkeli: the social democratic party could count on the support of between one-third and a half of the electorate in these areas, where the rival left-wing party barely managed to clear the 10 per cent level. In the north of the country, where SDP organization before 1917 had been rather weak, the pattern was reversed. Here, the SSTP took over the old party organization, and attracted far more votes than its rival, though not as many as the agrarian party. Isolated and impoverished, the small farmers and workers of these northern regions rallied to the SSTP in much the same way as their compatriots further south had done some twelve years earlier; the SSTP acted as the radical voice of their aspirations for a better life.

The break-up of the socialist workers' party virtually destroyed the last traces of a genuine, if unsophisticated native radicalism, and thereby strengthened the position of the illegal Finnish communist party (*Suomen Kommunistinen puolue* – SKP). The communist party had been founded in Moscow in August 1918 by exiled leaders of the abortive Finnish revolution. Racked by internal quarrels, it was unable to establish any sort of ascendancy over the SSTP, some of whose leaders showed a marked disinclination to follow the dictates of the exiles. It was amongst the younger working-class element that the Communist party gained its best recruits. The 'backwoods communism' of the northern periphery was more than balanced by 'industrial communism', for in towns with large-scale industrial enterprises such as Turku and Helsinki, the SSTP attracted more support than the SDP. The SDP enjoyed considerable support however amongst the textile workers of Tampere, and in towns where the local party was led by left-wingers.[6]

The success of the labour movement in the political arena stands in stark contrast to the relative weakness of the trade unions, which had failed to make much headway in establishing the principle of free collective bargaining before independence.[7] It was at the place of work that the class struggle was at its bitterest in post-civil-war Finland. The temporary gains made by the unions during the revolution of 1917, such as the eight-hour day, were eroded, and many employers were reluctant to take back any worker who had fought on the Red side in the civil war. The 'Red' worker was often a marked man in the factories and workshops. Similarly, those suspected of having 'White' sympathies were often given a rough time by their workmates, especially in lumber camps and on building sites. Poverty and indebtedness forced many small farmers as well as landless workers to seek work in the forests, on loading sites and log-floats. The existence of this large pool of rural labour also enabled the employers to recruit strikebreakers with ease. An unofficial dockers' strike early in 1919 prompted the employers' federation (STK) to take up the idea of recruiting strikebreaking volunteers, and in 1920, a general meeting of employers endorsed the idea. The strikebreaking organization which was subsequently set up (*Vientirauha*) was largely under the control of one man, Martti Pihkala, who could boast in 1925 that the word 'scab' no longer held any fears for workers who signed up with his organization. By the end of 1928, *Vientirauha* had over 20,000 men on its books. At the same time, membership of the unions affiliated to the national trade union federation (*Suomen Ammattijärjestö* – SAJ) had reached a peak of over 90,000. Some 30 per cent of the industrial workforce were unionized, but no more than 13 per cent of all workers.[8]

By 1920, the communists had succeeded in capturing control of most of the large trade unions, such as the woodworkers, transport workers and engineers; two-thirds of the delegates at the fifth congress of the SAJ voted in a communist majority on the executive committee. The overtly political tactics of the communist leadership of the unions in the early 1920s not only invited police repression and arrests, and the unremitting hostility of the employers, who refused to negotiate with communist-led unions: it also alienated many left radicals, who began to call for a breach with the émigré communist leadership. In the mid-1920s, the grip of the communists over the SAJ weakened. An accord was reached in 1926, whereby the decision to affiliate to Profintern (the communist Trade-Unionist International) was rescinded and the unions declared independent of political parties. A social democrat was elected chairman of the SAJ, though communists retained two-thirds of the seats on the executive committee. This relatively harmonious phase came to an end in 1928, when Comintern launched a new offensive against social democracy.[9]

The break-up of the fragile unity of the trade-union movement occurred against the background of two major labour conflicts, a lockout in the engineering industry in 1927 and a strike of dockworkers in 1928. Both conflicts were terminated by government intervention, on terms unfavourable for the workers. *Vientirauha* recruited over 15,000 men to break the dockers' strike, which was seen by the employers as a fight against communist influence. In May 1929, the social democratic minority broke with the 1926 accord and resigned all offices in the SAJ. By the end of the year, the social democrats had withdrawn from the SAJ and had set up their own rival organization. The communists, obedient to the call of Moscow, plunged the weakened union movement into a futile series of unsuccessful political strikes and demonstrations in the autumn of 1929, thereby playing into the hands of those who were clamouring for tough action against communism in the country.[10]

Between 1925 and 1928, the Finnish economy had experienced rapid growth. The number of industrial undertakings rose by one-fifth, the number of people employed in industry by 20 per cent, and the gross value of production by 33 per cent. The volume of foreign trade in 1928 was half as much again as it had been in 1913. This boom period began to come to an end in 1928, rather sooner than was the case elsewhere in Europe. In 1927, sawmills had had to pay high prices for timber, at a time when world prices were beginning to fall sharply. The dockers' strike in 1928 delayed shipments, and the re-entry of Russia into an already glutted world market forced down prices even more. As a consequence, the sawmill owners' association agreed to reduce output and to restrict timber felling. Stumpage prices paid to the farmers who owned much of the forested land fell sharply: a bad harvest in 1928 and falling world prices for agricultural produce also badly affected the small and medium-size farms which dominated Finnish agriculture.[11] Many farmers were burdened with short-term debts, and found themselves in severe difficulties, especially as the fall in land values affected securities for loans. Thousands of farms had to be sold up: in 1933, the peak year, 4,267 went under the auctioneer's hammer. The agrarian league was accused of having become an establishment party, indifferent to the plight of the small farmer, and a variety of protest movements sprang up around the country. The catastrophic crop failure in northern Finland in 1928 gave the communists an opportunity to organize the small farmers, in line with the 'third phase' decreed by Comintern, which sought to mobilize the peasantry into revolutionary action. A communist-led famine movement was organized, and sent representatives to the Berlin peasant congress in March 1930.

In spite of strenuous efforts to infiltrate and capture control of certain of the more promising 'depression movements', however, the communists achieved little success. Attempts to organize a national movement of peasant committees were soon stifled by the upsurge of a militant anti-communist movement and official suppression of all overt communist activities. The party leadership in exile failed to come up with a consistent strategy: its directives were often confused, leaving the agents in the field to cope as best they could. In addition, the party organized in Finland had been gravely weakened by arrests, and those still at large were under close surveillance not only by the police, but also the paramilitary *Suojeluskunta* and a variety of patriotic and anti-communist organizations.[12]

In the elections held in spring 1929, the socialist workers' and small peasants' electoral league won twenty-three seats, and in obedience to the new aggressive strategy of the Communist International, the new members lost no opportunity to attack the government. In the autumn, a new coalition headed by the agrarian Kyösti Kallio (who had been responsible for breaking up the socialist workers' party in 1923) began preparing legislation to deal with communist activity. At the end of November, a communist youth group, which had unwisely decided to hold a rally at Lapua, in the White heartland of Ostrobothnia, had their red shirts torn off their backs by outraged patriots. This incident was followed by a nation-wide wave of anti-communist rallies and demonstrations, many of them carefully stage-managed and financed by big business. Involuntary car rides to the Finnish–Soviet frontier were to become a favourite method of the Lapua movement for dealing with those whom it disliked, though the abduction in October 1930 of the former president of the republic, the liberal J. K. Stählberg, was an undoubted error of political judgement. Up until that time, the Lapua movement seemed to be carrying all before it. The Kallio government had banned the publication of all communist newspapers in June, and had all the communist members of parliament arrested on charges of plotting treason. In spite of his tough stand, Kallio was persuaded by the president to resign in favour of the hero of 1918, P. E. Svinhufvud. The avowed aims, if not the deeds of the Lapua movement were hailed by leading politicians in the agrarian and conservative parties, and the elections called after the government had failed to achieve the necessary five-sixths majority for the immediate promulgation of the anti-communist laws held in an atmosphere of violence and hostility towards the labour movement in general. The few communist candidates who stood for election received only a small fraction of the 1929 vote, and although the social democrats increased their representation by seven to sixty-six, this was not enough to block the passage of legislation designed to outlaw communist activity, and a revision of the electoral law. In 1931, Svinhufvud was narrowly elected president on the third ballot by the electoral college, after considerable pressure had been brought to bear on waverers by leaders of Lapua and the *Suojeluskunta*.[13]

With the communists effectively crushed, the men of Lapua now turned their attentions to social democracy. At the end of February 1932, a mob tried to break up a socialist meeting at Mäntsälä, a small town some thirty miles to the north of the capital. Attempts by the police to disperse the mob led to resistance, to which the Lapua movement gave its backing. Svinhufvud ordered the rebels to disperse, and the town was sealed off by army units. Lacking any effective support from the *Suojeluskunta* leadership or the army high command, the rebels meekly surrendered on 6 March, receiving remarkably light sentences for their indiscretion.

The failure of the Mäntsälä revolt exposed the bankruptcy of the Lapua movement, which was at bottom little more than a crude form of redneck anti-communism, lacking effective leadership or consistent aims. It was incapable of channelling and sustaining the economic grievances of the poor farmer or unemployed worker: several protest meetings were organized by the movement, but no organization ever grew out of these rallies. The Patriotic People's Movement (IKL) which was founded a month after Mäntsälä appealed to authoritarian nationalists of the educated élite, and failed to strike deep roots amongst the populace at large. The agrarian party, some of whose leaders had flirted with the Lapua movement, rallied in defence of constitutional democracy after 1932, and the conservative party also broke off its links with the IKL in 1934. The Lapua movement had served to crush communism and to cow the labour movement: having achieved this objective, it had become something of an embarrassment to its wealthier backers and to conservative politicians who had spent much of their lives extolling the virtues of the Finnish constitution.

The aggressive and crude tactics of the Lapua movement also offended the spirit of national reconciliation, which many intellectuals had espoused in the aftermath of the civil war. The campaigns to rally the people as a whole in defence of constitutional liberties in the early 1900s had revealed how little those who lived in poverty and isolation knew or cared about such values. The experience of civil war prompted many intellectuals to ponder over the 'maturity' of the Finnish people for independent statehood.[14] At a more practical level, national organizations such as the *Martta-yhdistys*, founded in 1899 to promote the message of self-help, sobriety and patriotism to working-class women, greatly expanded their activities: the *Martta-yhdistys* could claim a membership of over 30,000 by 1923.[15] Teachers in the elementary schools were in the forefront of attempts to inculcate national values, and the minutes of their annual district meetings provide a fascinating insight into what might be termed the front line of the struggle to integrate the 'deep ranks' of the people into the world of Finnish patriotic values.

There were however numerous obstacles on the path to national reconciliation, not least the parlous state of labour relations. What was really at issue in the dockers' strike was the principle of a national agreement, which the employers refused to concede, fearing that this would strengthen the unions. The 1924 law on collective bargaining remained virtually a dead letter, distrusted by employers and unions alike. Certain notorious industrialists, such as Rafael Haarla, one of the most prominent supporters of Lapua, pursued an openly anti-union policy. In 1930–31, legislation was pushed through parliament to enforce 'peace at the workplace'. Stringent controls were placed on picketing, and incitement to strike action, victimization of 'White' workers and the denunciation of strikebreakers were made punishable offences. Although few cases ever reached court, the legislation remained on the statute book until after the Second World War.[16]

The Lapua movement and mass unemployment crippled the already divided trade union movement. The SAJ was wound up by government order in the summer of 1930: the social democratic organization (SAK) had a mere 14,970 members at the end of that year, a figure which had only increased by 5,000 three years later. It is hardly surprising that *Vientirauha* was not called on once during these three years to intervene in labour disputes. On the other hand, attempts to set up 'independent' unions, with close links to the Lapua movement, failed to attract much support, and the relationship of the leaders of *Vientirauha* and the employers' federation came under some strain after 1932.[17]

The economic crisis put an end to a decade of vigorous industrial growth, and reduced the industrial workforce from a peak of 173,000 in 1928 to a low of 131,700 in 1932. Almost a quarter of the industrial labour force were registered as out of work in March 1932, when over 90,000 persons were recorded as unemployed. The Finnish state was ill-prepared to cope with the mass unemployment of the early 1930s. Unemployment relief rested with the local authorities, and many of the poor communes in the east and north were in no position to meet the demand. As a result, many men were forced to take to the road, and not a few crossed the eastern frontier in search of work in Soviet Karelia. Emergency work programmes, usually short-term, gave work to around one-third of the registered unemployed. The wages paid were poor, reflecting the general fall in earnings, which the SAK estimated in 1933 had declined by 30 per cent since 1927. The low wages paid in the paper industry caused some alarm amongst Finland's competitors, and attracted the attention of the Amsterdam-based trade union international, which carried out a survey of working conditions in Finland and the Baltic countries in 1933.[18]

The SAK ostentatiously aligned itself with the moderate international trade-union movement, but was still suspected of being under Marxist control by the employers. Although communists began to rejoin the unions from 1934, a tight control was maintained by the social democrats. Of the 72 full delegates at the 1937 SAK congress, only thirteen were communist: communist influence was largely confined to the metalworkers', transport workers' and building workers' unions. In comparison with Sweden, where nearly one million workers were organized in 1939, the SAK could only muster a membership of 70,000 in 1938, 20,000 fewer than the membership of the SAJ ten years earlier, in spite of a steady increase in the numbers of industrial workers from 1933 onwards. During the 1930s, the principle of free collective bargaining was firmly established in Sweden, and the anti-union attitudes of the Finnish employers were perceived by Swedish industrialists not only as a threat to their competitiveness in export markets because of the low wage levels of Finnish industry, but also as one of the serious weaknesses of Finnish society.[19]

The powerful position which Swedish social democracy was able to establish in the 1930s was an inspiration to the left in Finland, but was not easy to emulate. The legacy of the civil war – bourgeois suspicion and hostility, bitterness and constant reminders of the White victory – made it difficult for the SDP to break away from the past. The moderate Väinö Tanner, who dominated the party during the inter-war years, had hoped in the early years of independence to break up the bourgeois bloc and to find suitable allies on the centre-left, but no such alliance could be forged. Tanner had formed a minority social democratic government in December 1926, but had neither satisfied the demands of the labour movement for a more equable political balance – which would have involved curbing the powers of the paramilitary *Suojeluskunta*, the embodiment of the White triumph in 1918 – nor reconciled the right to full social democratic participation in public life. Within the SDP, there was a strong centre-left tendency which feared that excessive deviation towards a reformist path would drive the workers into the arms of the communists. Entry into government was accepted as preferable to the alternative, a right-wing coalition, but the centre-left held out little hope of achieving anything in office. Whereas Tanner and his supporters attempted to seek accommodation for the SDP within the bourgeois republic, those on the left like Karl Wiik, SDP secretary from 1926 to 1936, sought to maintain an unwaveringly class-conscious ideological line, and to rally the workers and small farmers to the movement.[20]

Falling membership figures and declining enthusiasm amongst the rank and file were matters of serious concern for the SDP. Recruitment drives in the mid-1920s helped stem the rot, but only temporarily. Party organizers blamed the decline – from a peak of 67,022 in 1919 to around 25,000 in 1925 and again in the early 1930s – on the disruptive activities of the communists, the indifference of workers and small farmers, and an inability to attract the young, who preferred sport and other forms of entertainment. The deleterious effects of illicit alcohol, smuggled into the country in vast quantities during the years of prohibition, was also widely held to have sapped the morale and class-consciousness of the workers. Many small rural workers' associations folded, though farmers and farm workers still constituted almost a quarter of the membership in 1931, slightly less than the proportion of industrial workers.[21]

Before independence, the labour movement had offered to thousands of manual workers an opportunity to use their leisure time in a wide range of cultural activities. The humble wooden workers' hall, usually built by the members themselves, was the focal point of this activity. During the interwar years, the fare of moral earnestness, sobriety and self-improvement of the early days proved to be less appealing and many workers' associations were obliged to rent out their premises for dances and other entertainments. Certain activities acquired their own organizational structure; workers' theatres, choral groups and bands were established in a number of the big towns: the workers' educational union supervised an extensive programme of educational and cultural activities: and sports clubs came together in 1919 to found the workers' athletics union (TUL). Within ten years, membership of the TUL had begun to outstrip that of the party, and continued to grow steadily throughout the 1930s. During the 1920s, the TUL had managed to remain outside the conflicts which divided the rest of the labour movement, in spite of the fact that the leadership was in the hands of left socialists. The communist party was slow to define its policy on sport, and when it did, the social democrats were more than ready to launch an attack to

Finland

capture control of the TUL. Although some 10,000 members were
dismissed from the TUL for defying a ban on participation in the
Moscow Spartakiad in 1928, the athletics union did not suffer the
same fate as the trade-union movement. During the early 1930s,
over 150 workers' sports clubs and a number of the district
committees of the TUL were disbanded under the anti-communist
laws, and the amount of financial aid provided by the state was cut.
Certain employers threatened to dismiss workers who participated
in TUL activities, and a number of sports clubs fell foul of the
1934 law banning the wearing of coloured shirts which could be
construed as politically provocative. In spite of these pressures,
membership remained above 30,000 throughout the Depression,
and from 1934 onwards, the fortunes of the workers' athletics union
markedly improved. Cautious moves towards co-operation with the
bourgeois athletics union (SVUL) were begun at the end of 1937.
The more relaxed political atmosphere, and the choice of Helsinki
as the host for the 1940 Olympics, helped bring the two sides closer
together, and although no official agreement was reached between
the two unions, sports contests were arranged between workers' and
bourgeois clubs in 1939.[22]

The fact that it took twenty years before a workers' football team
could play against opponents from a 'White' club is symptomatic of
the deep divisions within interwar Finnish society. The employers
continued to set their face against recognition of the principle of
free collective bargaining right up to the outbreak of the Second
World War. The paramilitary *Suojeluskunta* denied membership
to any member of the SDP and was a permanent reminder to
the working class of the bitterness of defeat in 1918. The social
democratic party still remained intact after the Lapua years, and
succeeded in increasing its parliamentary mandate to seventy-eight
seats in the 1933 elections: but it was politically isolated, and found
itself supporting politically unpalatable measures in order to keep
in office a minority government which it deemed preferable to a
right-wing coalition.

The SDP leadership also refused to consider any form of joint
front with the remnants of the communists and the left socialists.
Demands for a united front were made in 1933 by the party's young
radicals, organized in the Academic Socialist Society (ASS). Relations
between the ASS and the moderates grew increasingly strained, and
in 1937 the ASS was disaffiliated as a communist organization.
Those of its leaders who did not recant were expelled from the
party. Väinö Tanner's preferred strategy was coalition with the

53

agrarian party, and not a workers' and small farmers', alliance. The defeat of Svinhufvud in the 1937 presidential elections, after the social democratic bloc in the electoral college had swung their votes behind the agrarian candidate Kyösti Kallio, offered a more promising prospect to the party, which had won eighty-three seats in the 1936 elections. In March 1937, a coalition government of agrarians, social democrats and progressives, headed by the progressive A. K. Cajander, took up office.

The 'red-earth' Cajander government, which remained in power until the outbreak of the Winter War, was neither a 'popular front' government nor an alliance of the kind forged in 1932 between Swedish social democracy and the farmers' party. A number of social reforms, some of which had been prepared by previous governments, were passed, though these were modest by comparison with those achieved in Sweden. Above all, the restrictive laws governing trade-union activity remained on the statute book, and the appeals of the social democratic minister for social affairs for better labour relations evoked little response. In many important areas, such as the question of grain tariffs, there were serious differences between the social democrats and the agrarians: on defence, the SDP abandoned its earlier opposition to increased expenditure, and adopted a less hostile stance towards the *Suojeluskunta*.[23]

The 'red-earth' government nevertheless marked the first real step towards national reconciliation, at a time when a degree of modest prosperity was beginning to be experienced by the Finnish people as a whole. Average life expectancy had increased significantly, and the incidence of diseases of poverty and overcrowding such as tuberculosis was in decline. In 1901, the number of persons per room in the countryside was 2.4: by 1937, this had fallen to 1.8. The average family in 1940 could afford to spend proportionately more on clothing, entertainment and leisure than twenty years previously. There was a steady increase in the numbers of students in secondary and tertiary education, and although graduate unemployment had posed a problem in the early 1930s, the all-round raising of educational standards and the economic upsurge of the late 1930s gave a boost to social mobility. The emergence of a lower middle class of office workers, shop assistants and personnel in the service sector, and the doubling of the urban population between 1920 and 1940, made for a more varied social stratification and helped erode the features of a rural, patriarchal society of rank which had persisted well into the years of independence.[24] It is of course true that this was an uneven pattern: most of the country's industry and commerce was located in the south, where the farms also tended to be larger, and more mechanized than the smallholdings on the infertile northern and eastern periphery. But there were other developments which, if they did not lessen the divisions between prosperity and poverty, helped promote a sense of national identity. In this respect, the impressive and varied organizations of the labour movement, from savings banks and the consumers' co-operatives to the TUL helped integrate a working class still living under the shadow of the civil war.

Across the eastern frontier, the Karelian ASSR seemed to offer an alternative, or substitute, 'Red' Finland; but there was never a significant outflow of Finnish migrants to the socialist fatherland. The purges of the late 1930s, which scythed down much of the exiled Finnish communist leadership and effectively terminated their brief rule in Karelia, may also have dampened any residual enthusiasm for the Soviet alternative amongst the Finnish working class. It is in any event highly unlikely that the vast majority of Finnish workers and small farmers ever felt much loyalty for the Soviet system. Their main grievance was that they were treated as second-class citizens in the land of their birth. For some, communism was a way of hitting back: social democracy was a compromise with the system. There were however many within the social democratic party who also felt that the leadership was too willing to set aside principle in their eagerness to be accepted. Had the social democratic party passed entirely under the control of moderate reformists, the way would undoubtedly have been blocked to the many ex-left socialists and communists who were persuaded to vote for and even join the party in the 1930s.[25]

The brief but dramatic experience of the Winter War is generally seen as the moment when true national reconciliation was forged. Those in the Soviet Union who believed that the oppressed Finnish proletariat would welcome the Red Army as liberators were to be cruelly disappointed. Alone in a world of predatory great states, the Finnish people rallied without demur to the cause of national defence. Those intimately associated with 'White' Finland, from Marshal Mannerheim downwards, spoke warmly and appreciatively of the loyal and selfless sacrifices of the working class. In February 1940, the *Suojeluskunta* and SDP executive agreed to bury twenty years of mutual hostility and to allow socialists to join the paramilitary organization. A month earlier, after some behind-the-scenes pressure by the minister of social affairs, representatives of the SAK and the employers' federation issued a joint statement which acknowledged the significance of free trade-union activity in society and promised in future to negotiate as far as possible in a spirit of mutual understanding. Given that the employers had resolutely refused to make any such concession right up to the very outbreak of the Winter War, the so-called 'January engagement' was something of a breakthrough, even if it took a further four years before truly free and equal collective bargaining could begin.[26]

The euphoric spirit of national unity did not however long survive, though it probably helped Finland adjust to the harsh peace terms and the consequent urgent need to resettle thousands of refugees. Lack of access to raw materials and the export markets of Western Europe brought cutbacks in industrial production, with workers being laid off. Most of the regulations governing labour and production remained in force, and these, together with shortages of consumer goods and creeping inflation did little to relax tension. The SAK and social democratic leadership remained committed to the ideal of national unity, and were actively involved in the setting up of the Comrades-in-Arms League and the secret network of informers who provided the state information centre with weekly reports on the mood of the populace. Within the ranks of the labour movement, however, the autocratic control exercised by Väinö Tanner aroused discontent, and party policy came under fire from the 'group of six', three of whom were long-standing members of the centre-left opposition. The six were eventually expelled from the party and formed their own independent group in parliament. A more formidable oppositional organization was the Finnish–Soviet peace and friendship society, founded in May 1940 by left-wing socialists released from preventive detention. By the end of the year, the society could claim 40,000 members, in spite of the obstructions placed in its path by the authorities. There is little doubt that the supposedly non-political character of the society was gravely undermined from the start, and that the communists sought to use it for their own purposes, though the degree of support it achieved is indicative of a growing undercurrent of dissatisfaction with the SAK and SDP leadership.

When Finland re-entered the war in June 1941 in association with Germany, the authorities proceeded to ban the society and arrest its leaders. The six were also charged with treason and sentenced to long terms of imprisonment. Although there were instances of soldiers refusing to cross the old frontier during the advance in the autumn of 1941, the population as a whole, however, accepted the renewal of the war effort. Belief in a German victory remained strong even amongst social democratic voters until the end of 1942. The social democratic party endorsed the war aims of the government in which it was represented, and it was not until the second winter of the war that any noticeable opposition to the continuation of the war was heard in the party's ranks.[27] By the summer of 1943, that opposition had grown and had established contacts with like-minded non-socialists. In the last weeks of the war, the conflict between the Tannerites and the opposition, headed by the SAK leader Eero Wuori, became particularly fierce. Tanner's supporters were well-entrenched in the social democratic parliamentary group, which refused to join the SAK and party executive in calling upon the party's representatives to quit the government after an undertaking not to seek a separate peace had been signed by president Ryti in June 1944. Ryti's resignation in Marshal Mannerheim's favour at the beginning of August finally opened the way to peace talks with the Soviet Union, but Tanner still had sufficient support in the parliamentary group to head off an attempt to put forward the name of Eero Wuori as prime ministerial candidate.

The first real break with the past occurred on 7 November 1944, when the social democrats Wuori and K-A Fagerholm resigned from the government and precipitated its collapse. The reason given for their resignation was that the government, filled with compromised wartime figures, was utterly unsuitable for dealing with the allied control commission which had just arrived in Helsinki.[28] The new government formed by the aged conservative J. K. Paasikivi was a distinct break with the past, including one of the six imprisoned in 1941 and a communist. The communist party, now legal for the first time in Finland, sought to exploit the deep divisions in the ranks of the SDP. In this it was only partially successful. The 'six' and the communists formed the Finnish people's democratic league (*Suomen Kansan demokraattinen liitto* – SKDL) in November 1944, and under the SKDL umbrella, a range of auxiliary organizations were created. On the eve of the March 1945 elections, a section of the social democratic party joined SKDL after their pleas for an electoral alliance had been turned down by the SDP leadership. Two of the social democrats returned in the election subsequently joined the SKDL, making it the largest single group in parliament, with fifty-one members against forty-eight social democrats. This was, however, to be the furthest limit of the communist resurgence. Several of the leaders of the wartime opposition such as Wuori and Fagerholm remained in the social democratic party, and were to prove more than able at holding their own in the political and trade-union struggles of the late 1940s.[29]

CONCLUSION

The 1940s may be described as a watershed in Finland's history in a number of ways. Defeat in war, and the necessity of having to come to terms with the proximity of a great power, effectively put an end to the wilder excesses of nationalism. The experience of war had forged a great degree of national unity, and had helped efface the memory of the civil war. The war years had meant a great deal of hardship, but there had been full employment, and the pre-war divisions of class and income had been sharply eroded. The 'big three' government of social democrats, communists and agrarians which survived until 1948 instituted a number of valuable social reforms, but the truly significant shift occurred in the field of industrial relations. SAK membership had reached over 100,000 by the end of 1944, a figure which had more than tripled three years later. The general agreement hammered out with the employers' federation in 1944 provided the basis for a new era of labour relations, which saw the SAK become an integral part of the jigsaw of organizations and pressure groups. As rapid economic growth began to transform Finland from an agrarian to a highly successful manufacturing country, the trade unions were at last able to play a meaningful role, thereby bringing to an end the anomaly of deplorable industrial relations in a state where the political labour movement had enjoyed mass support for over three decades.

The social democratic party had attracted mass support after 1905 as a genuine party of the people (in contrast to the nationalist parties) and because political action seemed to offer the best means of realizing the demands of the leasehold farmer, the rural poor and the factory worker. The tragedy of the civil war served to reinforce that political choice. Those who had fought on or sympathized with the defeated Red side were easily identifiable in a predominantly rural landscape: they were unable to escape from the past. The agrarian party began to make inroads into the rural Red heartland in southern Finland, but the social democratic party could still command the loyalty of many thousands of former leaseholders. The legacy of bitterness and the sense of injustice felt at the treatment of the defeated helped keep alive this loyalty, even when social democracy no longer appeared to represent the interests of the small, independent farmer. The repression of communist activity also tended to preserve a tenacious loyalty, which resurfaced again after 1944: the strongholds of the SKDL were virtually the same as those of the SSTP in the 1920s. Above all, the civil war ensured that political action remained the most efficacious means for the working class to remedy their grievances – to achieve a degree of parity with employers at the negotiating table, to obtain state aid for cultural and sporting organizations, and ultimately, to be accepted as part of the nation. The tumultuous war years greatly changed the position of the working class in Finnish society, but this legacy of the primacy of politics as a means of articulating the demands of the working population remained deep-rooted, and has only begun to fade with the rapid socioeconomic transformation of the last three decades.

NOTES AND REFERENCES

1. *Suomen Virallinen Tilasto: Sosialisia erikoistutkimuksia xxxii:4.* Tutkimus metsä-ja uittotyöntekijäin oloista keväällä 1921, Helsinki 1923, pp. 2–3. A. Rytkösen matkaselostus 1929: Pohjolan Ammattillinen Piirijärjestö (Archives of the Finnish labour movement, Helsinki). Heikki Waris *Suomalaisen yhteiskunnan rakenne*, Helsinki 1948, p. 151.
2. Waris, 1948, pp. 183–5. Tapani Valkonen *et al. Suomalaiset, Yhteiskunnan rakenne teollistumisen aikana* Porvoo 1980, p 79.
3. Suomen Virallinen Tilasto: xxxii, Sosialisia erikoistutkimksia iii. Tutkimus Suomen maataloustyöväen oloista palkkausvuonna 1919–1920, Helsinki 1923 p. 95.
4. In elections to the 200-seat parliament between 1907 and 1916, the social democrats' mandate rose steadily from 80 to 103 seats. Hannu Soikkanen *Sosialismin tulo Suomeen* Porvoo-Helsinki 1961: David Kirby '"The Workers' Cause": Rank-and file Attitudes and Opinions in the Finnish Social Democratic Party 1905–1918' *Past and Present*, 111, 1986 pp. 137–50.
5. A. F. Upton, *The Finnish Revolution 1917–1918*, Minneapolis 1980.
6. Ilkka Hakalehto, *Suomen kommunistinen puolue ja sen vaikutus poliittiseen ja ammatilliseen työväenliikkeeseen 1918–1928*, Porvoo-Helsinki 1966 pp. 147–207: Pertti Laulajainen, *Sosiaalidemokraatti vai kommunisti*, Mikkeli 1979: David Kirby, 'New Wine in Old Vessels? The Finnish

The working class and politics

Socialist Workers' Party, 1919–1923', *Slavonic and East European Studies Review* (forthcoming).

7. Aarne Mattila, *Työmarkkinasuhteiden murros Suomessa* Helsinki 1969: Carl-Erik Knoellinger, *Labor in Finland*, New Haven 1959.

8. Markku Mansner, *Työnantajaklubista Keskusliitoksi, Suomen Työnantajan Keskusliitto ja sen edeltäjä Suomen Yleinen Työnantajanliitto 1907–1940*, Jyväskylä 1980 p. 263ff.

9. Hakalehto, pp. 208–69: Pirkko Ala-Kapee and Marjaana Valkonen, *Yhdessä elämä turvalliseksi, SAK:laisen ammattiyhdistysliikkeen kehitys vuoteen 1930*, Helsinki 1982.

10. Timo Helelä, *Työnseisaukset ja teolliset suhteet suomessa vv, 1919–1939*, (Vol. 2) Helsinki 1969 pp. 212ff.

11. Veikko Halme, *Vienti Suomen suhdannetekijänä*, Helsinki 1955, pp. 221–43, 261–7.

12. Matti Lackman, *Taistelu talonpojasta, Suomen Kommunistisen Puolueen suhde talonpoikaiskysymykseen ja talonpoikaislikkeisiin 1918–1939*. Oulu 1985, pp. 143–79.

13. For recent work on the Lapua movement, see: Juho Siltala, *Lapuan liike ja kyyditykset 1930*. Helsinki 1985. Risto Alapuro and Erik Allardt, 'The Lapua Movement: The Threat of Rightist Takeover in Finland 1930–32', in *The Breakdown of Democratic Regimes in Europe*. Juan Linz and Alfred Stepan eds., Baltimore 1978 pp. 122–41.

14. Cf. Volter Kilpi, *Tulevaisuuden edessä*, Porvoo-Helsinki 1918: Jaakko Forsman, 'Myöhästyneitä kansoja' Valvoja 1923, pp. 74–9.

15. *Martta-yhdistys 1899–1924*, Helsinki 1924 p. 63.

16. Marjaana Valkonen, *Yhdessä elämä turvalliseksi, Suomen Ammattiyhdistysten Keskusliitto 1930–1947*, Helsinki 1987 pp. 13–114. An excellent recent study of the difficulties of the labour movement in 1920s is by Pauli Kettunen, *Poliittinen liike ja sosiaalinen kollektiivisuus. Tutkimus sosialidemokratiasta ja ammattiyhdistysliikkeestä Suomessa 1918–1930*. Helsinki 1986.

17. Manser, pp. 383–400. Valkonen, pp. 141–62.

18. Valkonen, pp. 119–30.

19. Valkonen, pp. 209–23, 239–51.

20. Kettunen, pp. 283–315. Soikkanen 1975, pp. 445–60.

21. *Sos.-dem, puoluetoimikunnan ja piiritoimikuntien kertomukset vv. 1922–25*. Hämeenlinna 1925, pp. 85–142 for the detailed tales of woe provided by the district secretaries. Soikkanen 1975, pp. 531–2 for party membership figures.

22. For an excellent study of sport and politics, see Seppo Hentilä *Suomen työläisurheilun historia I Työväen Urheiluliitto 1919–1944* Hämeenlinna 1982.

23. Lauri Haataja *et al.*, *Suomen työväenliikkeen historia*, Helsinki 1977 pp. 211–19.

24. Heikki Waris, *Muuttuva suomalainen yhteiskunta* Porvoo-Helsinki 1968.

25. An analysis of communist voting behaviour in the 1930s is provided by Keijo Virtanen, *Vaihtoehtojen niukkuus. Kommunistisen liikkeen kannattajien äänestyskäyttäytyminen Suomen eduskuntavaaleissa 1930–luvulla*, Turku 1980.

26. Manser, pp. 445–50. Valkonen, pp. 276–83.

27. Hannu Soikkanen, 'Sisäpoliittiset rintamat jatkosodan aikana', in *Jatkosodan kujanjuoksu*, O. Vehviläinen, ed. Porvoo-Helsinki 1982 pp. 104–119.
28. Valkonen, pp. 394–412.
29. Upton A (1973) *Communism in Scandinavia and Finland. Politics of Opportunity.* New York. pp. 237–98.

CHAPTER FOUR

France

Roger Magraw

THE 'IN-BETWEEN YEARS' (1921–34)

The period 1921–34 long remained a wasteland in French labour historiography. Sandwiched between the heroic age of revolutionary syndicalism and the Popular Front it has been ignominiously labelled the 'in-between years'. (Y. Lequin). The labour movement appeared to lack vitality. If unemployment can be invoked to explain labour's defensive posture in the Depression of the early 1930s, the re-awakening of militancy after 1934, with the economy still in a trough, warns against any simple economistic explanation. Conservative political dominance and employers' industrial hegemony during the prosperous 1920s stemmed from the disastrous schisms in the labour movement resulting from the crushing of the labour insurgency of 1919–20.[1] Union membership declined from two million to below one million and was divided between the reformist CGT, the communist CGTU and the catholic CFTC. The schism in the Socialist Party (SFIO) in 1920 resulted in the emergence of the Communist Party (PC) which split the left-wing electorate between two rival parties. Workers were consigned to a political ghetto, excluded from the 'Republican synthesis' which rested on compromises between large-scale capitalist interests, represented by rightist parties, and the small businessmen, peasants and shopkeepers still loyal to the centrist Radical Party.

The chronic weakness of organized labour *may* be explicable in terms of the changing structures of the working class. By the 1920s the 'old' working class, the carrier of nineteenth-century syndicalist labour traditions – skilled craftsmen working in 'artisan'

workshops and living in *quartiers* with strong historic solidarities
– was dying, victim of the technological changes of the Second
Industrial Revolution accelerated by the First World War. As yet
no 'new' proletariat had matured. Within large-scale industry or
the new proletarian suburbs *(banlieues)* solidarities were not yet
forged. Employers were free to impose tight labour discipline,
'rationalization', and authoritarian paternalism, on a workforce
whose low levels of consciousness, solidarity and organization
permitted little concerted resistance.[2]

Between 1906 and 1931 the industrial labour force grew from
5.2 to 7 million. The proportion in plants with more than 100
workers rose from 25 per cent to 41.6 per cent. Coalminers
increased 75 per cent (to 300,000), car workers quintupled (to
over 100,000) and electrical-construction workers increased from
10,000 to 150,000.[3] A new industrial geography emerged. In Paris
the balance shifted from historic artisan *quartiers* to the sprawling
industrial *banlieues*. Bobigny's population grew 700 per cent between
1906 and 1931. Lyon and Marseilles were surrounded by satellite
industrial suburbs based on engineering and chemicals, while in the
south-east hydro-electric and electro-chemical schemes boomed in
the Alpine valleys.

Such shifts in industrial geography involving mass migration
and immigration may have weakened traditions, vital to trade-union
militancy, hitherto transmitted in specific crafts, workshops and
quartiers. Migration to new, 'history-less', *banlieues* engendered
disorientation, a profound 'rupture' in continuity of working-class
development. Thus in Lorraine memories of the bitter 1905 strikes
of steel workers and iron-miners were weakened by the scattering
of the population by the First World War.[4]

The strike wave of 1919–20 sparked off by pent-up feelings and
distant Bolshevik inspiration, proved the swansong of revolutionary
syndicalism's Sorelian myth of the General Strike and dreams of
workers' control. Twenty-thousand railway strikers were sacked.[5]
Annual strike levels declined from above 1,000 in the 1900s to
below 500 in 1921–34.[6] In 1931 58 per cent of all strikes and 70
per cent of those involving job-control issues were lost. In the *Nord*
two-thirds of all strikes were by relatively settled, long-established
textile workers. In Paris syndicalist traditions persisted only in small
metal-workshops – refuges for skilled craftsmen who resented the
disciplines of the assembly line – or in the shoe and furniture
workshops of the old Faubourg St. Antoine.[7]

Such structural determinism *can* be exaggerated. The allegedly 'passive', non-unionized, Paris metal-workers of the 1920s clearly included many active in the 1919 strikes. Migrants to the Paris *banlieue* included *Nord* miners, strongly unionized before 1914, and militants sacked by the authoritarian Schneider from his company town Le Creusot.[8] Did such workers forget all their previous experiences?

Possibly 'scientific management' allowed industrialists tighter control over an atomized, semi-skilled (*ouvrier-spécialisé*, OS) workforce. Here rhetoric must be distinguished from reality. Discussion of new production systems like 'Fordism' and 'Taylorism' became so fashionable that it is easy to be seduced into visualizing French large industry, as in René Clair's 1931 film *A Nous la Liberté*, as dominated by 'rationalized' plants in which robot-workers were slaves to assembly lines and time-and-motion experts. The debate about 'rationalization' was, however, laced with ironies. Reformist CGT leaders criticized the technological conservatism of French employers, urging a new deal in which unions would welcome 'American rationalization' in return for concessions on bargaining rights and shorter hours. How accurately the CGT, weak in blue-collar industry, reflected shop-floor opinion is questionable.[9] Conversely many employers dismissed Taylorism as costly, over-theoretical or as granting excessive control to engineers.[10] Even technocratic modernizers, such as E. Mercier of the electrical industry, argued that French workers needed to imbibe American dynamism *before* receiving the rewards of higher wages or shorter hours. Employers had, in general, viewed the eight-hour day – conceded in 1919 in an attempt to head off industrial unrest – as a threat to productivity rather than a stimulus to plant modernization.[11] There remained, too, fears that 'rationalization' would threaten smaller, less efficient, firms – the backbone of the middle class and of socio-political stability.

Nevertheless the 1926 slump did stimulate debate on 'rationalization'. If France had only five of the world's 201 fully-'Taylorized' plants, partial Taylorization occurred in car-plants, locomotive repair shops, petro-chemicals, electricals and military arsenals. In the 1927–29 boom, investment rose 28 per cent, labour productivity 8.7 per cent and mergers occurred at treble the rate of 1919–24.[12] After 1930 declining markets and price falls accentuated the need for cost cutting. Mechanization accelerated in textiles, footwear and food processing. Strict costing and timing exerted tighter budget controls. Planning agencies advised on how to switch workers rapidly between tasks (arsenals, agricultural tools). Time-and-motion and task subdivision were completed at Schneider–Creusot and Michelin and, more gradually, at Renault. One hundred and forty four firms adopted the Bedaux wage system. Workers thus faced technological redundancy, deskilling or the obligation to accept exhausting piecework bonus systems, speed-ups and fines for failure to meet production targets.[13]

State-regulated immigration offered a solution to labour shortages engendered by low birthrates, war deaths, the eight-hour day and the demands of post-war reconstruction. By 1930 immigrants comprised 14 per cent of the labour force, including 33 per cent of miners and heavy-metal workers and 20 per cent of building workers. Alongside older immigrant groups – Italians in Lorraine steel, Belgians in northern textiles – there were now 287,000 Poles in mining and agriculture and 471,000 North Africans.

What were the implications for French labour? By taking dirty, dangerous jobs, immigrants freed French workers to be white-collar employees or foremen in an ethnically segmented labour market. One hundred per cent of Lorraine iron-mine face-workers were Italians! Conversely immigrants not merely aided boom sectors by removing labour-supply bottlenecks but lowered overall wage levels. In the Pas-de-Calais, where coal output doubled between 1921 and 1926, Polish miners' wages were 40 per cent below French norms. Italian construction gangs, cut off from French union organizers by linguistic barriers, worked excessively long shifts. In company-towns employers provided segregated lodgings for immigrants and sponsored right-wing ethnic cultural/religious associations (the Polish ZRP; Italian *Opera Bonomelli*) to discourage contact between immigrant and French workers. The Miners' Union dubbed the ZRP *'agents provocateurs* of international fascism . . . delivering . . . Poles bound hand and foot to French capitalism'. Lacking the vote or basic civil rights, immigrants knew the perils of militancy. 'The fear of expulsion is the beginning of wisdom; it makes them submit more easily to the bosses', commented Longwy's police-chief.

Yet not all immigrants were docile pawns in employers' strategies. Many imported to do mining jobs 'escaped' to skilled employment in cities. Most remained outside the controls of company paternalism. Some Italians were political refugees from Mussolini. And if the CGT seemed preoccupied with excluding immigrants from skilled and white-collar jobs, the CGTU endeavoured to mobilize them, if with modest success – 25,000 Italians and 2,200 Poles – before 1933.[14]

A few case studies illustrate the problems faced by the labour movement in establishing footholds within the 'new' working class:

Industrial 'banlieues': Venissieux, outside Lyon, quadrupled its population between 1911 and 1931, attracting locomotive workshops, electrical construction, Berliet car plants. Of its overwhelmingly (80 per cent) proletarian population two-thirds were born outside the Lyonnais; half were immigrants – the targets of xenophobic right-wing denunciation as 'the excrement of all the races', spreaders of disease and crime who 'stole French jobs'. Unplanned urbanization multiplied problems of inadequate water supply, schooling, housing. Transport to Lyon was atrocious. Workers' culture remained inert, introverted. Oral witnesses evoke no memory of community identity – in sharp contrast to those from nearby Givors, an old glass-making town with a lively popular culture. Unionization was low. The regional CGT, dominated by Lyon's skilled workers, lacked empathy with Venissieux's unskilled proletarians. The socialist municipality, controlled by white-collar employees, was politically anodyne. Only in the 1930s did the PCs 'Red' Sports Festival tap an emerging *sociabilité* centred round workers' social clubs.[15]

The silence of the car-plants: Car-factories with their 'scientific' organization symbolized the new industry. Despite the uneven development of 'French Fordism' Citroën became a model 'modern' firm. Its glass-and-marble laboratory planned new techniques, for example interchangeable parts for its specialized plants like the Javel assembly line and the Clichy forges. Time-and-motion experts fixed productivity targets. Between 1921 and 1934 there were only three significant strikes. Unionization hovered around 1 per cent.[16]

A heterogeneous labour force weakened automobile unions. Among Renault's 30,000 workers at Boulogne-Billancourt seventeen languages were spoken on the shop-floor. With workers dispersing after work to the sprawling Parisian *banlieue*, community solidarities were minimal. Sophisticated hiring policies including references, finger-printing and blacklists weeded out militants. Attired in his Tsarist officer uniform, the White Russian security officer ran a network of shop-floor informers.[17] More paternalistic, Citroën cultivated an *esprit maison* via company holiday camps.

Relatively high wages were attractive to some semi-skilled workers; women wooed from sweated clothing trades, rural migrants who took macho pride in their productivity bonuses.[18] Yet undercurrents of resentment existed. Time-and-motion norms were often 'inhuman, absurd. Applied to sport [they] would demand a novice ... to achieve championship records'.[19] Semi-skilled workers developed ruses to slow the assembly line. Skilled toolroom workers, still one-third of Renault's workforce, retained job-control concerns. Since they remained the militant vanguard in the factories the CGTU was forced, despite its Leninist mistrust of the 'labour aristocracy', to adopt an increasingly hostile stance towards Taylorism and 'dilution'. While unionization remained extremely low – the CGTU had 60 members at Renault in 1934 – a hard core of activists was in place to exploit opportunities. When eight workers died in an explosion at Renault in 1933, the CGTU mobilized a demonstration of 20,000 to protest at their 'murder'.

Coalminers, immigration, rationalization: Northern mine-owners remained competitive through intensive rationalization. Major innovations were 'long-wall' mining, permitting mechanized hewing and extraction, and the 'Bedaux' payments system which allocated individual miners 'points' for subdivided work-tasks and disrupted the solidarity of workgangs which, hitherto, had received collective payments.[20] In the more difficult seams of southern pits the 'Fayol system' imposed rigid management hierarchies.[21] Miners complained that Bedaux norms were calculated on the performance of atypically strong pitmen working easy faces. ('The Bedu system, shit, it don't give the miner time to wipe the snot from his nose with his fingers' claimed one.) 'Long-walls' were noisy, dirty, dangerous – injury rates rose 66 per cent between 1932 and 1936.

Internecine union rivalries and lay-offs in the depression weakened miners' resistance. The Pas-de-Calais workforce fell by one-third between 1930 and 1935. Nonetheless there was a groundswell of demands for greater powers for elected safety delegates and for modifications of Bedaux. And though management played on the vulnerability of immigrants by introducing 'rationalization' into pits with Polish miners their 'docility' had its limits. In 1932, 4,000 Poles struck against the sacking of a union official. One oral history of northern pit-villagers suggests too that the disruption of community solidarities by war and immigration can be exaggerated. Interviewees recalled warmly the CGTU-run social and sports clubs which sustained a lively sociability into which the Poles were gradually absorbed.[22]

Men of iron, men of steel: In France's major iron-ore and steel-making region, Lorraine, unionism was feeble and conservative political hegemony unchallenged.[23] Within the steel-mills internal space was re-organized for smoother production flow and automatic

67

temperature controls rendered obsolete furnace-workers' skill in judging the steel's heat from flame colour. Older workers resented this 'progress', but offered minimal resistance.[24] An ethnically selective paternalism was perfected. Immigrants were lodged in filthy, overcrowded dormitories. By contrast most French workers were enmeshed from cradle to grave in a web of company crèches, schools, sports' clubs, houses, allotments and pension-schemes. An industrial apartheid segregated French employees – skilled, white-collar, supervisory – from immigrants.

Having thus imported immigrants during the 1920s employers responded to the Depression by inciting xenophobia against 'violent', 'oversexed' Italians who bore the brunt of the 40 per cent job cuts of 1931 to 1936. Police surveillance persuaded most immigrants to keep clear of labour politics, though the CGTU recruited some second-generation Italians. Since immigrant workers lacked the vote and 'loyal' French workers voted conservative in this Catholic, patriotic, frontier region employers could exploit their monopolization of municipal political control to disconnect water supplies from cafés unwise enough to host union meetings. While many steelworkers did regard company paternalism as an affront to their dignity, resentments rarely surfaced in organized protest. Nor was Lorraine unique, for authoritarian paternalism existed also at Schneider's Le Creusot and in some railway towns.[25]

In the 1920 schism the SFIO lost two-thirds of its members – young, radicalized, recent recruits – to the PC. War, Bolshevism and the labour unrest of 1919–20 shattered the fragile unity of a party which had never fully reconciled its internal divisions on issues such as national defence, Parliamentary reformism and relations with the unions. By 1932 it was – with 2 million voters and 131 Parliamentary seats – again the largest *left-wing* party, but scarcely a *workers'* party. Its 'typical' supporter was now a white-collar employee or petty *fonctionnaire* living in a small town in southern France. Symbolically, party leader Blum, a Jewish intellectual, lost his Parisian seat to the PC and took refuge in Narbonne where the SFIO was the party of wine-growing peasants.[26] Blum mixed *de facto* reformism with assertions of Marxist purity designed to parry Communist accusations that the SFIO had betrayed socialism. In turn, socialists denounced the PC less for being revolutionaries than for being obsessed with foreign rather than indigenous revolutionary experiences. Marxist phraseology preserved the loyalty of ex-Guésdists and of semi-Trotskyists, such as Pivert, but exasperated reformists who insisted that opportunities for social reform in alliance with the Radicals were being squandered. Blum, however, insisted that the 'occupation' of power was justifiable only to thwart right-wing dictatorship.

In 1920 the PC captured many of the SFIO's younger, proletarian supporters together with revolutionary syndicalists, angered by the impotent reformism of the CGT during the post-war labour unrest, and peasants radicalized by wartime experiences. Many early recruits were soon lost.[27] Capitalist re-stabilization punctured revolutionary hopes. Syndicalists resented the subordination of unions to party control, teachers and intellectuals found the PC's 'proletarianization' campaign crude. After 1928 the 'class-against-class' ultra-left strategy bewildered many staunch supporters. PC refusal to conclude second-ballot electoral deals with the SFIO handed victory to many right-wing candidates. Insistence that the Depression heralded the collapse of capitalism led to disastrous defeats in quixotic strikes and virulent antimilitarist propaganda led to the jailing of key party leaders. By 1932, reduced to 12 *députés*, 6.8 per cent of the electorate (795,000) and 30,000 members, the PC appeared a sectarian rump.[28]

Its members tended to be *young* authentic blue-collar proletarians. In the Cher, young workers from the huge Bourges arsenal, a sometime reformist stronghold radicalized during the War, seized control of the local PC from older ex-SFIO leaders. In the Paris *banlieue* skilled *métallos*, unable to secure effective union footholds in Taylorized factories, were prominent. So, too, were provincial railmen, as at Amiens, embittered by their brutally suppressed 1920 strike. The PC's 'factory-cell' strategy gave it advantages over the SFIO in blue-collar industry, but cells often succumbed to employer repression (e.g. Michelin 1929).[29] In Halluin, a northern textile town, the party compensated for its shop-floor weakness by imaginative adaptation of Flemish popular sociability. The communist municipality re-baptised streets, burned effigies of the *patronat* in carnival processions, and its choral groups maintained the tradition of popular protest songs.[30]

Crucially, the PC put down roots among the 'new' working class of the Paris *banlieue* whose population swelled by one million between 1918 and 1939. By 1932 one-third of the party's electorate and membership lived in this vast, sprawling area – engendering the press myth of the 'red belt' with its violent, brutal, dechristianized Bolshevised hordes. 'Municipal Communism' was a paradox because orthodox Marxist analysis criticized the idea of 'socialism in one borough' – as attempted by the SFIO in Bordeaux under Marquet

69

– as utopian illusion within a capitalist state, an analysis apparently confirmed when 'Red Vienna' collapsed to the assault of Dollfuβ in 1934. Eventually Communist Municipalities *did* establish clinics, sports facilities, etc. (e.g. Villejuif). Their trump card was their gut appeal to *banlieue*-dwellers: 'Our municipality has turned a swamp into a city' boasted the Villejuif PC.

The PC had supported a large Seine tenants' association protesting against high rents and poor maintenance.[31] Then in Bobigny communist mayor Clamamus became the champion of the *mal lotis* (inhabitants of *lotissements*, homes thrown up by speculators on land acquired from farmers) in their struggle for decent amenities and demands for state funding for workers' housing. In Bagneux it was the tenants of HBMs (apartment blocks) who gave the PC its social base. These had been constructed by major Parisian industrial firms to house 'respectable' workers, but the communists cleverly tapped the tenants' resentments at high rents, faulty central heating and at prying surveillance by ex-factory superintendents installed as *concierges*.[32]

By 1934 the combined membership of the CGT and the CGTU, at 755,000, was one-third that of the united CGT of 1920.[33] The CGT's strength lay in tertiary and public sectors (civil service; post; teaching). By 1929 it had 95,000 *fonctionnaires* members, but only 16,000 metalworkers. Abandoning their syndicalist heritage, its leaders sought legislative reforms via 'systematic presence' in national affairs. Their response to the Depression was to reject 'suicidal' industrial militancy and to espouse an economic 'Plan' for Keynesian public works, though low membership denied them sufficient leverage to influence policy making.

The CGTU had greater blue-collar strength among railmen, miners, metal, and building workers. But the Depression led to a 40 per cent fall in its membership through lay-offs, demoralizing strike defeats and the repatriation of immigrant members, though it had some success in organizing unemployment demonstrations. The defeat of the 1920 general strike convinced many syndicalists that the decentralist/anarchist strategies of revolutionary syndicalism were now an anachronistic luxury. Many joined the CGTU, only to leave disillusioned by the degree of communist-party control. The gradual and uneven pace of technological change and industrial concentration allowed craft groups still wedded to syndicalist ideals of job control, union autonomy and 'direct action' to survive among Limoges porcelain and shoe workers, Lyonnais building workers and Loire *métallos*.[34]

The 150,000 members of the Catholic CFTC are a reminder that not all organized workers were 'red' or anticlerical. The Flemish north, Alsace, Paris and the Lyonnais were its geographic bastions, white-collar employees its sociological base – though it also recruited textile workers, railmen and female clothing workers. It was patriotic, antisocialist, moderate – favouring negotiations and strike ballots – and defending 'family values' and Sunday rest. The efforts of the northern textile employers to persuade Rome to ban it suggest that leftist accusations that it was a 'yellow' bosses' union were somewhat unfair, and it *did* participate in some strikes. During the 1935 St Chamond armaments strike its members even collaborated with CGTU strikers. By then, however, the Popular Front had changed the entire mood of labour politics.[35]

LABOUR AND THE POPULAR FRONT – HOPE, VICTORY: 1934–36

The Depression *could* have served further to demoralize a weak and divided labour movement by eroding workers' bargaining position in the labour market. Instead there was a period in 1934–37 of unprecedented left-wing political vitality, union growth and industrial militancy as the 'fascist threat' prompted a 'Popular Front' political alliance of Communists, Socialists and Radicals, and CGT re-unification which in turn, boosted labour's self-confidence after years of division and defeat.

The French Depression was more a question of stagnation and slow paralysis than of severe collapse. Despite high unemployment in Paris and the *Nord* the Depression left less of a mark on French folk memory than it did in Britain and the USA – there was no French *Road to Wigan Pier* or *Grapes of Wrath* – but one peculiarity of the French Depression was its longevity. In 1937 car production was still 20 per cent below the 1929 peak, whereas in Britain by 1937 production levels had doubled. The sizeable peasant sector suffered severely from falling crop prices. Heavy export sectors like steel, where production fell 40 per cent in 1931–35, became obsessed with the need for deflation and cost-cutting to preserve markets. Though the industrial workforce fell by 1.4 million, including 400,000 in textiles, official unemployment figures reached 400,000 for those on relief. Four factors concealed the scale of job losses: the repatriation of one-third of the 3 million immigrant workers; the return of migrant urban workers to their families' peasant farms; the ineligibility of redundant married women workers (as in textiles) for dole; and extensive short-time working.[36]

The 'Fascist threat' which prompted the Popular Front mobilization was in part foreign. The fate of German and Austrian labour at the hands of Hitler and Dollfuβ was a grim warning. However, the anti-Parliamentary riots by the paramilitary leagues of the extreme right on 6 February 1934 highlighted the domestic dangers.[37] The existing political system rested on an alliance of dominant capitalist élites with the heterogeneous middle classes. Right/Centre coalition governments habitually pursued 'orthodox' financial strategies, resisted workers' social demands and compromised between economic modernization and the protection of small-scale businessmen who made up their electoral rank and file. This system was a potentially unstable compromise. The centrist Radical Party oscillated between the anti-collectivist and anti-communist economic instincts of its 'little-man' voters and their Jacobin-Republican heritage. Big business élites required the votes of an economic middle-class which was often suspicious of 'cartels' and 'trusts'.

After 1928 political destabilization was accelerated by two factors. First, Tardieu's attempts to create a conservative party wedded to 'modernization', economic collaboration with Germany and social welfare concessions, designed to woo the reformist CGT and marginalize the PC, alarmed many on the right – particularly in older industries and labour-intensive businesses, hostile to social welfare expenditure and to unions. Second, the Depression ruined Tardieu's hopes of collaboration with Germany, strengthened pressures for protectionism and for deflationary public-expenditure cuts. It reduced politics to a chaotic war of all against all and led to chronic cabinet instability. Radicals acquiesced in deflation, but faced a revolt from civil-service voters (resenting pay cuts) or peasant electors (demanding agricultural price support). Modernizing industrialists blamed 'traditional' sectors for structural economic weaknesses; export industries denounced the rise in tariffs; and small-businessmen criticized the political leverage of the 'cartels'. 'Fascism' thus appeared one solution to a crisis within the bourgeoisie. A 'strong' state could end parliamentary instability, mediate between factions of capital and ensure that it was the petty bourgeois and the workers who bore the brunt of the Depression by eliminating their Parliamentary and trade-union defences.[38]

To what extent was a labour revival already occurring? At first sight this seems implausible. Strike levels fell from 1,093 in 1930 to an average of 363 per annum in 1931–35; failure rates rose. Nevertheless there were signs of growing resentment against 'speed-ups' in many sectors, and that the 'new' proletariat was putting down roots, including immigrants who remained. The Depression reduced turnover rates in industry, forcing skilled workers to cling onto jobs in factories, to fight 'rationalization' rather than to 'escape' into small workshops. The network of tenant, unemployment and community groups established by the PC in the *banlieues* served to focus community concern on issues of public amenities, but could also act as the nucleus for 'anti-fascist' committees after 1934.[39]

Before analysing working-class experience between 1934 and 1939, some schematic overview is necessary of the political trajectory of the Popular Front. The riots of 6 February provoked an immediate, instinctive reflex of self-defence from labour's rank and file. On 12 February several million workers participated in demonstrations in 346 towns, with CGT and CGTU militants often marching together. In the succeeding months, governments' deflationary economic policies and apparent toleration of the paramilitary activities of the 'Fascist' leagues intensified calls for labour unity. The key breakthrough came with the PC's volte-face during the summer of 1934. Abandoning its 'ultra-left' stance it called for anti-fascist unity, a broad alliance of all voters of goodwill including Radicals and Catholics, and support for rearmament. Stalin's belated awareness of the need for a western alliance against Hitler was one reason for this shift – though the PC was certainly under strong pressure from its own supporters to change strategy.[40] An understandably suspicious SFIO responded only gradually to these overtures.

Labour confidence, boosted by the proliferation of anti-fascist committees and mass rallies, soared with the re-unification of the CGT. Key strikes, such as in the Marseilles docks in February, began to be won. Popular Front party and union leaders felt obliged, however, to distance themselves from the quasi-insurrectionary violence which led to several deaths in Brest and Toulon as arsenal workers, resisting public sector pay cuts, clashed with police.

An electoral pact was constructed. Socialists, Radicals and Communists would fight the first ballot on their own policy programmes, but would collaborate on the second ballot and on an agreed 'Popular Front' joint minimum policy. Paradoxically the

SFIO programme demanded structural economic reforms, such as nationalization, whereas the PC, keen to reassure centrist voters, suggested only a wealth tax on the rich.[41] The Radical Party's position was ambiguous; it joined the Popular Front, yet its own deputies had helped keep right-centre deflationary ministries in power during 1934–36, and some of its local Federations and candidates were openly hostile to the left.

Despite electoral indiscipline in 59 constituencies the Popular Front won by 378 seats to 220.[42] Blum's SFIO was the largest party and Blum formed a coalition government with the Radicals. The PC, whose vote had doubled to 1.5 million, declined to accept cabinet posts – illustrative of their ambiguous political strategy. On the one hand they wished to avoid the risk of Communist ministers alarming centrist voters or inciting their own proletarian followers to industrial militancy. On the other, they calculated that outside the cabinet they were positioned to tap workers' disillusionment should Blum fail to 'deliver' his promises.

Between Blum's election and the start of his ministry there occurred the largest wave of strikes in French history, in May–June 1936. In panic the employers' organization (CGPF) urged Blum to arrange a meeting with the CGT at Matignon on 7 June 1936 at which major concessions on pay, hours, union rights and annual holidays were made. Resisting far-left demands to turn these strikes into a revolution, Blum insisted that circumstances were not ripe for a socialist 'conquest of power'. The Popular Front's electoral mandate was for defence of Republican legality against 'fascism', not for structural reform. This scrupulous legalistic approach, it could be argued, spurned the only chance of translating unprecedented popular mobilization into a fundamental shift of power. Blum was incapable of turning the SFIO from an electoral machine into a mass party capable of harnessing mass protest.[43]

But there was little success even within Blum's reformist terms. The dissolved Fascist Leagues reappeared as political parties (PSF, PPF). The momentum and self-confidence of labour was undermined, returning the initiative to the *patronat*; and the failure to revitalize the economy or to achieve an effective anti-fascist foreign policy left the Popular Front in ruins by mid-1937.

The Spanish Civil War, begun by Franco's attack on the Popular Front's sister movement, aroused immense passion in the French labour movement. Nine thousand volunteers went to fight in Spain; Renault workers raised 164,000 francs in two months for Spain and 85 per cent of Paris *métallos* struck (7 Sept. 1936) to call for aid for

Spain. Fearing to annoy Tory London and centrist Radical voters, Blum accepted the League of Nations' call for non-intervention – a policy criticized by the PC and which split the SFIO and the CGT from top to bottom. Some arms were smuggled to Spain – but non-intervention shattered the morale of the grass-roots anti-fascism out of which the Popular Front had emerged.[44]

An effective economic strategy was essential to satisfy the aspirations of the Popular Front's working-class, peasant, and petty-bourgeois electorate, to remove the economic insecurities which nurtured fascism, and as a pre-requisite for anti-Nazi rearmament. There was little room for manoeuvre. Devaluation of the franc to boost exports had to be delayed until September 1936 in order to consult London and Washington to prevent retaliation. The Matignon wage and hours concessions, 'ransom paid to avoid civil war' (Blum), posed the threat of inflation and lower production. Blum's claim that higher wages would stimulate consumption, encourage production, and lower unit costs and unemployment as existing plant was fully utilized, proved over-optimistic. The economy failed to revive.[45] Instead rearmament stoked inflation and weakened the franc.

Conservative critics blamed the inflexible application of the 40-hour week, conceded at Matignon, for a shortage of skilled labour which crippled production. However, production *did* grow in arms-related sectors, such as engineering and chemicals, and stagnation in other sectors like construction stemmed from sluggish demand, lack of public works and the refusal of the *patronat*, implacably hostile to the Popular Front, to invest.

Blum was trapped between the need to revive the economy, the aspirations of his working-class supporters, conciliation of the Radical's petty-bourgeois voters, and the quest for the co-operation of capitalist élites. To woo them he 'practised economic liberalism more faithfully than any government in the past', limited nationalization to a few defence plants and in March 1937 announced a 'pause' in public works and social-welfare projects. Having failed to gain business confidence and increase capital investment, Blum finally sought from the Senate powers to curb capital outflow, and resigned when defeated – typically overruling left-wing socialists who urged mass demonstrations to overawe the Senate. A government born amidst unprecedented mass enthusiasm expired to the deafening sound of silence in the streets.[46]

Blum's defenders argue that his room for manoeuvre in

domestic politics, economic strategy and foreign policy was extremely limited. His conciliation of Conservatives, Radicals and capitalists was pragmatic and realistic. He did succeed in putting fascism on the defensive, whilst Matignon brought real, if limited, gains for labour. An alternative strategy of using mass mobilization to achieve fundamental socialist change would have brought economic and social chaos – and required a 'revolutionary mood' in the proletariat which was absent.

Leftist critics retort that scrupulous 'moderation' betrayed Spain, failed to secure a military alliance with the Soviet Union, predictably failed to win over an irreconcilable *patronat* and engendered only a 'Rooseveltism for Lilliputians' which failed to revive the economy. No anti-fascist Republican consensus emerged – indeed the Radicals' 'little-man' electorate joined the bourgeoisie in accepting appeasement and defeatism on the path to Vichy. The working class was left demoralized and demobilized. The year 1936 was a revolutionary opportunity which was squandered because left-wing leaders – the timid reformist Blum *and* the Stalinist PC – obsessed by the need for an alliance between the western bourgeoisie and the Soviet Union against Hitler, refused to seize the opportunity offered by a deep-seated crisis of bourgeois political hegemony and unprecedented proletarian mobilization.

Some light is cast on the scope of the Blum government for a more radical policy by an examination of the 1936 strike wave. The strikes began in provincial aircraft factories, spread to Paris engineering (27 May) before flooding across Paris and the provinces in early June. Many persisted for days or weeks after the Matignon settlement (7 June), indeed fresh strikes were still erupting in July. In June alone there were 12,142 strikes (74 per cent involving factory occupations), with 1.85 million strikers participating. Fearing revolution the *patronat* made unprecedented concessions on wages (12 per cent average increases), but, more fundamentally, on union bargaining rights – hitherto viewed by French employers as an intolerable loss of employer freedom and authority. In 1933, 29 collective contracts were signed, in 1937 3,064. Elected shop stewards were to be permitted within factories. Furthermore a 40-hour week and two weeks annual paid holiday were granted.

Most strikers were not union members – indeed the most heavily unionized sectors (rail, post, civil service) were scarcely involved in the strikes. But strikers now surged into the CGT which swelled to 4.5 million members. This process increased the influence of the communist ex-*unitaires* who controlled the blue-collar federations – metal, building, chemicals, textiles – which grew the fastest. Chemical-union membership grew 1,400 per cent. Communist organizers were younger and less supercilious towards new recruits than the reformist union leaders. Indeed, many strikers joined the PC, whose membership quadrupled to 284,000. At Renault the PC grew from 120 to 6,000. Lacking any syndicalist heritage, these neophyte semi-skilled unionists accepted centralized communist union directives.[47]

Among the strikers were elements new to the labour movement – technicians, department-store employees, and women. Though the relative stagnation of 'women's' jobs in textiles and clothing in the 1920s had reduced the percentage of women in the industrial labour force from 36 per cent (1906) to 27 per cent (1936), they had swelled the ranks of tertiary employees and of semi-skilled workers in Taylorized industries, such as light-engineering, electrics, and food processing. Twelve per cent of Renault workers were female, for whom youthful training as seamstresses often attuned them psychologically to speedy bonus-payment tasks. But in 1935 barely 8 per cent of union members were women. While photographs do attest to their presence in the June strikes, most strike delegates – even in the department stores whose workforce was predominantly female – were male. During factory occupations the CGT, fearing the impact of press stories of 'orgies', tended to evacuate women. To *some* extent this marked a watershed in the integration of women workers into the labour movement. The largely female Clothing Workers Union swelled from six to 100,000 and female delegates were prominent at the 1937 CGT congress. Yet the experiences of women workers still differed from those of men. Strike photos show male strikers playing cards, or football – while women, trained to accept domestic responsibilities, are knitting. CGT officials pressured feminist speakers *not* to raise issues of equal pay during the strikes. Many women workers lacked the one-year tenure to qualify for paid holidays, and doubtless for many the five-day week meant merely a chance to clean the house on Saturdays.[48]

Claims that the strikes were a 'communist plot' ignore the obvious concern of the PC's Stalinist leadership to end the strikes in the interests of national unity. Certainly communist factory cells at Renault or pit-safety delegates in the north acted as a leaven in the strikes. Yet many of the earliest plants to strike, such as the Nantes food-processing factories, were non-unionized. The banal

77

The working class and politics

explanation is that workers believed that Blum's election victory meant that for once strikers would not meet police and troop repression.[49]

The strikes were not primarily 'economistic', for many began without specific demands and persisted long after the Matignon wage concessions. There are two, partly persuasive, psychological explanations. One, that it was a 'revolt against work' will be discussed below.[50] Another views the strikes as a *fête*, suggesting the absence of revolutionary mood or demands. Enjoying the summer sunshine workers behaved as if on a picnic, their attitude that of children on holiday reluctant to see the vacation end.[51] B. Carcérès, building worker and autodidact, offers a utopian twist to this suggesting 'a *fête* of hope for a better world'. As musicians, actors, performed in occupied factories 'these mournful places . . . became places of creativity and joy. Work and *fête* met, once again in the workplace. Fragmented man became whole again'.[52]

Strikers rarely confronted the issue of political power, rarely challenged the authority of local municipalities, made few calls for nationalization and few demands for *autogestion* or attempts to run factories themselves. Nevertheless, some observations can be made.[53] First, *occupation* itself was an implicit challenge to property rights and employer authority. Foremen were often humiliated, forced to parade with red flags, and, once work re-started, no longer treated with the previous deference. Second, many workers ignored the Matignon settlement and CGT directives to resume work. In July there were 1,688 fresh strikes. Many local communist militants regarded the PC leadership's moderation as a clever ruse and actively encouraged further strikes. Third, there *was* a clear crisis of bourgeois hegemony. The 'Republican synthesis' was disintegrating, intermediate classes hit by the Depression were moving to the left or the far-right. Some capitalists were tempted by fascism – and the panic concessions of the CGPF at Matignon imply a fear of revolution.

The far-left (anarchist and Trotskyite) denounced the established left for squandering revolutionary opportunities. The Popular Front strategy was, they argued, fundamentally flawed. How could one defeat fascism, itself a product of capitalism, by parliamentary deals with bourgeois parties and military rearmament in alliance with the High Command and British Tories? That path could only lead to a new *Union Sacrée* as in 1914. They proposed a *Front Populaire de combat*, built up from below by factory committees and workers' militia, wooing the threatened petty-bourgeoisie away

78

France

from its Radical politicians. Although the Trotskyite, Hotchkiss shop steward F. Cherou, established a network of 280 factory committees, government attempts to blame Trotskyite agitators for June 1936 were implausible. Despite having sympathizers among the Pivertists in the SFIO's *Seine Federation* Trotskyites, barely 1,000 in number, were sectarian, inexperienced and lacked shop-floor credibility. While their analysis of the 'contradictions' and inevitable failure of the Popular Front proved perceptive, the radicalized workers who flocked into the labour movement still believed Communism to have an authentic revolutionary aura. Thus Trotskyites were physically assaulted by PC militants and denounced as *agents provocateurs*.[54]

Paradoxically in a world of Depression, Fascism and impending war, the subsequent 'image' of the Popular Front is amazingly sunny, epitomized by photographs of workers waving from excursion trains or paddling on beaches. When interviewed decades later, workers' recollections of 1936 centred on paid vacations. On trial under Vichy in 1941, Blum, evoking workers' access to leisure, boasted, 'I had a feeling, despite everything, of having brought a moment of sunshine into . . . drab lives'. B. Carcérès, himself a young building worker in 1936, claims that the surge of cultural vitality of the period is proved not merely by tourism but by popular audiences for radical theatre and cinema projects, travelling libraries, youth hostelling, museums.[55]

Emphasis on 'leisure' to provide a mystique for Republican social democracy was hastily improvised in 1936, for it played little part in orthodox leftist ideology – which, austerely, praised work culture and self-education – or in Popular Front programmes. Then Leo Lagrange, given the new post of minister for Leisure/Sport in Blum's cabinet, outlined an explicit leisure ideology. Fascism must not retain its monopoly on youthful vitality; socialism should encourage democratic participation in hitherto élitist sports to engender a healthy, happy (and productive) population and popular tourism to bring to workers a sense of the beauty of provincial France and contact with other classes. These themes had been prevalent hitherto only in the Alsace labour movement, influenced by the German SPD, which had long organized workers' rail excursions, sports festivals and musical groups, utilizing a utopian rhetoric which claimed that fresh air and healthy activity broadened the mind and freed spirits constrained by the daily factory grind.[56]

In August 1936 560,000 workers used cheap rail tickets ('billets Lagrange'). Labour newspapers printed emotional letters

79

from elderly workers enthusing over their first sight of the sea, while conservative journals responded with irate tirades from bourgeois whose Riviera vacations were ruined by the vulgarities of the proletariat at play. Lagrange encouraged the 'Red Falcons', a sexually mixed socialist scouting organization whose camps were dubbed 'Republics' and whose members sang revolutionary songs and revised children's stories to impart a socialist message. Youth hostelling was encouraged to increase contacts between workers, peasants and intellectuals. Such ventures challenged the previous hegemony of Catholicism over adolescent activities. Lagrange founded 255 sports projects, established Popular Sports' Certificates and a workers' sports federation grew to over 100,000, blessed by the PC hitherto dismissive of sport as an opium of the masses designed to train cannon-fodder for Imperialist wars. Since workers needed active minds as well as healthy bodies, travelling popular libraries, evening museum openings, art exhibitions in factories and radical popular theatre groups received support. Failure to bridge the gulf between workers and 'serious' culture would leave the proletariat exposed to the degraded values of Hollywood films and pulp-fiction.[57] However, the limitations of this *cultural* revolution need to be emphasized. Although 1.5 million '*billets Lagrange*' were issued in 1937, many workers took no holidays.

Street demonstrations and *fêtes* were the quintessential forms of mass mobilization of the Popular Front. Paris alone had 130 major demonstrations in thirty months.[58] These were led by PC and CGT dignitaries, followed by ex-servicemen, women and children, by metal-union rank and file, and the youth and sports groups. Carnival floats re-enacted scenes from 1789–93, the Commune and 1917 – symbolizing the Communists' appropriation of Jacobinism and the assimilation of the Bolshevik revolution into the French Republican heritage. During the Popular Front the First of May metamorphosed from a day of sporadic strikes to one of popular *fêtes*, whilst the *Fête de l'Humanité* matured as the annual Communist rally. The music featured at the 1936 *Fête* included Bizet's *La Patrie*, the *Marseillaise*, the *Internationale*, folk-songs – and Charles Trenet! Even in the Vienne, a largely agricultural *department* whose *chef-lieu*, Poitiers, was scarcely an industrial town, 1935–37 were years of extraordinary expressionist vitality. There were rallies for Spain. Agricultural labourers at hiring fairs wore hammers and sickles in place of traditional cars of corn in their buttonholes and waved red flags at St Jean midsummer bonfires; and strikers, dressed up as curés, ritually burned copies of the deflationary decree-laws of 1935! Such activities evoke M. Agulhon's classic portrait of the symbolic syncretism of peasant radicals in 1848.[59]

The most popular art-form, with 220 million attendances per year, was the cinema, whose potential for propaganda and education was appreciated by the left. In 1936 directors and technicians were active in the strikes, demanding state funding to save an ailing French film industry from foreign control. The *Ciné-Liberté* group (12,000 members) raised funds from trades unionists to make documentaries on Spain, on building workers and *La Vie est à Nous* for the 1936 election. Yet the vast majority of the 1,200 feature films made in the 1930s comprised military and colonial adventures, army comedies, Pagnol-esque rustic escapism and boulevard farces caught in a time warp. For much of the working-class audience of fleapit local picture-houses, the cinema was a place of escapism, a place to smoke, joke, and court.[60]

THE REVENGE OF THE PATRONAT AND THE DEFEAT OF THE POPULAR FRONT: 1937–39

Blum's hope that a period of industrial calm would follow Matignon, encouraging investment and economic recovery, was soon dashed as his government was trapped between a concerted employer backlash and a desperate worker struggle to maintain their recent gains. The CGPF, under the combative Gignoux, denounced the 40-hour week as 'insane'. Inflation accelerated as employers offset wage increases by raising prices and business funding of 'fascist' parties (PPF, PSF) increased. Tame 'yellow' unions (e.g. the *Syndicat Professional Francais*, SPF) were patronized as potential strikebreakers and union organizers were harassed.[61]

By autumn 1936, as employer provocation led to strikes and lockouts in northern textiles, Blum and reformist CGT leader Jouhaux urged new union members to show restraint and self-discipline. Jouhaux, seeking to protect workers whilst avoiding strikes, suggested a sliding scale linking wages to inflation and compulsory arbitration procedures. The PC was in a dilemma. Its official stance supported high productivity for national rearmament. Yet its local militants were ex-*unitaires*, with years of industrial agitation experience, or new members recruited amidst the euphoric radicalism of June. The leadership had obvious difficulty controlling its rank and file.

The working class and politics

In December 1936 Blum – against the wishes of the CGPF – introduced a Compulsory Arbitration law, a watershed in industrial relations. The 1892 law permitting conciliation of disputes by Justices of the Peace had rarely been invoked. However, Matignon insisted that employers negotiate with 'the most representative union', and 2,400 collective contracts were signed between June and December. The functioning of Compulsory Arbitration was soon under union attack for being slow, inconsistent in wage awards, deficient in enforcement machinery, and unclear in definition of 'collective disputes', for employers denied that the sacking of a shop steward came under this definition. A second law in Spring 1938 shortened delays, set up an Appeals Court, clarified definitions of collective disputes – but failed to meet CGT concerns over a sliding wage/price scale, sanctions against recalcitrant employers or control of dismissal procedures. Indeed by 1938–39 it was the unions who denounced the system, and the hitherto hostile CGPF which applauded it. Unions acquiesced to it to aid Blum's economic strategy – only to find it a weapon turned against them under subsequent governments. Arbitration decisions accepted employer statistics unquestioningly and gave pay awards well below the rate of inflation. Strikes fell from 3,600 in 1937 to 780 in 1938. In 1937, 37 per cent of disputes went to arbitration, by 1939 64 per cent – when only one of thirty-four employers found guilty by the Appeals Court of breaching agreements was punished. Courts denied protection to workers disciplined for 'political' strikes, viewed as a breach of contract.[62]

Blum's 'pause' in social reform projects and public works in March 1937 angered workers. Bitterness increased when police killed five workers involved in anti-fascist demonstrations in Clichy, provoking protest strikes in the Paris metal industry and accusations that the shootings were a ransom paid by Blum to appease the financiers.[63] Blum's fall, in July 1937, appeared to leave the labour movement indifferent.

Meanwhile 'rationalization' and speed-ups in Lorraine steel, car-plants, Lyon textiles, the coalfields and department stores provoked wildcat strikes and go-slows. Senior CGT officials preached moderation and 'productivism' but found their shop-stewards unwilling to act as agents of labour discipline.[64]

For M. Seidmann[65] these wildcat strikes were 'revolts against work'. Oblivious to harsh political reality, alienated by assembly-line work, semi-skilled workers sought escape in go-slows and shorter hours – deaf alike to CGT 'productivist' appeals and to the

82

job-control rhetoric of the far left. Briefly there was 'dual power' in factories as discipline was ignored and foremen insulted, with slowdowns, sabotage, and lax timekeeping. At the site for the Spring 1937 Paris Exposition 25,000 construction workers ignored government pleas for prompt completion of this prestige project, banned overtime and called a strike.

Is Seidmann's analysis convincing? Undoubtedly many workers found their jobs unsatisfying. Clearly they were prepared to exploit the favourable political situation. Nevertheless the choice of building workers is a poor example. Despite technological changes (cement mixers, spray paints, bulldozers) building retained a high proportion of skilled workers. G. Navel offers a portrait of this proud, undeferential workforce for whom union control of hiring and workpace constituted a continuation of revolutionary syndicalist aspirations, not a 'revolt against work'. Go-slows at *Expo 37* must, also, be viewed in the context of the 'pause'. Once the project was completed Paris building unemployment rose rapidly in 1937–38.[66]

Moreover, Seidmann also portrays an aviation industry moving towards mass production with a de-skilled workforce deaf to national-defence productivist pleas, regarding the 'battle against Fascism' with sectionalist selfishness as a battle to preserve the 40-hour week and lax labour discipline. However, there is evidence that many aviation workers *were* skilled and *did* imbibe CGT productivist and political concerns.[67] Until 1934 paternalistic aircraft firms had weak unions. The PC's volte-face on national defence improved the CGTU's recruitment prospects. Workers perceived that right-wing deflationary policies had reduced defence expenditure by one-third in 1931–35, whereas Popular Front anti-fascist rearmament would mean orders and jobs. In 1936–38 they showed strong commitment both to nationalization of defence factories and to workshop job-control, including union supervision of hiring and the elimination of piecework. What could be more left-wing and patriotic than building planes for anti-fascism in nationalized plants where militants strove for efficiency and workers' control? Many joined Lagrange's *aviation populaire* scheme to end élitist domination of flying by training working-class pilots. These years provided a crash course in rank-and-file union and political education, with the communist-run CGT ceaselessly active in negotiations with government and management over further nationalizations.

Elsewhere, Seidmann downplays the extent to which strikes were a desperate attempt to resist employer counterattacks. In northern pits miners' strikes won a partial victory over the Bedaux system, securing a return to payment by work-team and reductions in the number of time-and-motion experts. As productivity fell in 1936–37 management sought to make the working week more 'flexible' and provoked strikes by seeking to re-impose Bedaux in some pits. Ironically, communist CGT officials often urged miners to make Stakhanovite productivity efforts.

Renault workers were in the vanguard of the 1936 strikes, after which the CGT at Boulogne-Billancourt swelled to 25,000. Elected shop stewards asserted their rights – 'seeking to substitute themselves for management', claimed Renault. The tide soon turned. Management harassed union officials, used the fascist PPF to control its hiring policy, and introduced speed-ups. Union organizers had problems controlling the mass of new union members – unskilled, female, immigrant, young. Growing resentments against speed-ups and rising accident rates were in part tapped by the far left, critical of PC moderation. In December 1937 forty-two militants were sacked after a strike against lay-offs.

Nowhere were the 'contradictions' of Popular Frontism more exposed than in Lorraine. Though 90 per cent of Longwy steel-workers joined the CGT after June 1936 the *patronat*'s power was not easily shaken. Mobilizing its allies – clergy, engineers, foremen, ex-servicemen's organizations – it allied with the fascist PSF to play on the xenophobia of French workers in a region where 10 per cent of the workforce was now North African. During the 1928–34 period the PC alone had sought to attract immigrant workers. Now, in their new, moderate mood, communists bemused immigrants by adopting the rhetoric of *tricoleur* patriotism, singing the *Marseillaise* not the *Internationale*. As elsewhere, the CGT's productivist strategy made it reluctant to resist speed-ups.[68]

Despite Blum's brief second ministry in Spring 1938, the political landscape was dominated by a resurgent right. Prime Minister Daladier, Radical minister in Blum's cabinet, now metamorphosed into a 'strong man', symbolizing social order and national revival, determined to curb 'intolerable' union power and emerging – to his amazement – as a public hero by appeasing Hitler. His Radical party shifted back to coalition rule with the right, for its petty-bourgeois electorate had been alarmed at rapid communist growth, outraged by strikes and the costs of social concessions to workers, and terrified by the prospect of war with Hitler to save Stalin.[69] In by-elections, Radicals ran against the left, their rhetoric increasingly anti-Marxist, pro-colonial, and xenophobic. Asserting the need to 'put France back to work' Daladier allowed his Finance Minister, Reynaud, to issue decrees in November 1938 abolishing the 40-hour week which was blamed for obstructing economic recovery by creating shortages of key skilled workers.

The *patronat*, the backbone of Daladier's régime, was not politically homogeneous. Some favoured rearmament, others rejected this as inflationary; many were loyal to established conservative parties, some flirted with Fascism. But all favoured confrontation with the CGT.[70] Isère employers' organizations, already using PSF strikebreakers against their unions, made explicitly authoritarian appeals. 'Abandon all partisan politics, expel all undesirables. Repress all those who disrupt national unity. Make work obligatory once again. Laziness cannot be life's dogma, nor leisure its rule . . . Remoralize France!' New technocratic managerial groups, such as the *Cercle des Jeunes Patrons*, espoused a strategy of economic modernization, firm government, corporation and tougher managerial authority.

With four million members, the CGT remained a mass movement. In 1938 its congress made a show of unity against threats to the 40-hour week, viewed as a symbol of Matignon. Employers were blamed for provoking confrontation by refusals to renegotiate collective agreements and to accept unfavourable arbitration decisions. Management, it was claimed, should share the blame for low productivity, for failing to invest, exporting capital, refusing to train apprentices and for stripping nationalized arms plants (e.g. in Caen) of raw materials.[71]

But the CGT was in trouble. Dues paying had fallen by 15 per cent as unemployment rose. Employment in Paris rose 10 per cent in 1937, but fell back to 1936 levels in 1938. While the labour market for skilled male workers in defence-related industries expanded, older, unskilled and female workers in building, clothing, textiles, faced structural unemployment.[72] Ideological squabbles intensified. Jouhaux was critical of communist influence on blue-collar unions, but shared their aversion to appeasement. R. Belin's *Syndicats* faction, however – based on teaching, postal and civil-service unions – mixed reformism with virulent hostility to communist 'colonisation' of the unions and pro-appeasement pacifism. It won 30 per cent of the congress vote.[73] In April in St Etienne a *Syndicats* supporter had killed a communist in a union organizational dispute. *Syndicats* urged realistic, 'constructive' unionism, compromise with employers, and opposed strike resistance to Reynaud's decrees.

Although CFTC members had been drawn willy-nilly into

June strikes and though it approved of the 40-hour week, its relations with the Popular Front remained distant. It denounced CGT monopoly of collective contract agreements after Matignon. Its members swelled to 400,000 – and many of its new recruits were anti-communist 'moderates' rather than Catholics. Indeed its right wing flirted with the fascist PSF – and the CFTC militant who led an anti-CGT protest in Pas de Calais mines, P. Belange, was dubbed 'the Alcazar' (a reference to Franco's stronghold in the Spanish Civil War). The CFTC denounced the 'spirit of 36', urged class co-operation, national solidarity, productivism, a spirit of self-sacrifice ('spirit of 38') and welcomed compulsory arbitration.[74]

Sensing disarray on the left, government and employers forced the unions into a suicidal last-ditch stand. Reynaud's decrees were provocative – workers would be sacked for resisting the 6-day week and denied welfare benefits. They were introduced in a provocative way – at Hutchinson (Puteaux), the 44-hour week included a 9-hour Saturday. Jouhaux's appeal for negotiations was rejected. Wildcat strikes erupted – in Isère textiles, the northern pits and in metallurgy. There was a symbolic battle at Renault, the communist 'fortress', where strikers occupied the factory ('it was totally unlike 1936. Things appeared more serious. We anticipated Government repression. We bolted the gates . . .'). Four thousand five hundred police stormed the works. Strikers were forced to march out four by four giving the fascist salute whilst the police commander beat his shield with his truncheon chanting, 'One for Blum! One for Thorez! One for Jouhaux! . . .'[75]

Belatedly the CGT called a General Strike for 30 November by which time major strikes, as at Anzin, had been crushed. The government mobilized troops, used radio propaganda and headed off a transport strike by threats to call up railworkers. Two million workers did strike, over 70 per cent of textile, metal and building workers responded – but barely 3 per cent in *Syndicats'* postal and public service sectors, intimidated by threats of sackings and loss of pension rights. Systematic, massive, exemplary repression followed. Many, including 36,000 auto workers, were locked out, then selectively re-hired at lower wage rates. Twenty thousand were sacked, 10,000 of them in engineering, including many shop stewards. Renault workers now faced a 48-hour week (60 in defence-related sectors), lower wages and speed ups. CGT power was broken in the aviation factories, miners faced the return of the Bedaux system, and over 800 workers were jailed. At

Clermont-Ferrand, where strikers had beseiged the station, thirty Michelin workers were jailed and 500 sacked.[76]

Employers exulted as the Matignon humiliation was avenged. CGT membership plummetted to 2.5 million in September 1939, 1 million by May 1940. Strike levels declined. The split within the CGT widened as Belin and Dumoulin of *Syndicats* called for 'constructive' unionism in line with the wishes of the 'silent majority' who sought 'collaboration' with the *patronat* for economic revival. When, despairing of western appeasement, Stalin signed the Nazi-Soviet pact (August 1939), the PC's sudden denunciation of national defence and 'Imperialist' war gave Daladier the excuse to outlaw communist-led unions and close *L'Humanité*.[77] In many ways the tone of Vichy's industrial relations had, indeed, already been established before the war started.

No-one would claim Marseilles as a 'typical' French city. France's largest port – with its huge immigrant population, political gangsterism and clientelism – resembled a sort of Chicago-sur-mer. Yet in the transition from weakness and division to mass mobilization followed by disillusionment and defeat the experience of its labour movement epitomizes the wider history of the Popular Front. Until 1934 its politics were based on client groups and ethnicity. Political leaders (SFIO, Radical, Rightist) were 'bosses' who delivered the votes of the Italians and Corsicans by promises of municipal jobs. The SFIO was bourgeois-led, ideologically colourless, used its own tame gangsters and guaranteed municipal posts to naturalized immigrant voters. The CGT ran the municipal and dock unions but failed to penetrate the outer industrial suburbs.

The Popular Front revitalized the city's politics. Italian and Spanish immigrants, sensitive to the threat of Mussolini and Franco, were alarmed at the strength of Fascist leagues. A network of anti-fascist groups mushroomed in popular *quartiers* and arms were collected and smuggled to Spain. The PC, which made the running in the Popular Front mobilization, grew from 200 to 7,000 members. It penetrated the metal and chemical plants of the *banlieue* and sought respectability by crusading against gangsterism, prostitution and municipal corruption – though it was not averse to ensuring that only Algerians with party cards got waterfront jobs.

During 1936–37 the CGT clamped down on wildcat strikes, put its faith in Compulsory Arbitration and a sympathetic prefect – only to find that worker militancy could not easily be resurrected in 1938 when the political climate changed. Spanish non-intervention broke the momentum of anti-fascist enthusiasm, and by the time of

Munich public opinion was criticizing the PC as 'bellicose'. 'Militant anti-fascism appeared to fade back into the swamp of public opinion whence it had so mysteriously emerged' (D. Levy). In November 1938 50,000 workers struck. Then employers took revenge. In December 100,000 were locked out. CGT membership declined sharply to the benefit of the CFTC and a bosses' union headed by the PPF fascist gangster Sabiani.[78]

EPILOGUE: FRENCH WORKERS 1940–44 OCCUPATION, VICHY, RESISTANCE

The history of the working class in the 1940–44 period remains to be written. With rare exceptions studies of workers in particular regions or factories end in 1939.[79] The focus of the current historiography is, understandably, on Resistance networks. All of these had their distinctive ideological slant (Communist FTPF, socialist *Libération*, Christian-democrat *Combat*, etc.) but all had socially heterogeneous membership. Left-wing workers played a central role in the Resistance – but so too did professional people, army officers, cadres from a variety of centrist and right-wing traditions. And, undoubtedly, Resistance, however defined, remained a minority phenomenon, in a France where the majority seemed obsessed with food, survival and, in the south, convinced that Pétainism was the best shield against the Germans.[80]

Yet this period is a logical continuation of, not a break with, earlier conflicts. Pétain's claim to be 'above politics' was exposed as a sham, for Vichy's reactionary policies represented the revenge of the far-right not merely on the Popular Front but on the entire post-1789 Republican heritage. The Resistance was engaged in an ideological civil war.

Certainly, maverick renegade leftists found a place in the new régime. R. Belin, following the logic of his pro-appeasement and anti-communist views, was the Vichy Labour Minister who introduced the *Charter of Labour* (1941), which claimed to offer a future of social peace by replacing sterile class confrontation with management-labour collaboration in corporatist organizations Union Confederations (CGT, CFTC) had already been abolished. Individual, local unions were permitted, but not allowed to federate. 'Social Councils' of managers, cadres and workers were established in factories to discuss work grievances. The entire structure provided a façade for employer domination. No strikes or collective bargaining were permitted. Exhortations to employers to exhibit 'social responsibility' were an invitation to reassert authoritarian paternalism.[81] It was rejected as a charade even by many leaders of the CFTC who held several meetings with the Jouhaux wing of the CGT which agreed to attempt subversion of Vichy labour policies by infiltrating legal unions and to give union support to the *Libération-Sud* Resistance group.

Despite its clerical/reactionary tone, Vichy had its technocratic face. 'Modernizers' like Pucheu of *Comité des Forges* and Renault's nephew, Lehideux, frustrated by the weak executives and economic stagnation of the Third Republic, envisaged a rationalized, corporatist economy and technocratic management. SNCF bosses made plans for railway rationalization. The *patronat* emphasized productivity and profits. Berliet made tank-carriers for the *Wehrmacht* and Renault exported 90 per cent of its output to Germany. Industrialists who had urged Daladier to smash the unions in order to boost defence production now happily exported two-thirds of their aircraft to the *Luftwaffe*.[82] The first mass labour protest, the strike of 100,000 northern miners of May–June 1941, was against a *patronat* which had exploited the new policial *conjoncture* to restore payments systems and work-practices which the 1936 strikes had, briefly, succeeded in removing. Yet the slogan 'Long live the USSR' scrawled on the walls of the pit villages and the anti-German chants indicated the political element in this communist-led strike.[83]

Communist resistance pre-dated Hitler's invasion of the Soviet Union. The PCF's sudden switch in September 1939 from support for national defence to antimilitarism and denunciation of 'Imperialist war' gave the pretext for Daladier to purge communists from the CGT and persecute the PC. In 1940 the rhetoric of the official PC leadership remained ambiguous – it laid as much blame on London plutocrats as on Fascism for the war and, while denouncing Pétainism, stopped short of open calls for resistance to the Germans. However, the view 'from below' of local party members was rather different. Persecuted since September 1939 by the 'capitalist' state they often had their political views confirmed in 1940 when after months of 'phoney war' the 'patriotic' bourgeoisie appeared to capitulate overnight to the Nazis, then immediately start to collaborate enthusiastically with them. One railway worker at Oullins (Lyon), was actually impelled to *join* the PC. 'I saw that it was not really a war against Hitler . . . instead . . . communists were being arrested. I had taken part in the strike at Oullins in 1938 and ... seen the soldiers sent to occupy the factory ... so I knew it was another action against the working class.'[84] For such workers, Daladier, the police, Pétainists and the Nazis were virtually indistinguishable class enemies.

Local PC leaders such as Charles Tillon were critical of the official PC strategy in 1940–41 and actively involved in precocious resistance activity well before the invasion of the Soviet Union prompted Moscow's next volte-face.[85] The PC then entered its heroic age, becoming *the* hub of militant internal resistance at a time when socialist, Catholic and bourgeois Resistance groups 'did not like the idea of civil violence and preferred to keep the idea of rebellious action at arm's length. The working-class were more used to fighting for their rights. They wanted *action* and were prepared for violent conflict.' (A. Plaisantin, Catholic engineer involved in *Combat*.)[86] The PC's *'Front National'* strategy, calling for a patriotic war of national liberation involving all Frenchmen of goodwill, played down class war.[87] Its neo-Jacobin rhetoric portrayed the party as the authentic heir to the Republican-Revolutionary inheritance. Had not the élites in 1793 and 1871 treasonably allied with reactionary foreign governments? 'The only patriots are the workers and peasants of France, heirs to the French Revolution and the Paris Commune.' (*L'Humanité*, 29 May 1941.) The goal was a new France of equality and social justice – a leftist social Utopian vision which came to be shared by much of the Resistance.

Industrial action was central to PC strategy. In 1940–41, priority was given to the slow rebuilding of the party's shattered industrial organization. Then workers' economic grievances were used to stimulate protest. Lacking peasants' access to farm produce, and the bourgeoisie's influence in the black market, urban workers above all suffered from food shortages and price inflation. Deficiency diseases spread in urban areas and death rates rose. *L'Humanité des Femmes* played on working-class housewives' problems in feeding families. Food demonstrations occurred in southern cities, though the extent to which food shortages *per se* helped push workers into active Resistance is questionable.

B. Frâchon, the communists' labour leader, insisted on the need to rebuild a clandestine network, similar to the factory cells of the 1920–34 years – despite setbacks such as at Renault where the entire PC team were exposed and arrested. Equally he urged communist militants to infiltrate Vichy's official unions in order to subvert the influence of the 'traitors' who ran them.[88]

By 1941 'economic' but communist-led strikes broke out in Paris, Bourges, Rouen and, as seen above, in the northern coalfields. In 1942 the PC strategy emphasized armed struggle, but in 1943 it switched back to industrial conflict with big strikes in the mines of the north, St Etienne and Montceau, where coal trains and barges were sabotaged. The re-uniting of communist and Jouhaux-ist wings of the CGT in 1943 was a bonus because the PC had hitherto been denouncing Jouhaux for supporting the suppression of communist unionists after the Nazi-Soviet pact.

The Resistance helped cement solidarities between French and immigrant workers. Thus many Italians and Poles in the mines of Decazeville, the Gard and Carmaux were veterans of struggles against Mussolini and Franco and played a key role in the *maquis* and in the guerilla war of the Liberation. Poles in the northern mines had their own reasons for hating Hitler.[89] The *maquis* recruited heavily, too, among agricultural workers in the centre and south, areas with a history of rural radicalism. The greatest recruiting sergeant of workers for the *maquis* was, however, the '*Service de Travail Obligatoire*' – compulsory labour service in the *Reich*, introduced once the voluntary *Relève* system of 1942 failed to attract enough applicants. Up to 30 per cent of the workforce of some Loire firms were conscripted. Mass evasion ensued, despite police round-ups and shootings of deserters in Lyon. Around St Etienne there were 900 on the run by April 1943, thousands by 1944. The system, as the authorities confessed, had 'a disastrous effect on the population, who unanimously disapprove'. Over 50 per cent of known Resistance activists in the region were blue-collar workers.[90]

Three thousand workers at the locomotive works at Oullins (Lyon) in October led the first mass worker protest against labour service. Their example sparked sympathy strikes across the Lyonnais region, street demonstrations and led to 24 arrests. Railway workers had spearheaded the 1920 strikes and the growth of the CGTU in the 1920s but had been relatively quiet in 1936–38. Now their key strategic importance to the Nazi war effort gave them a vanguard role in the Resistance.[91] The clandestine *Tribune des Cheminots* encouraged strikes on work issues, such as excessive hours for drivers. Yet at the same time communist railmen established sabotage groups, derailed trains taking goods to Germany, and helped political refugees escape. They paid a terrible price for their actions – hundreds of communist railmen were shot by the Gestapo, including the inter-war union leader P. Semard. Mass protest strikes at rail depots at Dijon and Vitry greeted arrests of militants. Predictably, it was railworkers who played the key strategic role in disrupting the Nazis during the Liberation.[92]

The clandestine vitality of the PC in industrial struggles bore fruit in its capture of the CGT at the Liberation and in the huge growth of membership and voters in 1945.[93] Conversely the SFIO was less suited to clandestine militancy. It did regroup after the 1940 schism, when most of its deputies voted power to Pétain. But its Resistance activities involved relatively little grass-roots industrial agitation, though Liberation did recruit workers and a quarter of the party's voters in 1945 were working class. The earlier shifts in membership towards the liberal professions and teachers and geographical shifts towards the rural and small-town south were accentuated.

If, eventually, subordination to Stalin's global strategy led to the PC's squandering of this political capital, this 'party of a new type' had acquired huge prestige by its wartime achievements. G. Noiriel argues that the experiences of the Resistance (and of the quasi-insurrectionary strikes of 1947) built on the community and organizational solidarities of the 'new' proletariat which had gone through its baptism of fire in 1936. The 'classic' French proletariat reached its apogee in the 1936–60 period, until social and techno-logical changes and the ossification of Stalinist Marxism produced the present crisis of the blue-collar working class and of the PC itself.[94] For the PC the Resistance provided a heroic myth which legitimized it in the eyes of many workers. A sociological study of the 1970s investigating the 'radicalism' of French workers claimed that one major explanation lay in the war-time experience which confirmed workers' conviction that the French ruling class were not simply capitalist exploiters but unpatriotic pro-Fascist traitors.[95]

NOTES AND REFERENCES

1. A. Kriegel, *Aux Origines du Communisme Français 1914–21*, 2 vols, Paris, 1964.
2. G. Noiriel, *Les ouvriers dans la société française: XIXe et XXe siècles*, Paris, 1986. Much of this article relies heavily on Noiriel's analysis, although I find his pessimistic structural determinism slightly exaggerated.
3. Simultaneously service-sector workers increased by 80 per cent (to 1.45 m.) and white-collar employees by 150 per cent (to 560,000).

4. G. Noiriel, *Longwy: Immigrés et Prolétaires: 1880–1980*, Paris, 1984.
5. A. Jones, 'The French Railway Strikes of 1920: New Syndicalism and Emergent Communism' in *French Historical Studies*, Vol. 12, No. 4 (1982), pp. 580–40.
6. C. Tilly and E. Shorter, *Strikes in France 1830–1968*, Cambridge, 1974.
7. R. Michaud, *J'Avais Vingt Ans*, Paris, 1967 (the autobiography of an anarchist shoe-worker).
8. M. Massard, 'Syndicalisme et Milieu Social (1900–1940): Le Creusot' in *Le Mouvement Social*, No. 99 (1977), pp. 23–38.
9. M. Fine, 'H. Dubreuil' in *Le Mouvement Social*, No. 106, (1979), pp. 45–64; H. Dubreuil – *'Standards': Le travail americain vu par un ouvrier français*, Paris, 1929; M. Fine, 'Towards Corporatism: The Movement for Capital-Labor Collaboration in France 1914–36', University of Wisconsin Ph.D., 1971.
10. P. Fridenson, 'Un tournant taylorien de la société française' in *Annales: Economie, Société, Civilisation*, 42 année, No. 5 (1987); G. Humphreys, *Taylorism in France 1914–20*, New York, 1986.
11. G. Cross, 'The Quest for Leisure: Reassessing the 8-Hour Day in France' in *Journal of Social History*, Vol. 18 (1984), pp. 195–208; G. Cross, *Redefining Workers' Control: Rationalisation, Labor Time and Union Politics in France 1900–28*, in J. Cronin and C. Sirianni (editors), *Work, Community and Power*, 1983.
12. Y. Lequin, 'Le rationalisation du capitalisme français a-t-il eu lieu dans les années vingt?' in *Cahiers d'Histoire de l'Institut Maurice Thorez*, (1979).
13. A. Moutet, 'Une rationalisation de travail dans l'industrie française des années trente' in *Annales E.S. C.*, 42 année, No. 5 (1987).
14. G. Cross, *Immigrant Workers in Industrial France*, Philadelphia, 1983; P. Milza (editor), *L'immigration italienne en France d'une guerre a l'autre*, Paris, 1987; D. Reid, 'The Limits of Paternalism: Immigrant Coal Miners' Communities in France 1919–45' in *European History Quarterly*, Vol. 15, (1985), pp. 99–118.
15. P. Videlier, *Vénissieux de A à V 1921–31*, Lyons, 1983; P. Videlier, *La Restructuration de la main d'oeuvre: Le cas de Vénissieux* in *Université de Lyon II: Rapport de Recherche*.
16. S. Schweitzer, *Des Engrenages à la Chaine: Les Usines Citroën 1915–35*, Lyon, 1982.
17. J. Depretto and S. Schweitzer, *Le Communisme à l'Usine: Vie Ouvrière et Mouvement Ouvrier chez Renault 1920–39*, Lille, 1984.
18. P. Fridenson, 'Automobile Workers in France and Their Work 1914–83' in S. Kaplan and C. Koepp (editors) *Work in France*, Ithaca, 1986; A. Fourcaut, *Femmes à l'Usine: Ouvrières dans l'entreprise française de l'entre-deux-guerres*, Paris, 1982.
19. G. Navel, *Travaux*, Editions Stock, 1945.
20. O. Hardy-Hémery, 'Rationalisation technique et rationalisation du travail à Anzin 1927–38' in *Le Mouvement Social*, No. 72 (1970), pp. 3–49; A. Moutet, 'La rationalisation dans les mines du Nord à l'épreuve du Front Populaire' in *Le Mouvement Social*, No. 135 (1986), pp. 63–99.
21. D. Reid, *The Miners of Decazeville*, Cambridge, Mass., 1985.

22. C. Cubar, G. Guyot, J. Hedout, 'Sociabilité Minière et changement social à Sallaumines' in *Revue du Nord*, LXIV, No. 253 (1982), pp. 365–463.
23. G. Noiriel, *Longwy*, op. cit.; S. Bonnet, *L'Homme de Fer: Vol. I, 1889–1930*; *Vol. II, 1930–1959*, Metz, 1975–7; C. Noiriel, 'L'Histoire du Pays Haut Lorrain' in *Le Mouvement Social*, No. 115 (1981), pp. 77–87; M. Verret, 'Sur *L'Homme de Fer* de S. Bonnet' in *Le Mouvement Social*, No. 138 (1987), pp. 5–20.
24. See G. Navel, *Travaux*, op. cit.
25. J. Sherwood, 'Rationalisation and Railway Workers in France' in *Journal of Contemporary History*, Vol. 15, No. 3 (1980), pp. 443–74.
26. T. Judt, 'The French Socialist Party, 1921–36' in T. Judt, *Marxism and the French Left*, Oxford, 1986.
27. R. Wohl, *French Communism in the Making: 1914–24*, Stanford, 1966; A. Kriegel, *Aux origines*, op. cit.
28. R. Tierky, *French Communism: 1920–72*, New York, 1974.
29. J. Girault (ed.), *Sur l'implantation du Parti Communiste dans l'entre-deux-guerres*, Paris, 1977.
30. M. Hastings, 'Identité culturelle locale et Politique Festive Communiste: Halluin la Rouge 1920–34' in *Le Mouvement Social*, No. 139 (1987), pp. 7–25.
31. S. Magri, 'Le mouvement des locataires à Paris et dans sa banlieue 1919–25' in *Le Mouvement Social*, No. 137 (1986), pp. 55–76.
32. A. Fourcaut, *Bobigny, banlieue rouge*, Paris, 1986; J. P. Flamard, *La question du logement et le Mouvement Ouvrier Français*, Paris, 1981.
33. *Trade Union Membership:*

	Total	GCT	CGTU
1920	2 million	2 million	—
1921	837,000	488,000	349,000
1926	956,000	524,000	431,000
1934	755,000	490,000	264,000

34. K. Amdur, *The Syndicalist Legacy*, Illinois, 1986, Ch. 10, 11; K. Amdur, 'La tradition révolutionnaire entre le syndicalisme et le communisme dans la France de l'entre-deux-guerres' in *Le Mouvement Social*, No. 139 (1987), pp. 27–50.
35. M. Launay, *La CFTC 1919–39*, Paris, 1986.
36. G. Noiriel, *Les ouvriers*, op. cit.; J. Jackson, *The Politics of Depression in France 1932–6*, Cambridge, 1985.
37. I owe this analysis of French Fascism to Kevin Passmore, currently completing a Ph.D. thesis on the extreme Right in the Rhône in the 1930s at Warwick University. See also K. J. Müller, 'French Fascism and Modernisation' in *Journal of Contemporary History*, Vol. 11, No. 4 (1976), pp. 75–107.
38. Among those flirting with Fascism were 'modern' industrialists (e.g. Pucheu of the electrical sector) labour-intensive family firms hostile to unions and social-welfare costs and 'new' cadres such as engineers and managers.
39. G. Noiriel, *Les ouvriers*, op. cit.; B. Badie, 'Les grèves du Front Populaire aux usines Renault' in *Le Mouvement Social*, No. 81 (1972),

pp. 69–109; R. Hainsworth, 'Les grèves du Front Populaire: Le bassin houiller du Nord/Pas de Calais' in *Le Mouvement Social*, No. 96 (1976), pp. 3–30.

40. D. Brower, *The New Jacobins: The French Communist Party and the Popular Front*, New York, 1968; L. Derfler, 'Unity and the French Left' in *Science and Society*, Vol. 35 (1971), pp. 34–47.
41. J. Kergouat, *La France du Front Populaire*, Paris, 1986.
42. G. Dupex, *Le Front Populaire et les élections de 1936*. For a vivid example of the 2nd ballot 'betrayal' of the Popular Front by Radical politicians and voters see A. Bresle, 'Le Front Populaire à St. Etienne' in *Cahiers d'Histoire* (1966).
43. H. Gruber, L. *Blum, French socialism and the Popular Front: a case study in internal contradictions*, Ithaca, 1986. Among critiques of Blum from members of the SFIO far left see: D. Guérin, *Front Populaire: Révolution Manquée*, Paris, 1976 and C. Audry, *L. Blum ou la politique du juste*, Paris 1955; See also D. Noel Baker, 'The Politics of Socialist Protest in France: the left-wing of the Socialist Party 1921–38' in *Journal of Modern History*, Vol. 43 (1971) No. 1, pp. 2–41.
44. M. Moissonnier, *Nouvelles pratiques de la municipalité à Villeurbanne 1935–7* (unpublished conference paper).
45. *Industrial Production Index:*

1928	100
1929	109
May 1936	87
Sept. 1936	81
May 1937	94

46. J. Colton, 'Politics and Economics in the 1930s: The Balance Sheet of the "Blum New Deal"' in C. K. Warner (ed.), *From the Ancien Régime to the Popular Front*, New York, 1969; J. Amoyel, 'Les origines socialistes et syndicalistes de la planification en France' in *Le Mouvement Social*, Vol. 87 (1974), pp. 137–69; M. Margairaz, 'Les socialistes face à l'économie et à la société en juin 1936' in *Le Mouvement Social*, No. 93 (1975), pp. 87–108.
47. A. Prost, *La CGT à l'époque du Front Populaire*, Paris, 1964; M. Collinet, *L'ouvrier français: L'esprit de syndicalisme*, Paris, 1952.
48. S. Reynolds, *Femmes et Grèves de 1936* (unpublished conference paper). (This section rests heavily on this persuasive analysis.) See also S. Zerner, 'Ouvrières et employées entre la première guerre mondiale et la grande crise', Doctorat 3e cycle, Univ. de Paris X, Nanterre, 1985; A. Fourcaut, *Femmes à l'usine*, op. cit.; C. Rhein, 'Jeunes femmes au travail dans la Paris de l'entre-deux-querres', Doctorat 3e cycle, Univ. de Paris VII, 1977; M. Couteaux, 'Les femmes et les grèves de 1936: l'exemple des grands magasins', Mémoire de Maîtrise, Univ. de Paris VII, 1975.
49. There are obvious parallels here with the waves of strikes which had greeted the consolidation of Republican control of the State in 1879 and the appointment of the first ever socialist cabinet minister, Millerand in 1899; see M. Perrot, *Les ouvriers en grève 1870–90*, 2 vols., Paris, 1974.

50. M. Seidmann, 'The Birth of the Weekend and the Revolt against Work: Workers of the Paris Region during the Popular Front' in *French Historical Studies*, Vol. XIII, No. 2 (1982), p. 250.
51. A Prost, Les grèves de Juin 1936' in L. *Blum, Chef du Gouvernement 1936–7: Actes du Colloque*, Paris, 1967.
52. B. Carcérès, *Allons au devant de la vie: La Naissance du temps des loisirs*, Paris, 1981.
53. J. Kergoat, op. cit. (This section relies heavily on Kergoat's excellent analysis.) See also: J. Danos and M. Gibelin, *Juin 36*, Paris, 1972; G. Lefranc, *Juin 36: L'explosion Social*, Paris, 1966; G. Lefranc, 'Le probleme des grèves français de Mai–Juin 36' in G. Lefranc, *Essais sur les problemes sociaux et syndicaux*, Paris, 1970.
54. P. Broué and N. Dorey, 'Critique de Gauche et Opposition Révolutionnaire au Front Populaire' in *Le Mouvement Social*, No. 54 (1966) pp. 91–134; J. P. Rioux, *Révolutionnaires du Front Populaire*, Paris, 1973; J. Rabaut, *Tout est Possible*, Paris, 1974; T. Kemp, *Trotskyite and Left Critics of the Popular Front* (unpublished Conference paper); D. G. Berry, *The Hidden Popular Front: French Anarchism and the Front Revolutionnaire* (unpublished conference paper); N. Faucier, *Pacifisme et Antimilitarisme dans l'entre-deux-guerres*, Paris, 1983. Communist rail-union leader Semard insisted: 'This mass must be disciplined – and without giving it the impression that one is betraying its interests.'
55. J. Jackson, *Popular Tourism and Mass Leisure in the Popular Front's Cultural-Political Vision* (unpublished conference paper). This section relies heavily on this stimulating discussion; P. Ory, 'La politique culturelle du le Gouvernement Blum' in *Nouvelle Révue Socialiste*, (1975); B. Carcérès, op. cit.; S. Schweitzer, *Vous avez dit culture?* (unpublished conference paper); J. L. Chappal, *Les chemins de l'espoir ou les combats de Leo Lagrange*, Paris, 1983.
56. J. C. Richez and L. Strauss, *Tradition et renouvellement des pratiques de loisirs dans L'Alsace des années trente* (unpublished conference paper); M. de Veth, '*La politique culturelle des syndicats ouvriers pendant l'entre-deux-guerres*', thesis, Inst. Fr. de Utrecht, 1981.
57. S. Clouft, 'Les Faucons Rouges', thèse de Doctorat, Univ. de Paris X, 1983; W. L. Murray, 'The French Workers' Sports Federation and the Victory of the Popular Front in 1936' in *The International Journal of the History of Sport*, Vol. 4, No. 2 (1987).
58. D. Tartakowsky, *Manifestations, Fêtes et Rassemblements à Paris 1936–8* (unpublished conference paper).
59. N. Gérome, *Le Front Populaire et Les Loisirs à Poitiers en 1936* (unpublished conference paper); M. Agulhon, *The Republic in the Village*, Cambridge, 1983.
60. G. Vincendeau and K. Reader (eds.), *La Vie est à Nous: French Cinema of the Popular Front*, National Film Theatre dossier, No. 3, London, 1986.
61. J. Kolbloom, *La Remanche des Patrons: Le Patronat Français face au Front Populaire*, Paris, 1986.
62. J. Colton, *Compulsory Labour Arbitration in France 1936–9*, New York, 1951; J-P. Rioux, 'La Conciliation et l'arbitrage obligatoire des conflits

du travail' in R. Rémond and N. Bourdin (eds.), *E. Daladier, Chef du Gouvernement*, Paris, 1977.

63. For the failure of Blum to purge rightists from the bureaucracy see I. Wall, 'Socialism and Bureaucrats: the Blum Government and French Administration' in *International Review of Social History*, Vol. 19 (1974), pp. 325–46.

64. G. Noiriel, *Les ouvriers*, op. cit.

65. M. Seidmann, *The Birth of the Weekend*, op. cit.

66. On revolutionary syndicalism in the pre-1914 building union see M. McMechan, 'The Building Trades of France 1907–14', University of Wisconsin, Ph.D., 1974; N. Bavarez, *Le Front Populaire et le Marché du Travail* (unpublished conference paper); G. Navel, *Travaux*, op. cit.; M. Moissonnier, 'Le cartel lyonnais du bâtiment à l'heure de l'unification syndical' in *Cahiers d'Histoire de l'Institut de Recherches Marxistes*, (1983); C-A. Defer, 'La féderation du bâtiment CGT au moment du Front Populaire' Mémoire de maîtrise, 1971.

67. H. Chapman, 'The Political Life of the Rank and File: French Aircraft Workers and the Popular Front 1936–38' in *International Labour and Working-Class History*, No. 30, Fall (1986); H. Chapman, 'Reshaping French Industrial Politics: The Struggle for Control in the Aircraft Industry 1928–50', University of California. Ph.D. thesis, Berkely, 1980.

68. A. Moutet, *La rationalisation dans les mines du Nord*, op. cit.; G. Noiriel, *Longwy*, op. cit.; A. Mitzmann, 'The French Working Class and the Blum Government' in *International Review of Social History*, Vol. 9 (1964), pp. 363–90.

69. S. Berstein, 'Les classes moyennes contre la gauche' in *L'Histoire* (1984); P. Larmour, *The French Radical Party in the 1930s*, 1964; R. Remond and N. Bourdin (eds.), *E. Daladier, Chef du Gouvernement*, op. cit.

70. P. Fridenson, 'Le patronat français' in R. Rémond and J. Bourdin (eds.) *La France*, op. cit.

71. A. Prost. *La CGT*, op. cit.

72. N. Bavarez, *Le Front Populaire*, op. cit.

73. M-F. Rogliano, L'anticommunisme, dans la CGT: "Syndicats" in *Le Mouvement Social*, No. 87 (1974), pp. 63–84. Also see N. Greene, *Crisis and Decline: The French Socialist Party in the Popular Front*, Ithaca, 1969.

74. M. Launay, *La CFTC*, op. cit.

75. G. Bourdé, *La defaite du Front Populaire*, Paris, 1977; Depretto & Schweitzer. *Le communisme*, op. cit.; J. Kergouat, *La France du Front Populaire*, op. cit.

76. D. Avignon, 'La répression de la grève générale de Novembre 1938 à travers la presse', Mémoire de Maîtrise, Univ. de Paris VIII, 1975.

77. Belin, above all an anticommunist, shifted to support for national defence after the Nazi-Soviet pact – before becoming a Vichy Minister! R. Belin, *Du secretariat de la CGT au Gouvernement de Vichy*, (Mémoires 1933–42), (1978).

78. D. Levy, *Factors in the Organisation and Mobilisation of the Marseille Working-Class During the Popular Front* (unpublished conference

paper); J. Bailly, 'Le mouvement ouvrier à Marseille 1938–9', Diplôme d'études supérieur, Aix 1971; M. Tournier, 'Les grèves dans la Bouche-du-Rhone 1938–9', Mémoire de Maîtrise, Aix, 1974; A. Olivesi, 'Marseille et le Sud-Est' in R. Rémond & N. Bourdin (eds.), *Daladier*, op. cit.

79. Among the exceptions are G. Noiriel, *Longwy*, op. cit. and D. Reid. *The Miners*, op. cit.

80. H. R. Kedward, *Resistance in Vichy France*, Oxford, 1978.

81. M. Luirard, 'Les ouvriers de la Loire et la Charte du Travail', in *Révue de l'Histoire de la Ile Guerre Mondiale*, (1976).

82. J-P. Azema, *From Munich to the Liberation: 1938–44*, Cambridge, 1984.

83. E. Dejonghe, 'Problèmes sociaux dans les houillères du Nord et du Pas-de-Calais' in *Revue d'Histoire Moderne et Contemporaine*, (1970). German troops occupied the pit-heads. Dozens of strikers were arrested, many dying in German concentration camps.

84. H. R. Kedward, *Resistance*, op. cit.; H. R. Kedward, 'Behind the Polemics: French Communists and Resistance 1939–41' in S. F. Hawes & P. T. Whale (eds.), *Resistance in Europe 1939–45*, Harmondsworth, 1976.

85. C. Tillon, *On chantait rouge*, Paris, 1977. Tillon was later purged from party leadership – in 1952 – for this nationalist deviation, and eventually quit the party.

86. H. R. Kedward, *Resistance*, op. cit., p. 201.

87. Indeed left-wing socialists around the journal *L'Insurgé* in the Lyon region tended to think that the PC was giving too little weight to the class war: see N. G. Figere, *Mémorial de L'Insurgé*, Paris, 1968.

88. S. Courtois, *Le PCF dans la Guerre*, Paris, 1980.

89. D. Reid, *The limits of paternalism*, op. cit.; G. Sentis, 'Les communistes des bassins houillères de l'Aveyron et du Tarn à la Libération', Thèse IIIe cycle, Lille III, 1980. Italian second-generation immigrants in the Lorraine steel region had become the bedrock of the PC hegemony there in the post-1945 period, see S. Bonnet, 'Political Alignments and Religious Attitudes within the Italian Immigration to the Metallurgical District of Lorraine' in *Journal of Social History*, Vol. 2, No. 2 (1968), pp. 123–55.

90. M. Luirard, *La région stephanoise dans la guerre et dans la paix 1936–51*, St Etienne, 1980.

91. P. Durand, *La SNCF pendant la guerre*, Paris, 1968. The SNCF administration were mainly technocratic collaborators. The Resistance did get some support from cadres, engineers and stationmasters. On the Ouillins Strike, see G. Chauvy, *Lyon 40–44*, Paris, 1985.

92. J. Jacquet, *Les cheminots dans l'Histoire Sociale de la France*, Paris, 1967.

93. M. Sadoun, *Les Socialistes sous l'Occupation*, Presses de la FNSP, 1982.

94. G. Noiriel, *Les ouvriers*, op. cit.

95. D. Gallie, *Social Inequality and Class Radicalism in France and Britain*, Cambridge, 1983.

CHAPTER FIVE
Germany

Stephen Salter

INTRODUCTION

In considering the German working class and politics between 1929 and 1945, a distinction must be made between the political attitudes and behaviour of *members* of the working class (as revealed by voting behaviour, membership of political parties, politically affiliated organizations, or – where this may be established – worker opinion) and the strategies pursued by political and economic *organizations* which claimed to represent the interests of members of this class. This having been said, it must be borne in mind that large numbers of members of the working *class* were also active members of *organizations* claiming to act on behalf of the interests of the working class as a whole; and that the political behaviour and attitudes of workers who were not members of such organizations were often shaped by the strategies pursued by these organizations. Therefore, if one may not equate the political attitudes and behaviour of members of the working class with the strategies pursued by 'working-class' political and economic organizations, nor may the two be entirely divorced. Any account of 'the German working class and politics' between 1929 and 1945 must pay attention to both; and to the relationship between the two.

On the eve of the Depression, Germany was the world's second-largest industrial economy. Rapid industrialization from the mid-nineteenth century, but especially from the early 1880s onwards, had been accompanied by the creation of a large industrial working class: by 1925, 42 per cent of the working population was employed in industry and handicrafts. Over three-quarters of these were 'workers' according to the census statistics. To these workers in industry and handicrafts should be added the 1.44 m. 'workers' in the trade and transport sectors of the economy. These 11.7 m. or so workers, together with their dependants, made up the working class as a socio-economic category.[1]

The creation of an industrial working class was paralleled by the development of trade unions from the 1860s onwards. The change in the balance of power between workers and employers which had accompanied the collapse of the Imperial state in 1918, led to a marked expansion of trade-union membership. Membership of the trade unions peaked in the immediate post-war period at slightly under 9.4 m. in 1920, a figure which was to fall steadily throughout the 1920s: by 1929, 5.9 m. workers were members of trade unions. The largest group of trade unions were those grouped under the General Confederation of Free Trade Unions (*Allgemeiner Deutscher-Gewerkschaftsbund*, ADGB) and with more than 4.9 m. members, affiliated to the German Social Democratic Party (SPD); but there was also a significant 'Christian', i.e. Roman Catholic, trade-union movement (with 793,000 members) and a small group of liberal trade unions (with 169,000 members).[2] Whilst one cannot simply equate working-class political parties – the SPD and the German Communist Party, the KPD – with the working-class electorate, industrial workers were strongly represented at the political level by these two parties, which gained 40.5 per cent of the unspoiled votes cast in the May 1928 elections to the *Reichstag*[3]; as well as by the Centre party,which continued to attract the support of a significant number of Catholic manual workers.

DEPRESSION

The size of the German industrial economy and its heavy dependence on exports by the later 1920s ensured that the impact of the Depression would be particularly severe in Germany. Structural weaknesses within the economy – especially German industry's heavy dependence on foreign loans – compounded the German economy's vulnerability to a major downturn in the world economy. By 1932, national income had fallen to 62 per cent of its 1928 level; gross fixed investment to 30 per cent; industrial production to 61 per cent, with the capital-goods sector being more severely affected (50 per cent) than the consumer-goods sector (78 per cent). Unemployment had risen from 8.5 per cent to 29.9 per cent of the dependent working population. Yet a much higher percentage – 43.7 per cent – of trade-union members were unemployed.[4] The impact on the industrial working class and the labour movement was little short of catastrophic. Unemployment was particularly concentrated in those sectors of industry in which the workforce had been best organized in trade unions. The state unemployment insurance system broke down under the strain of having to cope with 6 m. (registered) unemployed; and the effects of the Depression also extended to those workers fortunate enough to have kept their jobs. At least 16 per cent of these were working part time by 1932; and the state of the labour market, together with wage cuts imposed by the Brüning government, increased tax and insurance contributions and an increase in the cost of living, combined to reduce the real wages of employed industrial workers by perhaps 18 per cent. Workers were forced to work harder in order to retain their jobs and found themselves competing with one another in the wake of mass dismissals: strike activity diminished rapidly, the number of working days lost as a consequence of strike activity falling from 8.5 m. in 1928 to 1.1 m. in 1932.[5]

How did the Depression affect industrial workers' political behaviour? Perhaps the first point to note is that the Depression was not accompanied by any general depoliticization in Germany. Participation in elections to the *Reichstag* in September 1930 (81.4 per cent), July 1932 (83.4 per cent) and November 1932 (79.9 per cent) was not only higher than in the May 1928 election (74.6 per cent), but was higher also than the previous record participation in the June 1920 elections (78.4 per cent).[6] The Depression also witnessed a marked radicalization in the electorate of the two parties of the Left, the SPD and the KPD, with a clear shift in support from the former to the latter. Whilst the share of the vote received by the SPD fell steadily after May 1928 to 24.5 per cent in September 1930, 21.6 per cent in July 1932 and 20.4 per cent in November 1932, that of the KPD increased to 13.1 per cent in September 1930, 14.3 per cent in July 1932 and 16.9 per cent in November 1932.[7] It is also clear that the Nazi Party (the NSDAP) was only a minor beneficiary of the general radicalization of the industrial working class which accompanied the Depression, despite strenuous effort by the party to win the allegiance of the majority of industrial workers from their traditional parties of the Left and from the Centre party. Traditional working-class environments remained remarkably resistant to Nazi electoral appeals; as did Catholic areas.

Throughout the Depression years, elections to the *Reichstag* saw a clearly negative correlation between the presence of industrial workers and the Nazi vote; and the Communist rather than the Nazi vote remained the strongest correlate of unemployment.[8] Nor was the NSDAP successful in large-scale recruitment from the industrial working class: whilst it is clear that a large proportion of recruits to the Nazi paramilitary, the SA, were unemployed, it is by no means clear that these should be equated with the *working-class* unemployed; and, although the NSDAP claimed that 32.5 per cent of the new members it gained between November 1930 and January 1933 were 'workers', it seems likely that the bulk of this membership was drawn from the non-industrial workforce in handicrafts and small-scale manufacturing.[9] The picture of an industrial working class strikingly resistant to Nazi appeals is confirmed by the poor performance of the embryonic Nazi trades union (the NSBO) in the factory-council elections of the Depression years and its limited success in recruiting members.[10]

Thus, the Depression saw both a marked radicalization of the industrial working class and the failure of the NSDAP to benefit from this radicalization. Why did the SPD lose support on such a large scale to the KPD? And why did the NSDAP fail to win significant electoral support from the industrial working class?

The electoral decline of the SPD during the Depression years may be attributed not merely to the unattractive political strategy that the party was forced to pursue, but also to the impact of the Depression upon its electoral constituency. The collapse of the last coalition government which commanded a majority in the *Reichstag* in March 1930 had been a direct consequence of the inability of the SPD and the German People's Party (DVP), which represented employers' interests, to agree on the means to fund the increasing demands being made of the state unemployment insurance scheme in the face of rapidly rising unemployment. The SPD initially mounted a vigorous opposition to the minority Brüning government but felt obliged to modify this strategy after the September 1930 elections, in which the NSDAP made significant gains and emerged as the second-largest party in the *Reichstag*. Henceforth, the SPD was to pursue a 'policy of toleration' (*Tolerierungspolitik*) towards the Brüning government, neither supporting it nor voting with the NSDAP and KPD in the *Reichstag* to bring it down, fearing a new surge in support for both the NSDAP and the KPD were new elections to be held. The party thus appeared to be acquiescing in the deflationary policies which the Brüning government implemented.

The SPD's own adherence to pre-Keynsian economics and the radicalization of its own members at grass-roots level prevented it from participating in government to modify the impact of Brüning's policies; fear of the likely outcome of new elections prevented it from bringing the minority government down. This was hardly a strategy likely to appeal to those of its supporters most directly affected by the Depression. The SPD was forced to stand by helplessly and watch the dismantling of many welfare provisions for whose introduction it had been responsible. Capable of no positive action, it appeared to have lost its political *raison d'être*. Its sober and realistic decision not to oppose the *coup d'état* carried out by Brüning's successor, Papen, against the Prussian *Land* government in July 1932, could easily be portrayed as political bankruptcy.[11]

Yet alongside the unattractiveness of its political strategy, the SPD also lost electoral support as the impact of the Depression led to a highlighting of divisions within the industrial working class. Bitter divisions opened up between the employed and the unemployed, strengthening the character of the SPD as a party of the employed, relatively skilled, privileged and 'respectable' working class, a character which had been apparent since the mid-1920s. The KPD, by contrast, increasingly came to be the party of the unskilled, semi-skilled, the young and, above all, the unemployed, who made up over 80 per cent of its membership by 1932. The KPD developed strategies more likely to appeal to the urban unemployed than those of the SPD such as rent strikes, prevention of evictions and the establishment of committees of the unemployed. The success of these strategies, and the perception of the SPD as a party of the relatively privileged, is confirmed by the strong correlation between unemployment and the communist vote in the elections of the Depression years.[12]

The failure of the NSDAP to make significant inroads into the industrial working class also needs to be explained both in terms of the political strategy pursued by the party and in social terms. After its refoundation in February 1925, the NSDAP had made determined efforts to break the hold of the SPD, KPD and Centre party over industrial workers in the urban centres of north and west Germany. Yet these efforts had, by 1928, been rewarded with little success. The 'urban plan' pursued by the NSDAP in the period before the 1928 elections failed to produce significant urban working-class support for the party: in the four electoral districts of the Ruhr, for example, support for the NSDAP was well below the 2.6 per cent of the vote the party secured throughout the

Reich as a whole. The reasons for this failure are not difficult to find. The NSDAP could offer workers little but slogans and its rabid nationalism was, if anything, a handicap when appealing to workers whose political consciousness – shaped especially by the SPD and the trade unions affiliated to it – was heavily influenced by the opposition of the principles of 'nation' and 'class', as a consequence of the long pedigree of the former as an ideological cornerstone of reactionary domestic politics. After the débâcle of the 1928 elections, the emphasis of NSDAP propaganda was to shift, with considerable success, to the middle classes disaffected with their traditional political representatives in the centre and right of the German political spectrum. Yet this was a two-way process, and the material interests of those social groups which came to form the core of the Nazi electoral constituency – the old lower-middle class and, to a lesser extent, the new lower-middle class – were to play a role in shaping the form and content of Nazi propaganda. Nazi propaganda advocated reduction of taxation, higher prices for food products, restrictions on consumer co-operatives and department stores, a reduction in wages and social services – a platform hardly calculated to make much appeal to industrial workers. Moreover, the formation by the NSDAP of a common front with the right-wing DNVP against the Young Plan in 1929 may have confirmed in the minds of many workers the traditional association between nationalism and the Right in German politics. This helps to account for the fact that the already pronounced inverse correlation between the presence in electoral districts of large numbers of manual industrial workers and the Nazi vote which had been apparent in the 1928 elections became more apparent in the elections of 1930 and 1932. Nazi appeals to the working class were not, however, entirely without success. By 1930, especially in Protestant areas, the NSDAP was attracting significant support from workers in the handicrafts and small-scale manufacturing sectors of the economy. Particularly important here seems to have been not the material position of these sections of the working class but rather the fact that they were not integrated into the organizations of the labour movement or into the working-class sub-culture associated with them.[13]

Mention of working-class *organization* leads on to the second main factor accounting for the relative lack of success of the NSDAP in winning large-scale support from the working class. For participation in the organizations of the labour movement was not simply a question of voting, but rather involved many aspects of everyday life in the working-class social environment, especially within the urban industrial strongholds of the SPD and KPD. Stigmatized as subversive 'outsiders' during the Imperial period, the urban working class had developed a remarkably dense associational network affecting almost every aspect of workers' lives. By 1914, this sub-culture embraced not only the SPD and unions but also a wide range of cultural organizations, sports clubs, housing and consumer co-operatives. Despite the upheaval of war and revolution, this sub-culture was to remain substantially intact; especially in the major urban industrial centres of the Ruhr, Saxony, Berlin and Hamburg. Even the division of the German Léft into the rival communist and social-democratic parties did not alter this picture significantly: indeed, as Detlev Peukert suggests, it may even have strengthened the comprehensive nature of the working-class milieu, as the KPD set up cultural organizations parallel to those of the SPD, thus duplicating a range of working-class organizations. Workers who abandoned the SPD during the Depression might easily be reintegrated into a politically rather different, but socially similar, sub-culture. Thus, working-class life was not characterized by any sharp division between the political and the non-political: rather, values, opinions and attitudes, political activity and everyday patterns of life were closely inter-woven. Whilst the NSDAP was able to recruit the support of workers *outside* of this milieu, it had little success in penetrating it. If workers *within* the political-cultural milieu of the organized working class were radicalized as a consequence of the Depression – and many were – this tended to benefit the KPD rather than the NSDAP.[14] Similar points might be made about the other major political sub-culture whose origins may be traced back to the Imperial period – the Catholic sub-culture – and Catholics were also to remain remarkably resistant to Nazi electoral appeals.

An examination of the July 1932 elections to the *Reichstag*, in which the NSDAP gained its highest-ever share of the popular vote in free elections (37.3 per cent), confirms this analysis. Whilst the NSDAP continued to concentrate its propaganda effort on the middle-class electorate, it did not abandon its attempts to win organized working-class voters away from the parties of the Left. Whilst much of its propaganda effort was directed at attacking the 'lies' of the SPD, underlining the failures of the SPD and the KPD, and trying to alter its image as a middle-class party, the NSDAP also sought to win workers' support through a determined attack on the von Papen government and advocacy of a large-scale public works programme and compulsory labour service for the young able-bodied unemployed. Yet even after three years of economic hardship, industrial workers do not appear to have abandoned their traditional parties for the NSDAP in significant numbers. Support for the NSDAP amongst industrial workers and amongst the unemployed remained weak. Moreover Nazi success in winning support from manual workers in the handicrafts and small-scale manufacturing sectors in the July 1932 elections had by and large disappeared by the November 1932 elections; a volatility which confirms the impression that it was the members of this socially amorphous section of the working class who were most likely to desert the parties of the Left for the NSDAP.[15]

DICTATORSHIP, 1933–1939

Before Hitler's appointment as Chancellor on 30 January 1933, the NSDAP had clearly failed to win the support at the polls of a significant proportion of the industrial working class. Yet the long-term foreign-policy ambitions of the Nazi leadership required the integration of the industrial working class into the 'national community' (*Volksgemeinschaft*): the possibility of a repetition of what the Nazi leadership saw as the 'betrayal of 1918' – supposed victory in an imperialist war being undermined by the disloyalty of the working class on the home front – must be eliminated. The NSDAP in power was consequently committed from the outset to the elimination of the trade unions as effective representatives of workers' interests as well as to the destruction of those political parties claiming to speak for the working class, the SPD and the KPD.[16] It seems clear, however, that the new government had no blueprint for the destruction of the trade unions and the parties of the Left: rather, the form assumed by and the pace of the government's policies towards the SPD, KPD and labour movement were to be shaped by a variety of pressures from below, principally the activities of the party and the paramilitary SA on the ground.

The government initially adopted the tactic of a gradual escalation of the political intimidation of the Left as part of its campaign against the SPD and KPD leading up to the *Reichstag* elections of 5 March 1933. This tactic was to some extent undermined by the employment of the SA as auxiliary police in Prussia from mid-February onwards; yet it was the wave of local party and SA activity which followed the *Reichstag* fire (27/28 February 1933) which marked the turning point in the government's policy towards the Left. The Nazi leadership appears genuinely to have believed that the *Reichstag* fire was a signal for a general communist uprising, and this belief led it to abandon its earlier strategy of postponing repression of the KPD until after the 5 March elections. On the basis of the Decree of the Reich President for the Protection of People and State of 28 February, which suspended the basic civil liberties embodied in the Weimar constitution, a full-scale terror campaign against the KPD was unleashed: large numbers of members of the KPD were arrested, KPD offices were occupied and the communist press was suppressed. The KPD had long made preparations for the eventuality of its being forced underground, yet these proved largely ineffective, not least because, if the party were to continue to contest the 5 March elections, any shift of the party organization to a clandestine footing could only be partial: in the two weeks following the Decree of 28 February perhaps 10,000 communists were arrested in Prussia alone. As early as 3 March, the leader of the KPD, Ernst Thälmann, and the group of functionaries with him, were arrested in Berlin; and the concentration of arrests on middle-ranking KPD functionaries resulted in a paralysis of the party.

The SPD was also subject to serious harassment from the SA and Nazi-party activists on the ground, as well as from the police, in the period leading up to the elections of 5 March. The widespread demoralization of ordinary SPD members in the face of mounting intimidation helps to explain the passivity of the party leadership when confronted by the Nazi 'seizure of power from below' in the *Länder* (regions) which followed the elections. An obsessive concern with the preservation of the organizational forms of the party, combined with the SPD's self-image and role as a democratic republican party and the incapacity of the trade unions to take effective economic action during a period of record unemployment, led the leadership to advocate purely constitutional opposition to the Nazi seizure of power.[17]

It is a testament to the resilience of the industrial working-class sub-culture outlined above that in the 5 March elections, the combined share of the vote received by the SPD and KPD fell by less than one-fifth, from 37.6 per cent (November 1932) to 30.4 per cent (March 1933), despite the fact that following the *Reichstag* fire many of the candidates of the two parties were arrested and press restrictions made effective electoral propaganda by the SPD

107

and KPD more or less impossible. The significance of the electoral losses sustained by the KPD and SPD in March 1933 is further diminished if it is recognized that the NSDAP was the principal beneficiary of the record turn-out (89 per cent) which characterized the *Reichstag* elections, as previous non-voters appear to have voted disproportionately for the NSDAP. In terms of absolute numbers of votes cast, the combined votes for the SPD and KPD declined only from 13.2 m. to 12.0 m. with over nine-tenths of this decrease being accounted for by the decline in electoral support for the KPD; no doubt largely as a consequence of the fearful pressures under which the party was working by this stage.[18]

Following the 5 March elections, the suppression of the left-wing parties was rapidly completed. On 10 March 1933, the SPD's property was confiscated and the social democratic press was suppressed; and following the call in early May by SPD émigrés for opposition to the new régime, the SPD was banned on 22 June. The Law against the Establishment of Parties of 14 July 1933 outlawed all political parties other than the NSDAP.[19]

This process of the exclusion of the political parties of the Left was paralleled by the destruction of the trade-union movement. At the beginning of March 1933, the Reich Labour Minister, Seldte, had plans drawn up whereby the role of the trade unions in the economy was to be gradually reduced. Yet the wave of local party and SA terror which followed the *Reichstag* fire extended beyond the parties of the Left to encompass the trade unions, and Seldte's plans were redundant almost before they had been drawn up. In early March 1933, the SA, SS and NSBO spearheaded attacks on union officials and the occupation of union offices, and by the middle of the month the trade unions could barely function in many large German cities. The SA and the NSBO took it upon themselves to replace representatives of the Free Trade Unions on factory councils. Yet despite this intimidation the NSBO was unable to secure a majority in the elections to the factory councils, and on 4 April, the régime suspended all such elections for six months.[20]

The lack of effective opposition by the trade unions to the terroristic campaign unleashed against them by the SA, NSBO and local NSDAP appears to have taken the Nazi leadership by surprise. When it became clear that the trade unions were as concerned as the SPD to seek to maintain their organizational existence through the pursuit of a strictly legal strategy, however, Hitler, Goebbels and Ley (the *Reich* Organization Leader of the NSDAP) decided to exploit the situation to settle the trade-union question quickly; and in mid-April

1933, plans were drawn up for the take-over of the trade unions. The government laid the foundations for the dissolution of the trade unions through a massive propaganda campaign co-ordinated by Goebbels, stressing the government's commitment to transcending class conflict and ensuring for workers a place of honour within the *Volksgemeinschaft*. The climax of this campaign came with the declaration by the government of 1 May as a public holiday for the first time ('Day of National Labour'). Early on 2 May, the SA, auxiliary police and NSBO functionaries occupied the offices of the Free Trade Unions throughout Germany, and a number of leading trade unionists were arrested: Ley announced the planned formation of a new organization intended to replace the trade unions, the German Labour Front (*Deutsche Arbeitsfront*, DAF). The coup of 2 May against the Free Trade Unions was in many respects of symbolic rather than real significance, since the majority of the trade union offices occupied on 2 May had in any case for several weeks only been able to function under the 'supervision' of the SA and NSBO. Pressure was now brought to bear on the liberal trade unions, which quickly subordinated themselves to the DAF; and with the dissolution of the Christian trade unions in late June 1933 (one of the provisions of the Concordat between the government and the Vatican) the last independent representative institutions of industrial workers disappeared.[21]

Thus, by the summer of 1933, German workers had been deprived of all independent institutions capable of representing their interests at the economic and political levels. This major shift in the balance of class power was soon to be embodied in law, as the essentially negative and destructive campaigns against the trade unions and the parties of the Left of spring 1933, gave way to a more positive consolidation of the 'reordering of class relations'. It rapidly became apparent that the DAF was not to act as a replacement for the independent trade unions; and the basic labour legislation of the Third Reich, the Law for the Ordering of National Labour of 20 January 1934, significantly strengthened the position both of employers at the expense of workers and of the Reich Ministry of Labour at the expense of the DAF. The factory councils of the Weimar period were replaced by so-called 'Councils of Trust', the regulation of working conditions was to be the responsibility of the regional officials of the *Reich* Ministry of Labour (the *Reich* Labour Trustees), and strikes were made illegal.[22] In this situation, labour in the Third Reich was essentially reduced to the status of a pure commodity, whose 'price' was to be determined principally by the

laws of supply and demand. The material experience of workers in
the period before the outbreak of war was thus shaped largely by
the global state of the labour market and the position of individual
industrial branches within the economy.

On Hitler's appointment as *Reich* Chancellor, unemployment
stood at 6.0 million. The new régime rapidly adopted plans to
reduce unemployment elaborated by the government of Hitler's
predecessor, von Schleicher, and supplemented these during the
summer of 1933 with a number of measures of its own. Yet it
was only during 1934, with the expansion of state contracts for
infrastructural projects to serve the rearmament programme, that
a long-term solution to high unemployment began to emerge. From
1936 onwards, manipulation of unemployment statistics was no
longer necessary as the massive rearmament programme launched
by the régime acted as the motor for economic recovery and a steady
reduction in unemployment. In March 1936, unemployment fell
below the two million mark; and during the remainder of the
pre-war period it was never again to rise above this level. In
April 1937, unemployment fell below one million: effective full
employment had been achieved.[23] Indeed, from mid-1938 onwards,
the German economy was characterized by a considerable labour
shortage, a labour shortage which soon began to jeopardize the
continuation of rapid rearmament, and workers were able to exploit
their relative market scarcity to secure significant improvements in
wages and working conditions during the later 1930s. Thus, whilst
wages and earnings were generally stagnant between 1933 and 1936
(and in some industrial sectors almost certainly fell), by 1939 real
hourly earnings had, according to the offical cost-of-living index,
risen to their 1929 level, and real weekly earnings had recovered
to their 1929 level a year earlier in 1938. Whilst the official
cost-of-living index almost certainly overstates the recovery of
real hourly and weekly earnings, it seems clear that real weekly
earnings had risen to their 1929 level by 1939, real hourly earnings
by 1941.[24] Moreover, whilst the evidence on working conditions is
not easily quantifiable, it seems clear that during the later 1930s
and especially during 1938–39, many employers, particularly in
the armaments and armaments-related sectors of the economy,
sought to improve working conditions as a means of attracting
workers in a tight labour market, especially ever-more scarce
skilled workers. The picture varied, of course, from industrial
sector to industrial sector: differentials in earnings between the
production-goods and the consumer-goods sectors of the economy

almost certainly widened between 1933 and 1936, for example; the inability of the Ruhr coal-mining industry (as a consequence of state-imposed price controls) to pass on higher labour costs in the form of higher prices seriously limited its capacity to compete with the adjacent armaments-related industries for scarce manpower by increasing wages, and the nature of mining meant that significant improvements in working conditions were difficult to achieve.[25] But the general picture of a recovery of real weekly earnings to their 1929 level by the outbreak of war, even if in large part as a consequence of a longer working week, remains.

By the summer of 1933, non-nazi working-class politics had effectively been forced underground. Any analysis of workers' oppositional political behaviour and values is, consequently, difficult. The first major problem is a definitional one: what behaviour may be considered 'political'? On the one hand, one might argue that only activity aimed directly at undermining the régime constitutes oppositional activity: on this reading, our analysis should concentrate on clandestine resistance activities. On the other hand, one may argue that, given the totalitarian aspirations of the Nazi régime, any refusal to subordinate one's interests to the overriding goals of the régime of imperialist expansion through war and to the economic and social measures necessary to the achievement of this goal, constituted a form of 'structural resistance' in so far as such 'resistance' limited the capacity of the régime to realize its goals, and so must be construed as political behaviour.[26] The second major problem is that any analysis which confines itself to *behaviour* alone runs the risk of ignoring the important area of attitudes and values, and so failing to take account of those elements of consent and dissent which did not result in political action (however this may be defined). An adequate discussion of 'the working class and politics' must take account of clearly political resistance activities; patterns of worker behaviour which, taken as a whole, indicated a refusal of workers to subordinate their interests to the objectives of the régime, and so might qualify as a form of opposition; and worker opinion towards the régime and its policies.

Working-class resistance to the Nazi régime was dominated by the underground activities of the KPD, which never abandoned its belief in the possibility of active conspiratorial opposition to the régime. Such resistance activity largely assumed the form of the printing and distribution of oppositional leaflets. In the years immediately following the Nazi seizure of power, communist oppositional activity was characterized by the participation of a high proportion of the

1933 party membership, perhaps half of whom undertook some illegal political activity in the period 1933–35. Yet the attempt to maintain a mass underground resistance was a hopeless one given the effectiveness of the *Gestapo* (state secret police) in penetrating resistance organizations; the horrifying dangers which confronted participants in clandestine oppositional activity being magnified by the pyramidal structure which the underground KPD sought to maintain. On numerous occasions, the capture by the Gestapo of middle- or high-ranking functionaries within the underground KPD organization led to the arrest of dozens or even hundreds of ordinary underground workers; and in 1935–36, in particular, the Gestapo was able to make mass arrests which did immense damage to the underground resistance. During the later 1930s, the KPD was both to reorganize its underground units, in an attempt to contain the damage which followed the arrest of individual members of the resistance, and to place greater emphasis on the penetration by members of the resistance of Nazi organizations such as the DAF. Whilst this 'Trojan horse' strategy reduced the number of underground workers arrested by the Gestapo, there is little evidence that it was any more successful than outright opposition to the régime had been; and by the later 1930s, the bulk of the former KPD membership appears to have been resigned and inactive.[27]

Resistance activity by the SPD was on a much smaller scale, and the party rapidly abandoned any attempt to maintain an active underground organization. This decision was, to a large extent, the consequence of a much more sober and realistic assessment than informed the strategy of the KPD both of the danger inherent in the attempt to maintain clandestine activity in a police state and of the likelihood of mass discontent leading to the overthrow of the régime from within. The SPD increasingly saw its task as one of attempting to hold together former party members in informal meetings; and the party leadership in exile gradually came to see defeat in war as the only means whereby the régime could be overthrown, confining its underground activity to the maintenance of a network of contacts within Germany and the gathering of information on economic, social and political developments.[28] In practical political terms, therefore, social-democratic and communist resistance to the Nazi régime was of little significance; and, by the later 1930s, the bulk of the former membership of both parties was politically inactive, as the régime's security service (SD) noted.[29]

How far may the refusal of workers to subordinate their material interests to the goals pursued by the régime be seen as constituting a form of opposition? Clearly, any conflict within society over the distribution of power and resources is political in some sense, and the approach of those historians who emphasize the notion of 'structural resistance' (*Resistenz*) by workers to the Nazi régime has the merit of avoiding an unnecessarily rigid (and probably unsustainable) distinction between political conflict on the one hand and economic conflict on the other. But, having conceded this, there are clearly limits to the helpfulness of construing economic conflict as a form of political action. Industrial workers certainly sought to exploit their market scarcity during the later 1930s to secure improvement in their earnings and working conditions, and did not shy from evading the attempts of the régime to restrict labour mobility and contain wage increases. Yet perhaps the most significant feature of the 'economic class conflict' which 're-emerged in Germany on a broad front after 1936' is that it generally assumed the form of attempts by *individual* workers to improve their material situation through *individual* action, principally through changing their jobs; and whilst the widespread occurrence of frequent job-changing, falling productivity and increasing absenteeism rates, created difficulties for the régime in maintaining the pace of the rearmaments programme in the later 1930s, there is little evidence to suggest that such phenomena were politically motivated.[30] Moreover, if the notion of 'structural resistance' – ignoring the intentions of actors and concentrating on the consequences of their actions – is to be applied consistently, then it follows that one should ask just how far such patterns of worker behaviour prevented the régime from realizing its goals. Here the evidence seems to suggest that, whilst the overheating of the economy as a result of the armaments boom and the problems associated with this seriously worried some sections of the Nazi leadership, the net effect was to push the régime in a direction in which it was in any case determined to go.[31]

Mention of the intentions which lay behind workers' attempts to defend and improve their earnings and working conditions in the later 1930s, leads one naturally on to workers' attitudes and values. In the absence of any free and independent channels through which workers might voice their attitudes, and given the omnipresent threat of savage reprisals against the expression of dissident opinions, one must of course proceed cautiously in trying to chart worker opinion. Yet the widespread availability of régime-internal assessments of popular opinion from a variety of institutions which may be set alongside one another, together with the invaluable and generally reliable reports on conditions within Germany published by the SPD in exile, make at least a preliminary assessment of worker opinion possible.[32] From this material, a picture emerges of a working class which, while largely (and perhaps prudently) desisting from overt acts of resistance, was never positively integrated into the Nazi *Volksgemeinschaft*. By and large, workers maintained a profound scepticism about the régime's claims to have transcended class conflict and 'reordered class relations' in such a fashion that workers and employers now worked hand in hand for the realization of the régime's goals.[33] Yet, in the absence of any possibility of collective action by workers to advance their interests, the German working class seems to have undergone a process of atomization, along skill and gender lines, as a consequence of the fact that the route to improvement of one's position was essentially an individual route. This process of atomization at the economic level was reinforced by the destruction of the dense working-class associational life which had been characteristic of the Imperial and Weimar periods, facilitating Nazi ideological penetration of the working class after 1933.[34] The 'Führer myth', the belief in Hitler's elevated standing 'above politics' and in his quasi-superhuman powers, seems to have been almost as widespread amongst workers as amongst other sections of the community; and the bulk of German workers were also in the mainstream of German popular opinion both in acclaiming the foreign-policy successes of the régime in the pre-war period and in their conviction that no foreign policy issue was worth going to war for.[35]

WAR

The outbreak of war saw a further tightening of restrictions on labour mobility and the introduction by the régime of a series of measures initially to depress, then to freeze and to contain increases in earnings.[36] Neither of these sets of measures was entirely successful. Collusion between employers and workers, especially skilled workers, against the attempt to plan manpower allocation, together with the failure of the régime to implement much more than *ad-hoc* labour-direction policies, resulted in extensive labour mobility. Similarly, the willingness of many employers to seek to circumvent wage restrictions in the attempt to recruit scarce labour, and the inability of the authorities to police firms' wage policies effectively, led to significant increases in both real hourly and real weekly earnings between 1939 and 1941, moving the Reich Economics Chamber to write in May–June 1940 of 'war profiteering on the part of workers'.[37] Only with the shift of the war against Germany, were more effective labour-mobilization measures introduced, from January 1943 onwards. Such measures coincided with the transfer of many contracts in the armaments and armaments-related industries from a cost-plus to a fixed-price system, giving employers in these industries a material incentive to contain wage increases; and with the weakening of workers' bargaining position as the prospect of the withdrawal of 'reserved worker' status (determined effectively by employers), and consequent conscription, became steadily more unattractive.[38] After 1942, most workers in industry experienced a stagnation of their nominal hourly and weekly earnings and a sharp fall in their real weekly earnings as the cost of living continued to rise and the black market expanded. Whilst the exploitation of occupied Europe enabled the régime to secure a high level of nutrition for the civilian population down to 1943, from 1944 onwards the deterioration in rations was significant and in the winter of 1944/45 the average daily calorie intake of the civilian population on standard rations fell below the long-term nutritional existence minimum.[39]

Worker *opinion* on the outbreak of war was dominated by disorientation and anxiety – the memories of the slaughter of the First World War concentrated many workers' attention on the hope that they would not be conscripted; and during the exceptionally harsh winter of 1939/40, workers' morale was depressed by the inadequacies of the rationing system, a *Reich*-wide coal shortage, and the absence of any prospect of a rapid end of the war despite the conquest of Poland. The cautious mood of the bulk of German workers in early May 1940, however, rapidly turned to astonishment at the successes of the *Wehrmacht* in the west: Hitler's personal standing amongst all sections of the population reached its highest point ever with the conclusion of the armistice with the French government in mid-June 1940, and the popular-opinion agencies of the régime noted the massive integrative effect of the victories in the west. It seems clear that much of this euphoria was grounded in hopes for an early peace rather than in enthusiasm for military conquest as such; and as the promised invasion of Britain failed to materialize, and the population faced a second war winter, civilian morale fell. The invasion of the Soviet Union in June 1941 took the civilian population entirely by surprise and, after the initial successes of the *Wehrmacht*, the failure of the *Blitzkrieg* and the entry of the United States into the war combined to produce the first real crisis of confidence in the régime during the war. Worker morale fell further during 1942, with the disappearance of any prospect of an end to the war in the east, significant ration cuts, widespread bitterness about the injustice of the burgeoning black market and the beginnings of the allied air offensive in the west. The catastrophe of Stalingrad made plain to large sections of the civilian population that the war was lost; and worker opinion during the last two years of the war was shaped by the extension of the allied air offensive, the drive for a total mobilization of Germany's human resources for the war effort, and by an increase in working hours in combination with inadequate supplies of food, clothing and housing. The turn of the war against Germany had disastrous consequences for the prestige of the régime: the influence of the régime's propaganda became weaker and was gradually replaced by foreign radio stations, letters from relatives at the front and rumours as the main source of information about the war for the civilian population. In spring 1944, the branch of the security services responsible for monitoring popular opinion, the SD, concluded that the bulk of the population had given up any attempt to analyse the military situation and was demoralized and easy prey to all kinds of rumours, and whilst the *Reich*-level popular opinion surveys of the SD do not go beyond July 1944, regional and local material suggests that it was in a mood of increasing fatalism and disorientation that the working population experienced the last months of the Third Reich, concerned only to survive the inevitable collapse of the régime.[40]

If enthusiasm for the victories of the *Wehrmacht* during the early stages of the war, bringing as they did hope of an early end to the war, and the emergence from 1942 onwards of a basic defensive patriotism were undoubtedly characteristic of most workers, this should not be equated with the achievement by the régime of any positive integration into the *Volksgemeinschaft* of the majority of the German working class. Whilst Hitler's personal popularity amongst workers, as amongst other sections of the community, remained high until 1941–42 and was to prove an effective integrative factor until 1943, worker opinion during the war was characterized to an even greater extent than had been the case during the pre-war period by marked scepticism about the reality of the *Volksgemeinschaft*.[41] The popular-opinion reports of the régime noted time and again workers' resentment at the unequal distribution of the burdens imposed by the war, such resentment emerging most clearly over the inadequacies of the

116

rationing system and the growth of the black market and over the issue of conscription of women outside the labour market for war work.[42] In conjunction with this, the continuing efforts of workers to maintain and improve their earnings and working conditions and the poor work-discipline and high absenteeism of female and young male workers as well as of workers directed to projects distant from their homes, belie the propaganda image which the régime sought to project of a working population which stood foursquare behind the régime and which was willing to subordinate its material interests to the imperialist goals of the régime and the policies these dictated.[43] The general lack of respect which characterized workers' attitudes towards the NSDAP and the DAF suggest that affective solidarity stopped short of any reconciliation of workers to the dictatorship as such.[44] This is not to suggest the existence of any widespread and coherent, let alone politically articulated, opposition to the régime amongst workers; but rather to argue that the relationship between the régime and the working class during the war – as during the later 1930s – is better seen in terms of *containment* of working-class discontent rather than any enthusiasm for the régime and its policies.[45]

The argument for regarding the relationship between the régime and the German working class during the war in these terms is strengthened if the major extension of the state coercive apparatus directed against workers during the war is borne in mind. Whilst the basic criminalization of labour law had taken place before the outbreak of war, the early years of the war saw a dramatic increase in the number of warnings issued to workers by the *Reich* Labour Trustees, requests from employers to the Trustees to authorize the arrest of workers for labour-discipline offences, requests for prosecution of workers through the courts, requests for transferral of workers to concentration camps or (more commonly) to 'labour education camps'; all disciplinary measures bolstering the unchallengeable position of employers *vis-à-vis* their employees. If the attention of the state authorities – especially of the Gestapo – was to turn after 1942 mainly to foreign workers and prisoners of war employed in German industry, it is nevertheless significant that the number of German workers arrested each month for labour discipline offences rose by 52 per cent between 1941 and the first half of 1944 (in the latter period over 2,000 German workers were being arrested *each* month), and that from 1942 onwards employers were to develop additional disciplinary procedures designed to maintain work discipline within the factories.[46]

The relative quiescence of workers during the war, and especially during the second half of the war, despite widespread criticism of the régime and its policies amongst the working class, clearly owed a great deal to the existence of an ever-more brutal and autonomous terror apparatus as well as to the increasing absorption of most workers with the problems of day-to-day existence. These factors were largely responsible for the insignificance of communist resistance activities during the war: following the Molotov–Ribbentrop pact of August 1939, which cut the ground from under the feet of the underground KPD, resistance activity was to revive only with the invasion of the Soviet Union and the massive influx of foreign workers into Germany after 1941, and was never to embrace anything but a tiny proportion of the German working class.[47]

Yet, alongside terror and the mounting daily concerns of wartime existence, it seems clear that the gradual process of atomization and disorientation which had characterized working-class experience during the pre-war period was extended further by the war. Conscription and evacuations and the impact of the allied air offensive served not least to disrupt solidarity between workers, as did the widening of differentials in earnings between German workers and the fostering by employers and the state of structural divergences of material interest between German workers and foreign workers.[48] By the later stages of the war, faced with ever-mounting burdens, many German workers appear to have withdrawn completely into the sphere of purely personal concerns; and the workplace seems to have become one of the few stable points in a collapsing world – a fact which helps to account for the relatively good work discipline of adult male German workers down to 1945.[49]

Terror and atomization thus worked in the same direction, undermining the few possibilities for collective action by workers which had survived the destruction of independent working-class economic institutions and of the left-wing parties. The defeat suffered by the German working class in 1933 was enormous by any standards, and must ultimately be traced back not only to the deep political divisions which characterized the German working class before 1933 but also to the devastating impact of the Depression on the labour movement and the parties of the Left. From 1933 onwards, German workers were to become largely the objects of the regime's policies, effectively deprived of any capacity for independent collective action. The essential precondition for the restoration of democracy in Germany and for the reconstruction of

118

the German labour movement – the destruction of the Nazi régime – was to be supplied from outside.

NOTES AND REFERENCES

1. Petzina, D., Abelshauser, W., & Faust, A. (eds) *Sozialgeschichtliches Arbeitsbuch III. Materialien zur Statistik des Deutschen Reiches 1914–1945* (Munich, 1978) table 9(e), p. 57.
2. Ibid. table 22, p. 111. Union density figures can be calculated with reliability only for 1925, when approximately 42 per cent of 'workers' in industry, handicrafts, trade and transport were union members. It seems very likely that union density never exceeded 50 per cent during the Weimar years, after the Great Inflation of 1922–23. In addition to *Sozialgeschichtliches Arbeitsbuch III*, tables 9(e) and 22, see also: G. S. Bain and R. Price, *Profiles of Union Growth. A Comparative Statistical Portrait of Eight Countries* (Oxford, 1980) table 6.1, p. 133.
3. M. Broszat, *The Hitler State* (London, 1981) p. 1.
4. Accessible accounts of the impact of the Depression on the German economy are provided by: K. Hardach, *The Political Economy of Germany in the Twentieth Century* (Berkeley & London, 1980) and D. Petzina *Die deutsche Wirtschaft in der Zwischenkriegszeit* (Wiesbaden, 1977). Unemployment statistics in *Sozialgeschichtliches Arbeitsbuch III* table 25, p. 119.
5. T. W. Mason, *Sozialpolitik im Dritten Reich* (Opladen, 1977) pp. 89ff; *Sozialgeschichtliches Arbeitsbuch III*, table 23(a), p. 114.
6. D. Geary, 'Unemployment and Working-Class Solidarity: The German Experience 1929–33' in: R. J. Evans & D. Geary (eds) *The German Unemployed: Experiences and Consequences of Mass Unemployment from the Weimar Republic to the Third Reich* (London, 1987) pp. 261–80; here, p. 261. Electoral turn-out figures in: V. R. Berghahn, *Modern Germany. Society, economy and politics in the twentieth century* (Cambridge, 2nd ed, 1988) table 42, p. 301.
7. T. Childers, *The Nazi Voter. The Social Foundations of Fascism in Germany, 1919–1933* (Chapel Hill & London, 1983) pp. 141, 209, 211.
8. Ibid. pp. 178–88, 243–57.
9. Geary, 'Unemployment and Working-class Solidarity', pp. 263–5.
10. Mason, *Sozialpolitik*, pp. 69–72; Childers, *Nazi Voter*, p. 244f; for the factory council elections in the Ruhr mining industry, see K. Wisotzky, *Der Ruhrbergbau im Dritten Reich* (Düsseldorf, 1983) p. 24f.
11. On the political strategy pursued by the SPD during the Depression years, see: E. Matthias, 'Die Sozialdemokratische Partei Deutschlands' in E. Matthias & R. Morsey (eds) *Das Ende der Parteien 1933* (Düsseldorf, 1960); H. Schulze 'Die SPD und der Staat von Weimar' in M. Stürmer (ed) *Die Weimarer Republik. Belagerte Civitas* (Königstein, 1980) pp. 272–86; H. Mommsen 'Die Sozialdemokratie in der Defensive: Der Immobilismus der SPD und der Aufstieg des Nationalsozialismus' in H. Mommsen (ed) *Sozialdemokratie zwischen Klassenbewegung und Volkspartei*

(Frankfurt/Main, 1974) pp. 106–33; H. A. Winkler, 'Spielräume der Sozialdemokratie – Zur Rolle der SPD im Staat und Gesellschaft der Weimarer Republik' in V. Rittberger (ed) *1933. Wie die Republik der Diktatur erlag* (Stuttgart, Berlin, Cologne, Mainz, 1983) pp. 61–75.

12. Geary, 'Unemployment and Working-Class Solidarity', pp. 265–72.
13. Childers, *Nazi Voter* is the standard account of the Nazi electoral constituency. But Mason, *Sozialpolitik* Chapter II is also perceptive.
14. D. J. K. Peukert, *Inside Nazi Germany. Conformity, Opposition and Racism in Everyday Life* (London, 1987) p. 102; Dick Geary, *European Labour Protest 1848–1939* (London, 1981) p. 167.
15. Childers, *Nazi Voter* pp. 255–6; J. W. Falter 'Unemployment and the Radicalisation of the German Electorate 1928–1933: An Aggregate Data Analysis with Special Emphasis on the Rise of National Socialism' in: P. D. Stachura (ed) *Unemployment and the Great Depression in Weimar Germany* (London & Basingstoke, 1986) pp. 187–208; T. Childers, 'The Limits of National Socialist Mobilization: The Elections of 1932 and the Fragmentation of the Nazi Constituency' in T. Childers (ed) *The Formation of the Nazi Constituency 1919–1933* (London & Sydney, 1986) pp. 232–59, here p. 241f.
16. This is the theme of Mason, *Sozialpolitik* Chapter I. An earlier version of his argument is: T. W. Mason, 'The Legacy of 1918 for National Socialism' in A. J. Nicholls & E. Matthias (eds) *German Democracy and the Triumph of Hitler* (London, 1971).
17. The standard account of the Nazi seizure of power is: K. D. Bracher, W. Sauer & G. Schulz *Die Nationalsozialistische Machtergreifung* (Köln & Opladen, 1960). A brief, accessible account of the Nazi monopolization of political power is Broszat, *The Hitler State* Chapter 3. The strategy of the KPD is examined in S. Bahne, *Die KPD und das Ende von Weimar* (Frankfurt/Main, 1976). Detlev Peukert's regional study of the KPD under National Socialism, *Die KPD im Widerstand. Verfolgung und Untergrundarbeit am Rhein und Ruhr 1933 bis 1945* (Wuppertal, 1980) pp. 79–97 illustrates the impact of the Nazi terror on the KPD in early 1933. On the SPD, see Matthias, 'Die Sozialdemokratische Partei Deutschlands' in Matthias & Morsey (eds) *Das Ende der Parteien.* J. Noakes & G. Pridham (eds) *Nazism 1919–1945. vol. 1: The Rise to Power 1919–1934* (Exeter, 1983) pp. 138–9 gives examples of letters of resignation from SPD members in early 1933.
18. Bracher, Sauer & Schulz, *Die Nationalsozialistische Machtergreifung* p. 93; Berghahn, *Modern Germany,* table 42, p. 301.
19. On the demise of the SPD see Matthias in Matthias & Morsey (eds) *Das Ende der Parteien* p. 181. The text of the law of 14 July is available in translation in Noakes & Pridham (eds) *Nazism 1919–1945* vol. 1, p. 167.
20. Mason, *Sozialpolitik* pp. 82ff.
21. Ibid. pp. 85f; Broszat, *The Hitler State* pp. 138–140.
22. The text is available in Noakes & Pridham *Nazism 1919–1945* vol. 2, pp. 330 ff.
23. *Sozialgeschichtliches Arbeitsbuch III,* table 25a, p. 119; Noakes & Pridham, *Nazism 1919–1945* vol. 2, p. 359. On job-creation programmes, see Petzina, *Die deutsche Wirtschaft in der Zwischenkriegszeit* pp. 110–14.

24. By November 1938, according to the estimates of the Reich Ministry of Labour, there were a million vacancies in the German economy: Mason, *Sozialpolitik*, p. 215. On the development of nominal and real earnings, see G. Bry, *Wages in Germany 1871–1945* (Princeton, 1960) pp. 263ff. Bry's account must now be supplemented with T. Siegel 'Lohnpolitik im nationalsozialistischen Deutschland' in C. Sachse *et al.*, *Angst, Belohnung, Zucht und Ordnung. Herrschaftsmechanismen im Nationalsozialismus* (Opladen, 1982) pp. 54–139. Siegel's persuasive amendment of Bry's cost-of-living index is at pp. 103–6.
25. Examples of firms attempting to poach skilled workers from their rivals are provided by the reports of the Reich Labour Trustees to the Reich Ministry of Labour: T. W. Mason, *Arbeiterklasse und Volksgemeinschaft. Dokumente und Materialien zur deutschen Arbeiterpolitik 1936–1939* (Opladen, 1975) e.g. doc. 150, p. 900; doc. 156, p. 943. On the relationship between the general labour shortage and improvements in working conditions, see also: H. Yano, *Hüttenarbeiter im Dritten Reich* (Stuttgart, 1986) pp. 116–40. On the difficulties of the Ruhr mining industry, see: K. Wisotzky, *Der Ruhrbergbau im Dritten Reich* (Düsseldorf, 1983) pp. 179–213.
26. M. Broszat, 'Resistenz und Widerstand. Eine Zwischenbilanz des Forschungsprojekts' in: M. Broszat, E. Frohlich & A. Grossman (eds) *Bayern in der NS-Zeit IV. Herrschaft und Gesellschaft im Konflikt, Teil C* (Munich & Vienna, 1981) pp. 691–709, esp. p. 708. The notion of 'structural resistance' is implicit in Mason *Sozialpolitik* pp. 312–22 and is made explicit in T. W. Mason, 'The Workers' Opposition in Nazi Germany' in: *History Workshop Journal* 11 (spring 1981) pp. 120–37, esp. p. 120. See also: Peukert, *Inside Nazi Germany* pp. 118–20.
27. On communist resistance activity, see: Duhnke *Die KPD von 1933 bis 1945* (Cologne, 1971); Peukert, *Die KPD im Widerstand*; H. Weber 'Die KPD in der Illegalität, in R. Löwenthal & P. von zur Mühlen (eds) *Widerstand und Verweigerung in Deutschland 1933 bis 1945* (Berlin/Bonn, 1982) pp. 83–101; D. K. J. Peukert, 'Der deutsche Arbeiterwiderstand 1933–1945' in K-J. Müller (ed) *Der deutsche Widerstand 1933–1945* (Paderborn, 1986) pp. 157–81, esp. pp. 161–70; G. Plum 'Die Arbeiterbewegung während der nationalsozialistischen Herrschaft' in J. Reulecke (ed) *Arbeiterbewegung an Rhein und Ruhr* (Wuppertal, 1974) pp. 355–83, here pp. 371–8; H. Mehringer 'Die KPD in Bayern 1919–1945. Vorgeschichte, Verfolgung und Widerstand' in M. Broszat & H. Mehringer (eds) *Bayern in der NS-Zeit V* (Munich, 1983) pp. 1–286.
28. The secondary literature on SPD underground resistance activities within Germany matches the modest scale of such resistance. The articles by Peukert and Reulecke mentioned in note 27 above are helpful; but see also P. von zur Mühlen 'Sozialdemokraten gegen Hitler' in R. Loẅenthal & P. von zur Mühlen (eds) *Widerstand und Verweigerung*. The 'Germany Reports' of the SPD in exile are now available: K. Behnken (ed) *Deutschland-Berichte der Sozialdemokratischen Partei Deutschlands (SoPaDe) 1934–40* (7 vols., Frankfurt/Main, 1980). A recent regional study is: H. Mehringer 'Die bayerische Sozialdemokratie bis zum Ende des NS-Regimes. Vorgeschichte, Verfolgung und

Widerstand' in Broszat & Mehringer (eds) *Bayern in der NS-Zeit V* pp. 287–432.

29. I. Kershaw, *Popular Opinion and Political Dissent in the Third Reich: Bavaria 1933–1945* (Oxford, 1983) pp. 105–10; D. Peukert 'Der deutsche Arbeiterwiderstand 1933–1945' in D. K. Bracher, M. Funke & H. A. Jacobsen(eds) *Nationalsozialistische Diktatur 1933–1945. Eine Bilanz* (Bonn, 1983) pp. 633–54, here pp. 642ff. On the SD assessment of SPD and KPD resistance activities see: H. Boberach (ed) *Meldungen aus dem Reich. Die geheimen Lageberichte des Sicherheitsdienstes der SS 1938–1945* (Herrsching, 1984) vol. 2, 'Jahreslagebericht 1938' pp. 53–64 ('Marxismus'): significantly, the report for the first quarter of 1939 (pp. 215–330) contains no reference to left-wing opposition. The monthly and quarterly reports from the regional Gestapo offices for late 1938–early 1939 confirm this impression. They are gathered in Bundesarchiv Koblenz R58 file 446. See also: J. Schadt, *Verfolgung und Widerstand unter dem Nationalsozialismus in Baden. Die Lageberichte der Gestapo und Generalstaatsanwalts Karlsruhe 1933–1940* (Stuttgart, 1976) pp. 194–218.

30. The formulation is Mason's: see Mason, 'Workers' Opposition', p. 120. On the individual nature of workers' attempts to improve their material situation, see: Wisotzky *Ruhrbergbau* pp. 238–42; M. Zimmermann '"Ein schwer zu bearbeitendes Pflaster": der Bergarbeiterort Hochlarmark unter dem Nationalsozialismus' in D. Peukert & J. Reulecke (eds) *Die Reihen fast geschlossen* (Wuppertal, 1981); Peukert *Inside Nazi Germany*, pp. 103–18. The similarity between (individual) workers' action to improve their material situation in Germany in the later 1930s and in the UK during the Second World War (or, more generally, in the post-war capitalist economies enjoying full employment) was noted by a perceptive reviewer of Mason's work: H. A. Winkler 'Vom Mythos der Volksgemeinschaft' in *Archiv für Sozialgeschichte*, vol. XVII (1977) p. 484–90.

31. I. Kershaw, '"Widerstand ohne Volk?". Dissens und Widerstand im Dritten Reich' in: J. Schmädeke and P. Steinbach (eds) *Der Widerstand gegen den Nationalsozialismus* (Munich, 1985) pp. 779–98, here esp. pp. 785f. The debate surrounding the role of economic pressures and anxiety about extensive worker discontent as contributory factors to Hitler's increasingly desperate foreign-policy initiatives in 1938–39 is now extensive. Representative are: L. Herbst 'Die Krise des nationalsozialistischen Regimes am Vorabend des Zweiten Weltkrieges und die forcierte Aufrüstung. Eine Kritik' in *Vierteljahrshefte für Zeitgeschichte* 26 (1978) pp. 347–92; J. Dülffer 'Der Beginn des Krieges 1939: Hitler, die innere Krise und das Mächtesystem' in *Geschichte und Gesellschaft* 2 (1976) pp. 443–70; R. J. Overy 'Hitler's War and the German Economy: a Reinterpretation' in *Economic History Review* 2nd series 35 (1982) pp. 272–91; R. J. Overy 'Germany, "Domestic Crisis" and War in 1939' in *Past and Present* no. 116 (1987) pp. 138–68. I. Kershaw *The Nazi Dictatorship* (London, 1985) pp. 78–81 strikes a sensible balance.

32. M. Broszat, E. Fröhlich & F. Wiesemann (eds) *Bayern in der NS-Zeit* (Munich, 1977) pp. 193–202 discuss the source materials. See also: I.

Kershaw, *Popular Opinion and Political Dissent in the Third Reich: Bavaria 1933–1945* (Oxford, 1983) pp. 5–10.

33. Kershaw, *Popular Opinion and Political Dissent* pp. 66–110. The analysis offered by D. Schoenbaum, *Hitler's Social Revolution: Class and Status in Nazi Germany 1933–1939* (Anchor Books edition, New York, 1967) esp. pp. 73–112 must now be regarded as having been superseded.

34. Peukert, *Inside Nazi Germany* pp. 108–18.

35. I. Kershaw *Der Hitler-Mythos. Volksmeinung und Propaganda im Dritten Reich* (Stuttgart, 1980) esp. pp. 46–71 & 111–26; I. Kershaw, 'Alltägliches und Ausseralltägliches: ihre Redeutung für die Volksmeinung 1933–1939' in Peukert & Reulecke (eds) *Die Reihen fast geschlossen* pp. 273–92, esp. pp. 285–91.

36. Mason, *Arbeiterklasse* Chapters XIX–XXI; W. F. Werner, *'Bleib Ubrig!' Deutsche Arbeiter in der nationalsozialistischen Kriegswirtschaft* (Düsseldorf, 1983) pp. 34–44; M-L. Recker, *Nationalsozialistische Sozialpolitik im Zweiten Weltkrieg* (Munich, 1985) pp. 26–37, 58–63.

37. Bundesarchiv Koblenz, R11/77, p. 183; Werner *'Bleib Ubrig!'* pp. 58–72, 81–108; Recker, *Nationalsozialistische Sozialpolitik*, pp. 37–53, 63–81, 155–61.

38. Werner, *'Bleib Ubrig!'*, pp. 220–41, 274–92, 318–34; Recker, *Nationalsozialistische Sozialpolitik*, pp. 161–93.

39. Werner, *'Bleib Ubrig!'*, pp. 194–241, 329–35; L. Burchardt, 'The Impact of the War Economy on the Civilian Population of Germany during the First and Second World Wars' in W. Deist (ed.) *The German Military in the Age of Total War* (Leamington Spa, 1985) pp. 40–70.

40. On workers' morale during the war see: I. Kershaw, *Popular Opinion and Political Dissent* pp. 296–315; M. Steinert, *Hitlers Krieg und die Deutschen. Stimmung und Haltung der deutschen Bevölkerung im Zweiten Weltkrieg* (Düsseldorf, 1970); Boberach (ed.) *Meldungen* (see note 29); M. Broszat, E. Fröhlich & F. Wiesemann (eds) *Bayern in der NS-Zeit* (Munich, 1977) pp. 228–325, 592–664.

41. On the continuing integrative force of the 'Hitler myth' see: Kershaw *Hitler Mythos*, pp. 123–94.

42. D. Winkler, *Frauenarbeit im Dritten Reich* (Hamburg, 1977) pp. 135–38; H. Boberach (ed) *Meldungen aus dem Reich. Auswahl aus den geheimen Lageberichten des Sicherheitsdienstes der SS 1939–1944* (Neuwied & Berlin, 1965) pp. 373, 470f; Werner, *'Bleib Ubrig!'*, pp. 194–220, 329–34.

43. S. Salter, 'Structures of Consensus and Coercion: Workers' Morale and the Maintenance of Work-Discipline, 1939–1945' in D. Welch (ed.) *Nazi Propaganda. The Power and the Limitations* (London, 1983) pp. 88–116, here pp. 96–103; Werner, *'Bleib Ubrig!'* also deals with this at length. Winkler, *Frauenarbeit* pp. 92–6 examines the work-discipline of female workers during the early years of the war.

44. On workers' attitudes towards the NSDAP and DAF, see: Kershaw, *Hitler Mythos*, pp. 142–48, 179ff; Broszat, Fröhlich & Wiesemann (eds) *Bayern in der NS Zeit*, p. 617.

45. T. W. Mason, 'Die Bändigung der Arbeiterklasse im nationalsozialistischen Deutschland' in Sachse *et al.*, *Angst, Belohnung, Zucht und Ordnung* pp. 11–53, here p. 34.

46. Salter, 'Structures of Consensus and Coercion', pp. 103–9; Werner

The working class and politics

'*Bleib Ubrig!*', pp. 72–80, 171–92, 318–28; Winkler, *Frauenarbeit*, pp. 96–101.
47. Peukert, *KPD im Widerstand*, pp. 326–417; Plum 'Die Arbeiterbewegung', pp. 378f. See also the regional studies indicated at notes 27 and 28 above.
48. Peukert, *Inside Nazi Germany*, p. 117 stresses the increasing individualism of workers.
49. Broszat, Fröhlich & Wiesemann (eds) *Bayern in der NS Zeit* p. 319; Seebold *Stahlkonzern*, p. 272; G. Hetzer 'Die Industriestadt Augsburg. Eine Sozialgeschichte der Arbeiteropposition' in M. Broszat, E. Fröhlich & A. Grossmann (eds) *Bayern in der NS Zeit III* (Munich, 1981) pp. 1–234, here pp. 129f; Werner, '*Bleib Ubrig!*', pp. 350–8.

CHAPTER SIX
The United Kingdom

John Stevenson

INTRODUCTION

By the end of 1945 with a Labour government in power, a
welfare state in process of creation and a powerful trade union
movement intimately involved with the structure and decisions of
the governing party, the years since the onset of the depression
could be interpreted as marking the triumph of the interests of
the British working classes, broadly defined. Overall, the period
since the 1920s could be characterized, too, as witnessing gains
in real living standards and the development of a broadly social
democratic ethos in public policy which brought benefits in the
form of redistributive fiscal policies and social-welfare legislation.
Such an outcome, however, was by no means certain. During the
inter-war years Britain was to experience the most severe economic
depression of modern times, the effects of which were still being
felt in some quarters right up to and even beyond the outbreak
of the Second World War. Further, in the aftermath of the First
World War and during the inter-war years, organized labour was to
suffer humiliating defeat in many of its attempts either to challenge
the power of the State or deflect the major consequences of the
depression in terms of job losses and reduced bargaining power.
In addition, the most severe phase of the depression, after 1929,
was indirectly to have a devastating impact on the major party which
claimed to represent working-class interests, destroying the Labour
Government of 1929–31 and effectively depriving the Labour Party
of the possibility of forming a government for the remainder of the
decade. Finally, from 1939 Britain experienced six years of the most

intensive military involvement in her history, led by a Conservative premier who retained a massive personal popularity right up to its end. To many observers the most likely political outcome of the war would be, as in 1918, a confirmation in power of the leader who had seen the country through to ultimate victory and a perpetuation of pre-war Conservative government.

The aim here is to ask two important and related questions. First, to what extent did the experience of depression and war affect the political behaviour of the British working classes? Secondly, to what extent was the outcome in the form of their political responses and the repercussions of them out of line, in so far as can be detected, with patterns already set. In order to answer these questions, it is important to recognize that working-class political expression was not synonymous with either organized labour, the Labour Party, or other parties of the left. For most of this period, there were large numbers of the working class who were beyond the reach of the organized labour movement, including the unoccupied – still comprising the great majority of women – the unemployed, and large numbers of non-unionized workers. Similarly the working class contained a large group of Conservative voters and activists, as well as those who supported the Liberals, nationalists or other groupings. Most frequently ignored are the indifferent and apathetic, whose interests and experiences are the most difficult for historians to penetrate.

THE LEGACY OF THE 1920s

Even before the onset of the worst phase of the depression after 1929, a number of features had established the boundaries within which the political responses of the working class could be articulated. The first of these was the experience of the First World War. The war had been embarked upon with a national solidarity and a patriotic fervour remarkable in its scale and effects; alone of the combatants, Britain found the majority of her fighting forces from volunteers. Although the introduction of conscription in 1916 was testimony to the extent that the fund of willing volunteers was insufficient to meet the continuing needs of the armed forces, there is little evidence even by 1918 that morale either on the home front or amongst the armies in the field had reached breaking point. Although there was a severe crisis of defeatism in the winter of 1917–18, it was followed by what has been called 'a revival of working-class patriotism highly reminiscent of the early months of the war' in response to the German spring offensive and determined Government attempts to extend rationing and moderate food prices. The prospect of victory in October 1918 brought a renewed mood of popular chauvinism. Britain entered the post-war era undefeated: while 'victory' might have been a somewhat hollow term given the size of Britain's casualty lists and the effects of the war upon her economic position, the war had also elevated national consciousness, including potent symbols of unity like the Royal family and the Remembrance Day ceremonial.[1] A corollary of this was that the British polity entered the post-war decade with its apparatus of government unimpaired and even strengthened. In the immediate aftermath of the war the first election based on full manhood suffrage and that of women over 30 confirmed in office the Conservative-dominated coalition led by Lloyd George. Backed by a clear constitutional mandate, the post-war British state was in full command of all the resources necessary to defend itself in the post-war world. Strikes in the police were met by a mixture of repression and concessions, while the incidence of mutiny and unrest in the armed forces on either side of the armistice were primarily the result of specific grievances which were soon resolved.[2]

But the war also had important repercussions for the working class. The single most important social effect of the war was to raise the real wages of the unskilled part of the labour force, compressing the earnings differential between skilled and less skilled workers. By the inter-war years, social surveys noted that there was a growing conformity in material standards and cultural norms amongst the working class as a whole. Although the skilled worker could still usually command a premium for a 'trade', the relative gains by the unskilled and semi-skilled as a result of the war, compounded by longer-term changes in the structure of industry and family size, reduced the extent to which the artisans formed a separate social sphere. By 1935 Rowntree's second social survey of York had to include a modification of his pre-war social ranking of the working classes to include a top echelon, some 36 per cent of the working-class population, half of whom were unskilled and semi-skilled workers.[3] The war, too, reinforced a sense of solidarity within sections of industry by the practice of industry-wide, national wage awards negotiated with the representatives of organized labour. In doing so, wartime industrial relations gave impetus to the incorporation of the working class into a more institutionalized form of bargaining. Of necessity, government acquired a 'working commitment' to the official trade-union movement which, in turn, was expected to deliver industrial peace.[4]

Within this context organized labour had emerged from the First World War in many ways strengthened. Trade-union membership rose from just over 4 m. members in 1914 to just over 6.5 m. by 1918. By 1920 trade-union membership stood at its highest ever level with over 8.25 m. members. In part, the continued rise of union membership reflected a great upsurge in strike activity. Although the early months of the war had been marked by a TUC-backed 'strike truce', industrial action was gathering pace in the latter years of the war. Disputes over 'dilution', a revival of syndicalist activity, continuing pre-war patterns amongst groups such as the miners and engineers, and a favourable bargaining climate led to a resumption of the levels of strike activity seen immediately prior to the war. The Bolshevik Revolution in Russia added for some a heady mood of optimism and enthusiasm and helped to encourage a more militant socialist movement in places such as Clydeside, South Wales, Sheffield, Merseyside and London. The end of the war and the removal of government controls led to rapid price rises and a rising spiral of industrial disputes as unions attempted to consolidate and defend the advances made during the war. Strikes broke out in numerous industries, but most seriously affected were the railways, mines, and engineering works. Working days lost through strikes rose to almost 35 m. in 1919, over 26 m. in 1920, and to 85 m. in 1921. The pre-war Triple Alliance was re-formed by the miners, railwaymen, and transport workers, capable, were it so to wish, of inflicting massive disruption upon the whole economy. Although talk of a General Strike was in the air, it was upon 'Red Clydeside' that attention focused when a local general strike was called in support of the engineering workers' demand for a forty-hour week.

'Red Clydeside' has come to occupy a central place in the mythology of Britain's 'failed' post-war revolution, but in spite of the adoption of the Bolshevik cause by some of its leaders and the politicization of some parts of the workforce, a combination of force, piecemeal concessions, and internal conflicts undermined the position of the more militant shop stewards represented in the unofficial Clyde Workers' Committee. Few unions were prepared to give official backing to the Forty Hours' strike and several crucial groups of workers refused to join in the strike call. Faced, too, with a show of force by the police and the army even some of the more militant leaders were unwilling to push ahead into further open confrontation with the authorities. As a result, the strike fizzled out with its leaders arrested.[5] Clydeside was significant in that it demonstrated the ability of the authorities to deploy both coercion and concessions to defeat a major industrial and political challenge; it also showed, in one of the main centres of industrial militancy, the triumph of essentially reformist and sectional concerns over the more radical aspirations of a minority. The collapse of the Triple Alliance in 1921 when the railwaymen and transport workers failed to act in support of the miners, served only to confirm the failure of the post-war phase of militancy to become an effective threat to the government.

But if the story of the immediate post-war period were to be interpreted solely as one of defeat it would misread the position of workers in these years. First, crucially, union militancy in the short-term consolidated the gains in living standards made during the First World War. Secondly, whatever the readiness of the Government to react to threats to its ultimate authority, it also pursued an extensive policy of social reconstruction. Although truncated by the fiscal crisis of 1921 and the 'Geddes Axe', the post-war period was to see the first major housing acts, education reform, and a wide extension of national insurance. Gains in social provision were made which though only hesitantly extended between the wars, none the less provided a baseline which governments were reluctant to erode. Thirdly, although it was industrial militancy which captured the headlines in the aftermath of the war, there was a powerful undercurrent of conciliation and arbitration which did much to consolidate the position of the trade unions as an estate of the realm.

Major industrial confrontation had long been a matter of concern for the government, not just at the level of preparing for the disruption caused and maintaining public order, but also in calling forth intervention and arbitration. This was enshrined in the Whitley Report of 1917 proposing the setting up of joint industrial councils, made up of representatives of employers and workers, on national, district, and works level, to resolve labour questions. Although a full scheme of Whitley Councils was never established they were set up in a number of minor industries. Their most extensive application came in government employment, such as in the Civil Service and the Post Office. The Industrial Courts Act of 1919, gave the Ministry of Labour power of conciliation and inquiry, although without power of compulsory arbitration. In 1921 the Railway Act instituted an arbitration procedure and agricultural workers were covered by the Agricultural Wages Act of 1924. In all, thirty-three new Trade Boards were set up between 1919 and 1921 to provide a compulsory system of wage fixing in industries without formal negotiating machinery. A further ten Boards were added between 1922 and 1939, representing by that date some 1.5 m. workers. Between 1919 and 1934 the Industrial Court made over 1,700 awards and was given further jurisdiction in specific industries during the inter-war years, as in the Sugar Industry Act of 1936 and the Road Haulage Wages Act of 1938. This theme of arbitration and industrial conciliation remained a feature of the inter-war years, strongest perhaps in the years immediately after the First World war, but resurfacing in the Mond–Turner talks of the late 1920s, and again in the 1930s.

For some unions at least the possibility of establishing themselves in a routine system of arbitration had growing attractions after the ending of the post-war boom in 1920–21. Growing unemployment and pressure on wage levels, gave less scope for militancy. Unemployment doubled in the winter of 1920–21 and had reached over 2 m. by the summer of 1921. Almost immediately the number of strikes fell; as did union membership. In effect, from the end of 1920 many unions were on the defensive: thus in 1922 the engineering workers were forced to return to work after a three-month lock-out with their funds exhausted. In coalmining Lloyd George's proposed return of the industry to its private owners led not only to the break-down of the Triple Alliance in 'Black Friday' but also to a lock-out of the miners which forced them to accept major cuts in wages. The engineers and the miners were only the two most prominent groups of workers to be hit by the new, harsher climate of industrial relations. Skilled workers, especially groups like railwaymen, engineers, and textile workers were the ones to witness the greatest decline in their bargaining power and wage levels. Its effects were shown in a decrease of union membership by almost a third between 1921 and 1924.

Fluctuating demand for coal, within a context of serious structural weaknesses in the industry, a strong tradition of militancy, and a seemingly inevitable conflict of interest between the coal-owners and the unions set the scene for the confrontation of the General Strike of 1926. Its importance is easy both to overestimate and to underestimate. On the one hand it demonstrated the ability of the trade-union movement to call upon the support of millions of working people, at least some of whom knew they were putting their jobs at risk in the event of the strike's failure. It showed, in that sense, the permanence of some of the solidarities built up and the ability of the unions to count upon the allegiance of large numbers of workers. On the other hand, it confirmed conclusively what had been evident since the peak of the post-war strike wave, that in a contest between organized labour and the government, the latter had most of the cards stacked in its favour: including emergency powers and the use of force when necessary, extending to some 8,000 arrests and the use of troops to move essential supplies. More important even than the full use of state power to defeat the strike was the evident reluctance of the TUC to use the General Strike as a political weapon. Trapped by their loyalties to the miners and outmanoeuvred by the Government, the TUC found itself involved in a game it had no wish to play.[6] The TUC's climbdown, leaving the miners to carry on the dispute on their own was seen as a humiliating defeat for organized labour. In fact it was less a turning point than a confirmation of processes already evident in the early 1920s. Trade-union membership and strike levels had been falling *before* the General Strike, trends which were now accelerated. The essentially conservative stance of the trade-union leadership had been apparent before 1926, the events of that year served only to confirm it and to strengthen the argument for a new strategy on the part of organized labour. First, this required a defensive stance on the industrial front, involving an abandonment of the rhetoric of 'General Strike' and a readiness to rebuild the status of the unions as a necessary part of the normal processes of industrial bargaining. Secondly, the General Strike reinforced, in so far as reinforcement was necessary, the need for the trade unions to seek political means to advance their members' interests. Evidence of this strategy lay in the participation of the TUC in the Mond–Turner talks in 1928. A group of employers, including Sir Arthur Mond of ICI, persuaded a number of fellow-industrialists to participate in discussions with the TUC. Opened in February 1928, the talks took their name from Mond and Ben Turner, the veteran textile workers' leader and chairman of the TUC who, with Ernest Bevin and Walter Citrine, were the chief participants on the TUC side. The talks ranged over various areas of business–union co-operation and although producing little practical result in the short term have been regarded as having significant long-term influence on both Bevin and Citrine in their increasingly pragmatic and moderate view of the role of the unions in their current situation.[7]

The 1920s had also witnessed the rise of a political vehicle for the expression of working-class interests at parliamentary level. The grass-roots growth of Labour in constituency parties and affiliated organizations from before the First World War has been well-documented, as has the improvement of its parliamentary fortunes as a result of the First World War and the extension of the franchise in 1918.[8] The dramatic increase of the electorate from approximately 7 m. voters to nearly 20 m. coincided with the preparation of a new Labour Party constitution, formally committing it to a socialist programme. Labour's share of the vote rose from under 8 per cent in the two elections of 1910 to 22 per cent in 1918. In 1924 Labour formed its first, minority, Government on the basis of a 30 per cent share of the vote and 191 seats, overtaking the Liberals in votes and seats. The General Election of 1924, although reducing Labour representation to 151 seats, witnessed an increase in its share of the vote to 33 per cent and, more emphatically, saw a huge fall for the Liberals to 17 per cent reducing them to a mere 40 seats. The theme of the 'three-party' situation in the 1920s was the gradual decline of the Liberals as an effective national political force and the establishment of the Labour Party as the principal opposition. In 1929 the coming to power of the second Labour Government with 288 seats and almost 40 per cent of the total vote, with the Liberals reduced to a mere 59 seats in spite of an attractive and revamped programme, seemed to confirm a major realignment of political forces.[9]

It would be dangerous, as we shall see, to overstress the identification of the working-class vote solely with the Labour Party. Both the Conservatives and the Liberal Party drew a large vote from the working class. Traditions of working-class Toryism remained strong in some areas of the country, notably in Lancashire and the West Midlands, while strong non-conformist traditions still influenced Liberal support in the Celtic fringe, rural areas, and in parts of the north-east. Moreover, the Labour Party had competitors to its left; the Independent Labour Party retained some influence, though dwindling, while one legacy of the militancy of the post-war years was the formation of the British Communist Party whose core of activists were a focus for loyalty and commitment for the revolutionary left. None the less, the success of the Labour Party in the 1920s in establishing itself as a party of government was critical. Combined with the defeat of industrial militancy in 1921 and 1926, it provided an alternative route for organized Labour to press its claims in the polity as a whole.

THE GREAT DEPRESSION

One of the features of Britain's economic position in the 1920s was the continued weakness of the 'ailing giants' of coal, shipbuilding, textiles, and iron and steel. Although the late 1920s saw some economic revival, Britain did not experience the late-1920s 'boom' to the same extent as either the United States or Germany. Unemployment remained obstinately over 1 m., a tenth of the insured workforce, and heavily concentrated in the old staples. Faith in a cyclical upturn solving the problems of some of the areas affected had already been largely put aside. Although the Labour Party maintained that tariffs and a limited programme of public works could assist the areas affected by heavy unemployment, studies by the Board of Trade and others were already talking the language of structural 'surplus' and of the need for rationalization.

Labour's plans to deal with the 'intractable million' were soon swept aside in the devastating economic and financial consequences of the Wall Street Crash. At its lowest point in June 1929 unemployment had stood at just over 1 m., by January 1930 it had reached over 1.5 m. and, by the end of the year, 2.5 m. The Labour Government's attempts to cope with the effects of a world-wide depression have been discussed many times. Widely condemned for its failure to break out of the straitjacket of orthodox financial advice, the Labour Cabinet has been treated more sympathetically by other historians who have argued that there was little firm evidence on which Labour could base an alternative economic strategy to the one being offered to it by the Treasury and financial experts.[10] A prisoner of conventional wisdom, the Labour Cabinet found itself torn between its socialist commitments to maintaining levels of welfare, especially unemployment benefit, and the pressure to secure sufficient economies to satisfy financial opinion. The Cabinet split in August 1931 and the resignation of the Labour Government to be replaced by a National Coalition led by the ex-Labour Premier and his Chancellor of the Exchequer marked a reversal of fortunes since 1929 of almost unprecedented proportions. On the left, there were cries, still echoing to this day, of 'betrayal' by a Labour Prime Minister. The vilification of MacDonald and his 'National Labour' colleagues was to reach fresh heights with the General Election of October 1931. A massive vote of confidence for the National Government completely altered the distribution of forces in Parliament, reducing the Labour Party to a mere fifty-two seats.

Explanations for Labour's defeat lay easily enough to hand. A lacklustre performance in Government, culminating in the breakdown and split of the August crisis, followed by the 'treachery' of its leader and an election in a mood of national emergency, left little scope for Labour to do well. However, the most remarkable feature of the 1931 election, overshadowed by the result in terms of seats, was that the Labour party managed to do so well following such a catalogue of disasters. It still managed to field 516 candidates, virtually the same number as it had in 1924, and only 50 less than in 1929. In spite of its difficulties, Labour in 1931 continued to show at the grass roots considerably more vitality than the rapidly disintegrating Liberal Party, whose various factions were only able to put up 160 candidates. It was Liberal weakness, as much as Labour's record in office which did much to shape the outcome of the election in terms of seats won and lost. The greatly reduced field of Liberal candidates together with Conservative support for Liberal National and National Labour candidates meant that Labour's opponents were more united than ever before. There was a massive reduction in three-cornered contests compared with 1929, only 98 as opposed to 447, so that in over 400 constituencies Labour found themselves faced with a straight fight against united opposition.[11]

The party still polled over 6.5 m. votes – a third of the total and more than it had polled in either 1923 or 1924. The fall in Labour's share of the vote was only 6 per cent from 1929, but the effects were magnified out of all proportion by the operation of the 'first-past-the-post system' and the collapse of the Liberal challenge, a combination of circumstances which exaggerated the scale of Labour's defeat. No less significant was the evident failure of any rival parties for Labour's role of major opposition party. The combined Liberal total of about 2.25 m. votes was 3 m. *less* than in 1929. In the 51 seats contested in 1929 and 1931 by all three parties, the Liberal vote slumped. Only where no Conservative candidate took the field were the Liberals able to make gains. As significant, other rivals for the allegiance of voters did not find themselves attracting significant support. Mosley's New Party, formed as a breakaway movement in 1931 deliberately setting out to offer an alternative economic strategy from that of the 'old gang', fared disastrously. The party fielded twenty-four candidates, all but two of whom lost their deposits. Sir Oswald himself, at Stoke, contesting his wife's ex-seat, was one of the only two New Party candidates to poll respectably with 24 per cent of the vote. The Communist Party fielded twenty-six candidates but failed to take advantage of

Labour's difficulties, twenty-one candidates lost their deposits and the total vote for all their candidates totalled only 75,000.[12]

Although Labour could take some comfort from the failure of its rivals, the shattering defeat of the parliamentary party did, however, raise the issue that Labour might lose the allegiance of its working-class supporters, especially as unemployment rose inexorably to new levels, reaching almost 3 m. by the end of 1932. As governments all over Europe began to be threatened by extremists of both left and right, how real were the fears that Britain's electorate would show the same volatility or that the patience of the unemployed would snap?

ROUSING THE WORKING CLASS?

On the left, the Communist Party entered the trough of the depression ill-equipped to turn itself into a party of mass appeal. With under 4,000 members in 1929, half of them concentrated in the mining areas of South Wales and Scotland, the party had just embarked upon the 'class-against-class' policy, severing its connections with sympathetic organizations such as the ILP and reserving its fiercest attacks for social democratic and reformist organizations like the Labour party and the TUC. Its denunciation of the Labour Party as 'social fascists' and its attempt to set up the Minority Movement as a rival organization to established trade unions effectively ensured that during the worst phase of the depression the Communist Party had walled itself into a ghetto of its own making. By November 1930 its membership was down to 2,500. Although membership was to rise as the economic crisis worsened, it still stood at only 6,000 in 1932. Its paltry vote in the elections of 1931 was a fair reflection of the Party's influence at this time – negligible. Only in the coalfields could the Communist Party count upon anything like a sizeable following. Even here, however, as militant a union leader as A. J. Cook had found the intransigence of the Communist Party at variance with his instincts as a trade unionist.[13] Both in terms of membership figures and electoral support at parliamentary and municipal level, there was no evidence in the trough of the depression of the Party gaining anything like the levels of support it required to make a significant impact upon politics. The hostility of the Labour movement and the TUC, repaying the Communist Party's attacks upon them in kind, meant in most cases that communist influence was treated with suspicion, if not positively prohibited as in the TUC's 'Black Circular' of 1934, banning communists from holding trade-union positions. Moderate trade-union leaders like Bevin wielded their influence to curtail communist-led branches of their own union, as in the case of the London Busmen's strike of 1937, when the TGWU leadership intervened to revoke the powers of the strikers' committee, the Rank and File movement, and expel its leaders from the union.[14]

Although the Communist Party developed strong roots in parts of South Wales, Scotland, London, and other industrial centres, in the early 1930s it was as a 'cadre' party, undoubtedly drawing in some men and women of ability and commitment, but essentially a fringe movement in a political situation which had failed to develop into one of revolutionary upheaval. Of the industrial districts, South Wales was one in which the Communist Party did develop wider support both in local elections and via the South Wales Miner's Federation.[15]

South Wales was an exception however, and even there the strength of the Communist Party tended to be concentrated in particular areas and villages. The militancy of the 'Little Moscows' of Maerdy and Bedlinog should not be writ large over an area which voted overwhelmingly Labour and whose most famous political sons and daughters sought careers in Labour politics. Indeed, the important study by Stuart MacIntyre of those localities which earned a reputation for militancy in the inter-war years like Maerdy, Chopwell in County Durham and the Vale of Leven in Dumbartonshire is strongly suggestive of their peculiarity, drawing their militancy from a combination of local conditions and the strength of local leadership.[16] The expansion of Communist influence dates less to the depression years than it does to the middle and late 1930s when the adoption of 'united-front' tactics and growing concern with the growth of fascism made communism the fashionable creed of the 'Red decade'. Influential converts to fascism amongst writers and intellectuals, however, and the wider penumbra of those drawn in via the Aid to Spain movement, the opposition to domestic fascism, and the Left Book Club, does not alter the minority status of the Communist Party throughout the decade. The Party was to achieve its highest membership in the late 1930s, but even then it did not have more than 18,000 members, with much of the increase coming from middle-class and metropolitan recruits.[17]

Electorally, the Communist Party was unable to achieve a significant breakthrough. As seen earlier, their widest parliamentary challenge, in 1931, was not very successful. Only in two of the twenty-six constituencies contested, Rhondda East and West Fife, did the Party win more than 20 per cent of the vote. There was little evidence after 1931 that the situation was any different. In the six parliamentary by-elections contested between March 1932 and June 1934, only in one, Rhondda East in March 1933, did the Party make a significant showing, elsewhere, even in industrial seats like Merthyr Tydfil, it achieved only a fraction of the total vote. In local elections too, although they had successes in some parts of the country, notably South Wales, the general record was poor; the Party never came near to widespread electoral successs at either parliamentary or municipal level. In the 1935 General Election the Party chose to contest only the two seats where it had been most successful in 1931, a strategy which led to it winning West Fife with 29 per cent of the poll, and narrowly failing to win Rhondda East. The total Communist vote of 27,117 in the two seats was a creditable showing, but it is doubtful whether a wider electoral challenge would have brought them success in similar degree elsewhere given their record since 1929. In electoral terms, it appeared there was only strong support for the Communists in a handful of constituencies, more general electoral challenges were beyond their reach.

In terms of reaching out to a working-class following, the most successful Communist strategy was the formation of the National Unemployed Workers' Movement (NUWM). Set up under the auspices of the Communist Party in 1921 it was specifically designed as an instrument for mobilizing and politicizing the unemployed. The NUWM's approach was potentially fruitful. It took a lead in organizing 'Hunger Marches' to publicize the plight of the unemployed and in acting as a pressure group for improvements in benefits; on the ground, it also acted as a form of 'claimants' union', providing often much-needed advice on unemployment benefits and representing claimants before tribunals.[18] As many as 400,000 people may at one time or another have passed through the ranks of the NUWM between the early 1920s and the late 1930s, but few stayed in it for any length of time. Recent research on the NUWM, using its internal membership accounts, has suggested a maximum weekly membership in the early 1930s of around 20,000, falling from this peak to as low as 10,000 in late 1934 with the recovery of the economy, though rising again to more than 20,000 during the campaign against the Unemployment

The working class and politics

Assistance Board Scheme early in 1935. Thereafter, numbers fell off once more to under 10,000 by 1938.[19] Thus even at its peak, the NUWM only mobilized a fraction of the unemployed as members, a point accepted by its leader Wal Hannington in 1936, for which he blamed the opposition of the Labour party and TUC to what they perceived, correctly, as a Communist front organization, the general 'apathy' of the unemployed, and the tendency of many unemployed to refuse to join an organization which effectively branded them as unemployed while they remained themselves hopeful of obtaining a job.[20]

Certainly there is evidence that all these factors operated to prevent the mobilization of the unemployed by the organization specifically designated by the Communist Party for the purpose. People who joined the NUWM frequently left once they had secured assistance with their dole claim or when they obtained a job.[21] In turn, the practical help and support which the NUWM gave the unemployed seems to have been its main attraction. Indeed some tension became evident between the NUWM activists and the Communist Party precisely because the latter recognized that the organization was becoming bogged down in 'trade-union legalism' and failing to politicize the unemployed.[22] This was palpably the case, the NUWM proving incapable of converting the hundreds of thousands of unemployed into converts to communism.

The most serious challenge the NUWM seemed to offer to the conventional political parties lay in its programme of 'Hunger Marches' and demonstrations as the depression worsened after 1929. Building upon the precedents of the 1920s, the Communist Party urged the NUWM to mount a militant campaign of mass demonstrations, marches and propaganda. This phase of activity culminated in a 'National Hunger March' in 1932, in which contingents from different parts of the country converged upon London bearing a million-signature petition against the Means Test. This march and further national ones in 1934 and 1936, as well as locally mounted demonstrations, certainly led to a degree of mobilization of the unemployed and some alarm in government circles, but the resulting confrontations with the police and mass demonstrations were not of such a scale, or backed by sufficiently broad support, either to shake the political system or to wrest the loyalty of the working-class electorate and activists from the trade unions and the Labour Party.[23] The most successful agitation in which the NUWM played a part, in forcing the National Government to halt its introduction of nationally based, unemployment benefit rates

138

early in 1935, was, significantly, one in which large-scale backbench opposition in parliament was involved – an opposition drawn from within conventional politics which forced concessions from the Government in a pre-election period.[24] Finally, the irony was that although the NUWM made the device of the 'Hunger March' its own, the march which was to go down in history as synonymous with the 'hungry thirties', the 'Jarrow Crusade' of November 1936, was the smallest, least political, and the only march not organized by the NUWM, but by Jarrow's Labour MP Ellen Wilkinson and the local town council. In the political economy of Britain in the 1930s it was the eminently respectable Jarrow marchers who gained favourable publicity and access to the House of Commons, not the NUWM.[25]

If marches and demonstrations for the left occupied only a fraction of the unemployed, British fascism was virtually a non-starter as a force in mobilizing working-class support. Founded in October 1932, the British Union of Fascists' rallies and marches only got under way on a large scale after 1933 when the worst phase of the depresssion was ending. At its peak, Mosley's BUF may have had as many as 40,000 members but neither in terms of members nor in electoral support was it a significant force.[26] Like the Communists it was a 'vanguard' party waiting for crisis that never occurred. While there is evidence that some recruits were drawn from sections of the higher-paid working class who might also have been natural working-class Tories, they were never sufficient to turn the BUF into a mass movement. One partly successful card the movement had to play was protectionism, which gained Mosley some well-attended meetings in Lancashire and elsewhere, but even here the larger parties proved more adept at mobilizing support than Mosley. The BUF's original contribution to the politics of the 1930s, anti-semitism, also undoubtedly tapped a vein of support in areas of Jewish settlement like the East End of London, but suffered from the low-level of serious racial tension elsewhere in the country and the ostracism and opposition which the tactic produced. It is entirely likely, if almost impossible to prove, that the anti-semitic campaigns of the BUF actually mobilized more support for anti-fascist groups and the Labour Party than they ever did for Mosley.[27]

Why did the various political extremes fail to gather more recruits, especially from amongst the unemployed? Part of the answer undoubtedly lies in the nature of the British experience of the depression. At its peak, unemployment reached one in four of the insured workforce in the winter of 1932–33, with the worst phase of the depression occurring between 1929 and 1935. But parts of the country had suffered chronic unemployment from the collapse of the post-war boom in 1921–22. After 1929 the impact of unemployment was felt most heavily in areas which had been grappling with it for almost a decade. A corollary of this was that the slide into the trough of the slump after 1929 was less of a shock than in Germany and the United States where the boom of the late 1920s had been more evident. Although the rise in unemployment was rapid, it intensified an existing problem rather than bringing a new one. As in other countries, however, there was a measure of recovery after 1933, reducing the levels of unemployment as world trade picked up; a temporary reverse in 1937–38 being overcome by the onset of heavy expenditure on rearmament. One characteristic feature was that although the long-term unemployed tended to attract attention, the great majority of those out of work were short-term unemployed. The highest number of those out of work for twelve months or more was 480,000 in July 1933, representing less than a sixth of the total registered unemployed.[28] The typical experience of unemployment was of a spell or, quite commonly, spells of unemployment and periods of short-time working. While for the long-term unemployed apathy and fatalism may be an explanation for their failure to become politically active, for the great majority of the unemployed the more appropriate explanation lay in their not unrealistic hopes of obtaining work before too long.

Moreover, while large pockets of poverty and hardship undoubt-edly existed, not least amongst the unemployed, the great majority of the population saw some improvement in living standards by the end of the 1930s. It has been estimated that average real living standards for those in work rose during the 1930s by between 15 and 18 per cent, within a context which saw a rise in national income per head of approximately a third during the inter-war years. With never less than three-quarters of the population in work, most people in Britain were better-off by 1939 than they had been ten years earlier. With smaller families, cheaper food, and substantial economic recovery in the middle and late 1930s, the average family was better-off, healthier, and better-housed than it had been in 1929. Taking the longer perspective, the Ministry of Labour's budgetary enquiries in 1937–38 revealed that average family income in 1937–38 was more than double what it had been in 1913–14 and, at least as important, spread over a family only four-fifths the size. A clutch of social surveys, often making direct comparisons with the situation prior to 1914, demonstrated that the number of people falling below minimum standards of human needs was much reduced, averaging around one in ten compared with one in three prior to 1914.[29] Not least of the features involved was the ability of the British polity to continue to deliver a high level of social welfare benefits. Total spending on the social services rose from £101 m. in 1913 to £596 m. in 1938, representing an increase from 4.1 to 11.3 per cent of the gross national product. Although a proportion of this expenditure was paid for out of National Insurance contributions and indirect taxes, a study carried out in 1945 concluded that the redistribution of income from rich to poor by the late 1920s amounted to as much as £200–£250 m. a year, the bulk of the gain going to those earning less than £125 a year. The effect was to raise the incomes of the working classes by 8–14 per cent. Whereas before 1914 the working classes were contributing more in taxation than the cost of the social services from which they benefited, they contributed only 79 per cent by 1935–36. National Insurance, extended in 1921, improved pensions, and a succession of housing acts, contributing to the first large-scale Council house-building programmes in the 1930s, represented the tangible evidence of this spending.

Unemployment relief, although placed at exiguous levels and subject to humiliating tests, none the less provided the unemployed with a subsistence. In fact, the real value of unemployment benefit between 1920 and 1931 for a man, wife and two children rose by 240 per cent. Indeed, one of the few studies to use realistic working-class budgets, has confirmed that living standards amongst the unemployed were much worse in the early 1920s than subsequently because of the unfavourable effects of post-war price inflation. Even after the cuts of 1931, benefits were set at about the level of basic subsistence commonly found amongst those *in* work prior to 1914. For some, at least, these minimal levels were, by providing a regular income at rates higher than the lowest wages, actually providing a slightly higher standard of living than if they had been working.[30] Certainly, the extension of benefits to dependants in the twenties and a series of *ad-hoc* continuations of unemployment benefit beyond the insured period, created a major item of government expenditure by the early 1930s. While the provision of unemployment relief could itself provide the catalyst for protest, as over the Means Test in 1931–32 and the Unemployment Assistance Board Scheme of 1934–35, the dole was widely regarded as a palliative to discontent. The upsurge of discontent over the introduction of new relief scales in 1935 and the humiliating government climbdown – the only major reverse of government policy in this area between the wars – demonstrated that certain minimum conditions had to be maintained even in the absence of spectacular new initiatives to cure mass unemployment.[31]

THE CONSOLIDATION OF REFORMISM

Measured in sheer numbers, the trade unions and the Labour Party remained the 'big battalions' of working-class political allegiance. The defensiveness of the trade unions after 1926 was emphasized by the continued fall in their membership during the depression of 1929–33 reaching a low point of 4.4 m. members in 1933 when they represented a mere quarter of the workforce. Since 1920 the trade unions had lost 4 m. members and had declined from representing approximately one worker in two to one in four. As a result the trade unions in the 1930s never represented more than a minority of the working population. Union representation was strongest in the manual, male-dominated sections of industry, miners, railwaymen, shipbuilders, and iron and steel workers. It was much lower in white-collar occupations, and in many areas such as construction, agriculture, light industry, and the service and distributive trades often non-existent. For all groups, the slump acted to depress union representation. Even highly unionized groups like the miners, three-quarters of whom were in a union in 1921, saw membership slashed by just over a half by 1931 and the introduction of 'company unionism'. In less-organized areas of industry, like the food, drink and tobacco industries, levels of union membership fell as low as 15 per cent between 1929 and 1933. Amongst some groups, shopworkers for example, it was relatively easy for employers to maintain a 'no-union' policy.[32]

Union membership, however, revived substantially in the latter part of the decade, reaching 6.3 m. members in 1939. For example, the miners were able almost to eradicate 'company unionism' raising 'union density' in that sector to almost 80 per cent by 1939.[33] Elsewhere a major effort was made to unionize the new engineering and motor vehicle plants of the midlands and south-east in the more propitious circumstances of the economic recovery after 1933.[34] Better conditions for union organization assisted this recovery, namely falling unemployment and rapid economic growth. But a larger reality lay behind these figures. In their recovery from the defeats of the 1920s and the 'backs-to-the-wall' situation of 1929–33, the unions were only precariously represented in some central areas of the economy. In 1939 only 54 per cent of cotton operatives belonged to a union and only 35 per cent of engineering workers: in construction the figure was only 30 per cent and in the distributive trades a mere 12 per cent. Hence, even in major industries it was common, more common than not, for workers to be non-union. Moreover, these figures themselves tell only part of the story; women remained considerably less organized than men, union membership falling as low as 12 per cent of all women workers in 1933–34, and still stuck below 15 per cent in 1938.[35] Strike figures closely followed the pattern of union membership, falling to an inter-war low point in 1933–34. In place of the great set-piece confrontations of the early 1920s, more characteristic were the grim defensive battles of the cotton weavers in 1932 and the strikes to secure union recognition in the engineering trades during the mid-1930s.

In this situation the union leadership opted for a fuller involvement in the Labour party as the means of advancing the cause of the working class in the political arena. Although barely representing a majority even of the working portion of the working class, the unions were already in the habit of claiming to speak for the whole body. A continued process of amalgamation and bureaucratization confirmed the tendency of the unions to speak the language of piecemeal advance within the existing political system. Giant unions like the TGWU with 1.5 m. members in 1938 or the National Union of General and Municipal Workers, formed in 1924, with moderately reformist leaders like Ernest Bevin and Walter Citrine, sought to run well-organized disciplined unions which conducted collective bargaining on a national level, while pursuing longer-term aims for social, economic and political change through the Labour party. As Robert Shackleton has written, the political history of the unions in the 1930s is predominantly the history of the relations between them and the Labour party and that this was 'a matter of necessity, not choice'. While the unions settled down to living with the Tory-dominated National Government as best they could, they also 'turned back to the Labour Party as the central instrument for achieving their political aims'.[36]

Instead of shattering, the Labour Party retained the allegiance of millions of working-class voters. The 1935 General Election was fought by a Labour Party in which optimism was high and spirits considerably revived after the débâcle of 1931. Labour's 552 candidates compared with 516 in 1931 reflected the party's renewed confidence. Nor was this confidence entirely misplaced for Labour's electoral recovery since 1931 at municipal level had been substantial and swift. In 1932 Labour won 458 of the 836 council seats it contested, at 52.7 per cent, one of its highest success rates ever; while 1933 saw the spectacular by-election win in East Fulham when a substantial Conservative majority was overturned. In municipal election results, 1933 was one of the best years the party ever enjoyed, sweeping gains brought Labour to power in Sheffield, Norwich, Leeds, Bootle, Swansea and Barnsley; in 7 boroughs Labour gained a council majority for the first time. With 181 gains and only 5 losses Labour was once again a party to be reckoned with in municipal politics and had apparently resumed the progress interrupted in 1931. Labour's continuing recovery carried on into 1934 with by-election victories and widespread municipal gains, including the great prize of the largest local-government unit of the country, the London County Council.[37]

The 1935 General Election saw Labour achieve a measure of recovery at parliamentary level with 38 per cent of the poll and over 8,325,000 votes. The overall result, however, was disappointing with Labour securing only 154 seats. Labour's net gain of 94 seats displayed a worrying unevenness; only 20 seats in Scotland, a failure in industrial seats in the north-west like Salford, Stockport, Bolton, Oldham, and Preston, as well as in the north-east in places like Sunderland, Stockton and the Hartlepools, while not a single Labour MP was returned in Birmingham, Cardiff, Newcastle or Leicester. The psephological explanation of Labour's failure was its inability to win its marginal seats, many of them in working-class towns. A key reason here was less the failure of the Labour Party to secure its working-class vote than its inability to attract sufficient ex-Liberal voters. The Liberal result was a disaster, reducing the party to 21 seats, but its former voters deserted to the Conservatives in far greater numbers than to Labour. This affected not only middle-class voters but significant numbers of working-class voters who had once voted Liberal but were not yet ready to vote Labour.[38]

Writing in 1937, G. D. H. Cole recognized that the Labour Party's fortunes rested upon its relationship with trade unionism. Labour could rely upon the old industrial areas where trade unionism was relatively strong to bring out a solid vote in municipal and parliamentary elections. It was, in spite of the slump, in Cole's phrase 'an unbroken power'. The strengthening of links between the moderate leaders of the TUC and the Labour party in the 1930s ensured the Labour Party's survival and with it the frustration of the hopes of extremist politicians of the Left and Right who might have hoped to capitalize upon the demoralization and disarray produced in 1931. In that sense the single most remarkable feature of working-class politics in the slump was the continued loyalty of millions of working-class voters to the Labour Party. But there were important qualifications to this apparent strength. Regional variations cut across class lines. Lancashire retained a deviant pattern amongst the older industrial areas where the Labour Party only took 28 seats in 1935 as against 40 in 1929. There were no Labour seats in Birmingham, while the north-east retained distinctive features. Labour still suffered in 1935 from its incomplete erosion of rival loyalties amongst working-class voters. Large parts of the country were denied to Labour in 1935, outside Greater London it had only two seats in the whole of southern England. While many poorer voters still voted Conservative and some, a dwindling band, Liberal, many of the voters in the new industrial and suburban areas had also failed to come over to Labour. These, for Cole, were the doubtful voters:

> The larger army of clerks and typists, managers, shop assistants, garage hands, lorry drivers, attendants at cinemas, road houses, swimming pools and other places of amusement, hotel servants and restaurant workers and domestic servants. In short, they are all the host of workers in the industries which have been expanding as the older industries have declined. They are, in the vast majority of cases, non-Unionists.[39]

Cole's prescient categorization of the voters in the 'new England' of the 1930s as also those with less sense of class identification was to become one of the recurrent concerns of Labour in the post-war world.

Nor was it clear that the Labour Party had overcome the apathy or indifference of a sizeable portion of the working-class electorate. Apathy or indifference has yet to find its historian, but the issue of a working class indifferent to the appeals of politicians, whether of Left or Right, was not magically dissolved by the introduction of universal suffrage. Although the 'residuum' of those in absolute poverty was diminishing between the wars, the world of slum districts like 'Campbell Bunk' was as yet largely untouched by either organized labour or the Labour

Party. Municipal turnouts were often low, even Labour's assault on the LCC in 1934 was successful on the basis of a very low poll. Although there were very active Labour wards and constituencies with something approaching a mass membership, there were many others kept alive by only a handful of activists. At its peak between the wars in 1937 the Labour Party had 447,000 members, only 1.5 per cent of the total electorate. Moreover the depression did not seem to have increased the electorate's appetite for politics; turnout in 1931 was only fractionally greater than in 1929 and less than in 1924; in 1935 it was 5 per cent lower still at 71.2 per cent. Three out of ten electors did not bother to cast their vote. That a large proportion of non-voters were working class seems likely on the evidence of social surveys carried out during the late 1930s. When the Carnegie Trust published a study it had conducted in Liverpool, Cardiff, and Glasgow between 1936 and 1939 it reported that out of a total of 1,490 young unemployed only 20 were members of a political organization and at least 10 per cent did not even know the names of the various political parties: 'The overwhelming majority of the men had no political convictions whatsoever. When asked why, they invariably replied, "what does it matter?"'[40]

THE SECOND WORLD WAR

There is little evidence that a General Election in 1939 or 1940 would have brought Labour to power. The decisive period in . Labour's road to 1945 lay in the Second World War. Labour's place as part of the Coalition Government from 1940 brought it a power to influence policy it could not otherwise have expected at least in the short term. As in 1914, the war revolutionized the position of the trade unions when a state of dire national emergency made it essential to secure the full co-operation of organized labour. More pervasively, as a war fought almost from its outset to the full limit of national resources, it involved a deliberate effort to enlist the support and energies of the population at large. The great national emergency following the formation of the Churchill coalition, the fall of France, and the Battle of Britain was notable for bringing the language of reconstruction and a new post-war Britain to the fore much earlier in the conflict than had been the case in the First World War. By early 1941 pressure for a 'New Britain' was already being mounted by influential writers and broadcasters, of which

Picture Post's 'A Plan for Britain' in January 1941 might be taken as a particularly clear statement.[41] That the war gave an opportunity for the victory of progressive 'middle opinion' of which the Beveridge Report was the obvious symbol is incontestable.[42] Often, however, it is difficult to detect the voice and intentions of the working classes in the debates about their future and the extent to which we are, in fact, talking about a dialogue between pressure groups, civil servants, and politicians over the heads of the toiling and fighting masses. Certainly the Beveridge Report with its radical language of conquering the 'five giants' of Want, Ignorance, Squalor, Idleness and Disease aroused widespread interest. The Report was a runaway success, selling over 630,000 copies, and was widely discussed in radio broadcasts, newspapers, and in the armed forces through the Army Bureau of Current Affairs. Widely regarded as a blueprint for post-war reconstruction the 'Beveridge Plan' seemed to vindicate Beveridge's own pithy comment that 'the most general effect of war is to make the common people more important'.[43]

The Beveridge Report and like-minded schemes for post-war reconstruction received a crucial boost through an apparent left-ward shift of opinion. The formation of a new party called Common Wealth by Sir Richard Acland and a group of colleagues, mostly middle-class socialists, offered a challenge to sitting Conservative MPs at by-elections. Successes at Eddisbury in Cheshire in March 1943 and at Skipton in January 1944 confirmed that there was a tide running against the Conservatives. These were not, however, obviously working-class seats, nor could they necessarily be inter-preted as encouraging for Labour. Labour did, however, become closely identified with support for the Beveridge Report when it was debated in the Commons in February 1943. The hesitancy and caution of the Coalition spokesmen led the Parliamentary Labour Party to put down an amendment and divide the House for the one and only time during the Coalition years. Henry Pelling has argued that although embarrassing for the Labour ministers in the Coalition Government 'it did more than anything else in wartime to identify the Labour party with the widespread popular desire for social reform in the post-war world'.[44] By 1944 the reconstructionist tide with which Labour and progressive opinion was identified seemed to be flowing strongly. The Butler Education Act was passed and the Minister for Reconstruction, Lord Woolton, pushed through the critical White Papers on the health service, employment policy, and social insurance which were to lay the basis for the post-war settlement.

The infant science of opinion polling also provided some evidence that there was movement in opinion during the war. The Mass Observation surveys carried out during the Blitz revealed the significant finding that many people looked to a more 'classless' and socially just society after the war was over, a theme which received reinforcement from the mood of collectivism and common endeavour which was the staple fare of official wartime propaganda and reflected many aspects of the shared experiences of evacuation, bombing, national service, and rationing. Moreover, the Gallup polsters who began in 1943 to ask people how they would vote 'if a General Election were held tomorrow' generally showed the Labour party with a lead of 10 per cent or more over the Conservatives. These polls, however, were easily discounted because of their novelty and the still enormous popularity of Churchill as wartime leader which they also revealed.[45]

Beyond the general desire for a 'better tomorrow' and some evidence of increased support for Labour, the war had actually brought tangible benefits to the working class. Unemployment was eradicated and replaced by a scarcity of labour which forced the recruitment of hundreds of thousands of extra workers, many of them women. An effective system of rationing with special provision for children and pregnant and nursing mothers actually improved the general level of health in spite of war-time shortages of many items. Social provision was improved – the 'Means Test' abolished and a *de-facto* system of family allowances brought in, enshrined in legislation in 1945. To permit women to take up war work, nursery schooling and crèche facilities were radically expanded, while factory conditions were transformed by the provision of better canteen and medical facilities. For workers engaged in civilian employment there was a distinct measure of redistribution of income. Wages were generally high through the willingness of employers to concede almost any reasonable demands in return for increased production. In addition, overtime and piece-work payments swelled wage packets so that by 1944 average wage rates had risen 11 per cent above the cost-of-living index. Progressive income tax on higher incomes and an improvement in wage rates meant that the share of national income taken by wage-earners increased by about £900 m. between 1938 and 1947. According to one estimate, working-class incomes rose by more than 9 per cent as a result of the war.

In the conditions of wartime, organized labour was able to continue the process begun in the mid-1930s of expanding membership and consolidating their position. With almost 8 m. members in 1945 the unions had almost recaptured the position they had achieved a quarter of a century earlier. But in some ways they had done more. Through the wartime coalition, and with Ernest Bevin acting as Minister of Labour, organized labour was firmly within the circles of power. Moreover, while not trouble-free, the degree of strike activity in the Second World War was considerably less than in the previous conflict; the total number of strike days lost in six years of war being less than in just two years in 1917–18.[46] The quid pro quo was that via the Coalition Government, organized labour was able to stake its claims for a post-war settlement, while at factory level full employment before and after 1945 transformed the bargaining situation of workers, enabling the unions to consolidate their wartime advances in wages and recognition.

Labour's surprise victory at the polls in 1945 seemed to confirm that the war had transformed working-class politics. Labour won its first outright victory with 393 seats out of 640, far surpassing its previously best result in 1929. It was the beneficiary of the first-past-the-post system at a time when constituency boundaries were out of date, favouring Labour in the generally smaller, inner-city constituencies.[47] But in 1945 Labour undoubtedly consolidated the working-class vote in some key areas, such as marginals it had failed to take in 1935, and finally secured the bulk of the agricultural workers' vote. Clearly, too, Labour's success owed much to the swing of 'middle opinion' which enabled it to capture seats in southern England, especially in the London suburbs, denied to it in the 1930s. But the results could be read another way. Over 52 per cent of those voting had not voted Labour: many of them, by any definition based on income or occupation, were working class. Over a quarter of the electorate, almost 5 m. people, had not voted at all.[48] The lesson here, to be brought home in 1951 when Labour lost power, was that the histories of the Labour Party and of organized labour were not coterminous with either the working class or the workforce. Ferdynand Zweig's analysis *The British Worker*, based on work carried out in the late 1940s, indeed argued that the popularity of socialist ideas differed 'according to the industrial group, age, status, education, and upbringing'.[49] Similarly, unionization still only claimed a bare majority of the workforce, with substantial groups, such as women, the unskilled, and low-paid workers revealing very low levels of union membership even in 1945. Even for many union members, membership was lightly worn and in no sense implied active political involvement or commitment. In 1945

149

the Labour party certainly consolidated and increased its support, but it had not captured anything like all its potential constituency.

It would be unwise to overemphasize the war as producing the social reforms summed up in the 'welfare state'. These had their origins in the ideas and discussions between the wars amongst a broad spectrum of opinion. Even Labour's election manifesto of 1945 was largely the 1937 document, the 'Immediate Programme'. The war gave welfare reforms a decisive impetus, but what is striking is the extent of the consensus on which they were based. The essential elements had been accepted by the Churchill-led conservative-dominated coalition by 1945. Britain's adoption of a wider spectrum of social democratic policies was neither the product solely of the war nor of the Labour party. Although the war placed social welfare on the agenda of any government once the immediate crisis was over, it is worth recognizing the extent to which social reform grew out of what had been called a 'growing climate of social responsibility' of which the war proved the occasion not the cause. Moreover, the welfare state and the mixed economy are too frequently made to appear uniquely British currents of thought, but as Walter Laqueur observed, social reforms to the benefit of the working classes were carried out all over Europe after 1945. Almost everywhere, as before 1939, the trend was towards higher social spending to the extent that western European expenditure on social services quadrupled between 1930 and 1950. Strikingly, the phenomenon included non-combatants as well as combatants: Sweden's expenditure was six times higher in the latter year than in 1930.[50] For Britain the war emphasized but did not create a more social-democratic thrust in public policy.

In the longer term, Labour's difficulty in securing majority governments after 1951 is more explicable in view of its partial securing of the allegiance of the working class. As the continued success of the Conservative Party was to demonstrate, a significant minority of the working class looked elsewhere for political expression. Equally, a trade-union-backed Labour Party had proved strongly enough entrenched to weather the crises of the depression and to defeat challenges from the Left. Critically, too, Britain survived the Second World War, like the First, without the crises of defeat and occupation experienced elsewhere. Neither depression nor war fundamentally upset the evolution of a mildly reformist socialism nor prevented Britain surviving her first generation as a mass democracy.

NOTES AND REFERENCES

1. For the 'crisis of defeatism' and its ending, see B. Waites, *A Class Society at War: England, 1914–18*, Leamington Spa, 1987, pp. 229–35.
2. H. A. Clegg, *A History of British Trade Unions since 1889: volume II, 1911–1933*, Oxford, 1985, pp. 195, 286. J. Stevenson, *British Society, 1914–1945*, Harmondsworth, 1984, pp. 97–9.
3. Waites, *Class Society at War*, pp. 158–9, 176–8.
4. *Ibid*, pp. 30–3; Clegg, *British Trade Unions*, p. 209.
5. Clegg, *British Trade Unions*, pp. 270–1; T. C. Smout, *A Century of the Scottish People, 1830–1950*, London, 1986, pp. 264–7.
6. For a recent review of the General Strike see P. Renshaw, 'The depression years, 1918–1931' in B. Pimlott and C. Cook (eds), *Trade Unions in British Politics*, Harlow, 1982, pp. 108–11.
7. A. Bullock, *The Life and Times of Ernest Bevin*, London, 1960, vol. 1, p. 405; see also G. W. McDonald and H. Gospel, 'The Mond–Turner Talks, 1927–1933: a study in industrial co-operation', *Historical Journal*, 14, no. 4 (1973), pp. 807–29.
8. See especially R. McKibbin, *The Evolution of the Labour Party, 1910–1924*, Oxford, 1974, Ch. 7.
9. On Labour's electoral breakthrough see C. Cook, *The Age of Alignment*, London, 1975, Chs 3 and 4.
10. See especially R. McKibbin, 'The economic policy of the second labour Government', *Past and Present*, no. 68 (1975), pp. 95–123.
11. C. Cook and J. Stevenson, *The Slump: society and politics during the depression*, London, 1977, pp. 100–1; for a more recent analysis of the election see A. J. Thorpe, 'The British General Election of 1931', University of Sheffield Ph.D. thesis, 1988.
12. Cook and Stevenson, *The Slump*, pp. 130–1.
13. P. Davies, *A. J. Cook*, Manchester, 1987, pp. 163–7.
14. K. Fuller, *Radical Aristocrats: London Busworkers from the 1880s*, London, 1985, pp. 149–59.
15. H. Francis and D. Smith, *The Fed: a history of the South Wales Miners in the twentieth century*, London, 1980, chs 8, 10.
16. S. MacIntyre, *Little Moscows: communism and working class militancy in inter-war Britain*, London, 1980.
17. In 1927 only 16.8 per cent of the party's membership came from the metropolitan area, but by 1942 29 per cent; see K. Newton, *The Sociology of British Communism*, London, 1969, pp. 176–7.
18. The fullest history of the NUWM is now R. Croucher, *We Refuse to Starve in Silence: A History of the National Unemployed Workers' Movement, 1920–46*, London 1987.
19. See H. J. Harmer, 'The National Unemployed Workers' Movement in Britain, 1921–1939: Failure and Success', University of London Ph. D., 1987, Appendix B.
20. W. Hannington, *Unemployed Struggles*, London, 1936, pp. 322–3.
21. Harmer, 'The National Unemployed Workers' Movement', Appendix B; compare with Hannington's 'millions of workers have passed through membership of the NUWM', *Unemployed Struggles*, p. 323.

22. Croucher, *We Refuse to Starve*, p. 115; Harmer, 'The National Unemployed Workers' Movement', Appendix B.
23. See Cook and Stevenson, *The Slump*, Chs 10, 12.
24. J. Stevenson, 'The Politics of Violence' in C. Cook and G. Peele, *The Politics of Reappraisal*, London, 1975, pp. 146–65.
25. Cook and Stevenson, *The Slump*, pp. 184–90.
26. BUF membership figures remain elusive; but see D. S. Lewis, 'The Ideology and Politics of the British Union of Fascists', University of Manchester Ph.D. 1983, pp. 128ff for a review of various estimates.
27. See, for example, the number of anti-fascist meetings during the winter of 1936–37 in the East End of London, Mepo 2/3043: Report of fascist and anti-fascist activities, item 26A.
28. S. Pollard, *The Development of the British Economy, 1914–1950*, London, 1962, p. 247.
29. *Ibid*, p. 295 and J. Stevenson, *Social Conditions in Britain between the Wars*, London, 1977, pp. 65–120.
30. Pilgrim Trust, *Men Without Work*, Cambridge, 1938, p. 110; K. Nicholas, *The Social Effects of Unemployment on Teeside between the Wars*, Manchester, 1987, pp. 43–69.
31. See J. Stevenson, 'The Making of Unemployment Policy, 1931–5', in M. Bentley and J. Stevenson (ed), *High and Low Politics in Modern Britain*, Oxford, 1983, pp. 182–213.
32. See G. S. Bain and R. Price, *Profiles of Union Growth: A Comparative Statistical Portrait of Eight Countries*, Oxford, 1980, pp. 43, 45, 50, 51, 63, 67, 67–8.
33. D. Smith, 'The Struggle against company unionism in South Wales', *Welsh History Review*, 6, no. 3 (1973), pp. 367–81.
34. See R. C. Whiting, *The view from Cowley: the Impact of Industrialization upon Oxford, 1918–1939*, Oxford, 1983, p. 65.
35. Bain and Price, *Profiles*, p. 37.
36. R. Shackleton, 'Trade Unions and the Slump' in Cook and Pimlott, *Trade Unions*, pp. 120–1.
37. Cook and Stevenson, *The Slump*, pp. 116–19.
38. *Ibid*, pp. 250–7.
39. G. D. H. and M. J. Cole, *The Condition of Britain*, London, 1937, pp. 412–18.
40. Carnegie Trust, *Disinherited Youth*, Edinburgh, 1943, pp. 78–9.
41. See J. Stevenson, 'Planners' Moon? The Planning Movement and the Second World War in Britain' in H. L. Smith (ed.), *War and Social Change*, Manchester, 1986, pp. 58–77.
42. See R. Macleod, 'The Promise of full Employment' in Smith, *War and Social Change*, pp. 83ff.
43. See J. Harris, 'The Debate on State Welfare' in Smith, *War and Social Change*, pp. 247–54; W. Beveridge, *The Pillars of Security*, New York, 1943, p. 108.
44. H. Pelling, 'The Impact of the War on the Labour Party' in Smith, *War and Social Change*, p. 136.
45. T. Harrison, *Living Through the Blitz*, London, 1976, p. 315; Pelling, 'The Impact', pp. 140–1.
46. H. Pelling, *History of British Trade Unionism*, 3rd edn, 1976, pp. 294–5.

47. Pelling, 'The Impact', p. 145.
48. Turnout was 72.7 per cent.
49. I owe this reference to J. Benson's forthcoming *The British Working Class*, London, 1989; F. Zweig, *The British Worker*, London, 1952, p. 187.
50. W. Laqueur, *Europe since Hitler*, 2nd edn, London, 1982, p. 248 cited by P. Addison in *Contemporary Record*, vol. 1. no. 2 (summer, 1987), p. 15.

CHAPTER SEVEN
ITALY

Paul Corner

An essay on the working class in Italy in the years following 1929 runs the risk of being principally prologue and epilogue. Prologue, in the sense that, for Italy, 1929 is hardly a significant year; the depression had begun earlier, with the revaluation of the lira in 1926–27, and the consequences were already evident. More important, fascism had been in power since 1922; the political terms on which the working class would react to international recession were, therefore, already defined well before the onset of the international crisis. Epilogue, in the sense that the massive popular reaction against fascism, which became evident with the strikes of March 1943 in the factories of the north, appears to have come from almost nowhere. From the point of view of working class politics, we seem to be in the presence of an end and a beginning, but there is something of a vacuum in between.

The reason for this impression is fairly obvious. The working class in Italy had been defeated, and defeated very badly, during the 1920s; fascism dominated the scene for more than twenty years. The situation in Italy after 1929 was, therefore, totally different from that in Germany, where a strong working class movement continued to exist after the advent of the crisis. To understand what happened in Italy, and to appreciate the causes of the relative quiescence of the Italian working class during the crisis, it is necessary to go back at least a decade – to the years of the First World War and the *biennio rosso* or 'red years' of 1919–1920 which were crucial to the formation of the Italian labour movement. Here it is also essential to point out that this essay deals only with the industrial working class; the problems of the large numbers of landless labourers (the *braccianti*) were very different and would require separate treatment.

THE LEGACY OF THE 1920s.

As in most belligerent countries, the First World War brought radical changes to the working class in Italy. The main industrial centres remained those of the 'triangle' of Turin, Milan, and Genoa, but the character of these centres altered profoundly. The war required an enormous expansion of the workforce; many firms saw a massive increase in the number of workers employed. Ansaldo, one of the principal iron, steel, and engineering concerns, increased its workforce from 6000 in 1915 to 111,000 in 1918; Fiat from 4000 to 40,000. This increase was achieved largely by drafting in new workers from the provincial hinterlands, many of whom were women and children of peasant families undergoing their first experience of industrial work.

The expansion of the workforce clearly created problems for long-established workers; 'dilution' was a common complaint, although it appears that, in the circumstances of the war, solidarity rather than conflict characterised working class attitudes. Solidarity was engendered, at least in part, by the savage industrial legislation of the war. Workers were subjected to the harsh military regime of the *Mobilitazione industriale* whereby the minimum of protest could result in the dissenting worker being dispatched to fight at the front. Within the factories workers were overseen by soldiers or *carabinieri* (armed police); disputes were reviewed by arbitration committees on which the military were heavily represented. The first factory experience of most of the new working class of the war was, therefore, of an exceptionally harsh regime, characterised by state intervention largely favourable to employers, where protest carried high risks and promised few returns. It is indicative of the situation that the most prominent figures in protest were women, precisely because they could not be condemned to fight at the front.[1]

In post-war conditions the solidarity engendered by the conflict proved difficult to maintain. The *biennio rosso* undoubtedly demonstrated many of the strengths of the Italian labour movement, which was able to win great improvements in working conditions and wages; but it also showed up certain of the weaknesses of the movement. In the process of reconstruction the traditional skilled workers of the cities often attempted to regain their positions of relative privilege. There was resentment against immigrants from other areas who attempted to settle in the cities. At the same time, the new workers often demonstrated the very shallow roots of their

industrial origins. A new class of commuters had been created by
the war; many – the women in particular – were often members
of families which still carried on agricultural activities in the rural
hinterland. As 'worker-peasants' their political position was liable to
be different from that of the long-established urban worker. Their
principal concerns remained those of the revision of agricultural
contracts or the purchase of small holdings. In this, of course, they
found few points of contact with factory workers.

This kind of fragmentation of the working class, provoked
largely by the vast industrial expansion of the war years, rendered
the class very vulnerable to attack. Events made other weaknesses
evident. The Occupation of the Factories, in 1920, served in part
to demonstrate the extreme isolation of the northern industrial
working class from the rest of the country. Turin remained a
very localised centre of revolt, reflecting its very specific social
composition and political background. It had not proved possible
to carry the generalised protest and discontent of the war years into
a sustained and united popular movement in the post-war period.
The advent of economic crisis in 1921, with an increase in levels of
unemployment, promoted further fragmentation and emphasised
isolation and political differences within the working class.[2]

Industrialists, on the other hand, had learned a great deal from
the experience of the First War. Wartime legislation had provided
them with almost everything they could wish for in terms of social
control within the factory. This was the aspect they remembered,
and, with fascism, attempted to restore. In one important respect,
however, industrialists hoped to improve on the situation of the war
years. The *Mobilitazione industriale* had also subjected industrialists to
a certain measure of state control, and this had been regarded with
suspicion. Not surprisingly, industrialists insisted that the special
legislation of the war years be repealed at the end of the conflict,
precisely because they wished to be free of state controls, but their
position thereafter remained fairly clear. While they welcomed
legislation which permitted them to control the workforce, they
wanted that control to be enforced – within the factory – by
themselves. Fascism provided them with precisely that kind of
solution.

If the initial successes of the fascist movement were realised
against the *braccianti* of the Po Valley in late 1920 and early
1921, the physical violence of fascism was never very far from
the factory gates of the northern cities. Employers ensured that
fascist thugs only rarely entered the factory, but socialist party and

union leaders were regularly identified and beaten up when they emerged from their work shift. Yet physical violence was perhaps less important in turning the tables on the working class than was the knowledge, among workers, that government had permitted the fascist onslaught on the rural proletariat and that the rural workers had been severely defeated. This defeat produced a change in the overall political equilibrium which the urban working class was unable to ignore. Politically undefended by the state, economically subject to the blackmail of unemployment, workers were forced to recognise – well before Mussolini's March on Rome in October 1922 – that there remained few defences against fascism.[3]

The period between the March on Rome, the advent of the first coalition government of Mussolini, and the legislation of 1925 which fully established the fascist regime as such, confirmed the initial implications of defeat. Repression of workers' rights and wage reductions were felt most strongly in heavy industry and in the textile industry, always characterised by paternalist and authoritarian attitudes. The more advanced mechanical and engineering companies were less ready to use crude repressive measures, preferring mediation with the workforce and attempting to take advantage of the new political situation to arrive at a reorganisation of the work process. In a sense, employers were most interested, during this first phase of fascism (a phase of economic expansion), in re-establishing the control of the workforce which they had seemed to lose during the *biennio rosso*.

THE FASCIST ERA

Fascist syndicalism plays only a limited part in the overall picture of the conditions of the working class in the 1920s and 30s. Created in order to replace the socialist unions, the syndicates were never in a position to do what the socialists had done before them. They were forced into the stance of arguing for 'class collaboration' rather than class conflict, but were never able to assert themselves against employers who collaborated only nominally. The struggle between fascist syndicates, fascist party, and employers is one which concerns more appropriately the history of the fascist movement *per se* rather than that of the working class. What is evident is that the efforts of Edmondo Rossoni, the syndicalist leader, to realise his concept of 'integral syndicalism' which would involve employers as much as unions were destined to fail from the start. The fascist unions may have achieved a limited following among workers – simply because there was no alternative and often no option – but neither employers nor fascist party wished to see the recreation of a strong union organisation.

With the Pact of Palazzo Vidoni between employers and the regime in 1925 and the anti-strike legislation of 1926, fascist unions effectively gained a monopoly of worker representation. But there was little they could do with it. In the years between 1926 and 1928 the unions did make efforts to assert a certain autonomy, sometimes calling strikes, more often denouncing malpractices of employers, but the poor results reflected the fact that industrialists could simply go over the head of the unions and appeal directly to government, in the knowledge that Mussolini was not prepared to risk his alliance with the industrialists. Botched agreements sometimes permitted the unions to cry victory, but the reality was always that of a worsening of the conditions of the working class. With the division of the unified corporative organisation into seven separate bodies in 1928 (the so-called *sbloccamento*), even the tension within fascist syndicalism was destroyed, and the fascist unions remained little more than the overseers of the urban working class.[4]

Well before the international crisis of 1929, therefore, almost the whole structure of worker organisation and worker defence had been destroyed. The major union organisations had been forced to bow to force majeure; within the factory, worker representation had ceased with the abolition of the *commissioni interne* (workers' factory councils) in 1925. And, in parallel with loss of representation, workers were confronted with the massive reorganisation of the workforce, which, if in some ways it had begun with the war, was greatly intensified in the course of the 1920s. The introduction of new systems of production served to disorientate workers, undermining the role of the skilled workers and creating new divisions within the working class. If a few workers saw their role enhanced, the great majority found themselves deskilled. Employers clearly used these techniques to try to break down the old solidarity of class. The new organisation of the factory had all the virtues of being more efficient, less costly, while at the same time fracturing the old loyalties of the workforce.[5]

It was in these circumstances that the fascist government determined on the stabilisation of the lira – the so-called 'quota 90'.[6] This very high level of revaluation implied massive internal deflation, and it seems unlikely that such a decision could have been taken without the knowledge that the political conditions favourable to deflation already existed. Wages were reduced across the board by decree – by 18 per cent in 1927 alone – with the official justification that revaluation would provoke a corresponding fall in the cost of living. Employers often took advantage of the situation to impose much greater wage cuts, a fact recognised by both prefects (provincial governors) and provincial chambers of commerce. Agricultural workers suffered most, but industrial workers were also often forced to accept reductions well in excess of official figures – without seeing a very marked or immediate fall in the cost of living. Reductions were particularly severe in the textile industry – an industry which had lost its competitiveness in export markets as a result of revaluation. The impact of this crisis is immediately apparent in any of the statistical tables which show levels of consumption of basic foodstuffs.

Discontent and protest were widespread, as police reports make clear. But there is no indication of concern for the fate of the regime; the special legislation of November 1926 was clearly capable of dealing with outbreaks of unrest. The only official path for popular protest remained that of the fascist union, and – if the unions did attempt to exploit the situation in order to reinforce their position – their ambiguous stance in respect of employers and fascist party made their efforts totally ineffective. They were equally ineffective in opposing the other major consequence of revaluation – an increase in unemployment. From 1927 onwards the generally lower level of economic activity became dramatically apparent on the labour market. Many firms virtually collapsed. The motor manufacturers, OM of Brescia, for example, who employed 1500 workers in January 1927, had reduced the workforce to 163 by June 1928, and most of these were only employed part time.[7] Here again, the fascist unions proved powerless to intervene on behalf of the workers they claimed to represent.

THE DEPRESSION YEARS

This much represents prologue to the international crisis of 1929. Italy entered that crisis already suffering the consequences of a drastic deflationary policy which had had serious effects on both exports and imports, and in many ways prefigured what was to become the official policy of autarky. This tendency to reduce economic links with other countries was, of course, no protection for Italian workers, who, with international recession, saw a further worsening of conditions, particularly in respect of wages and employment. Wages, which had fallen consistently after the revaluation of 1927, continued to fall after 1929. Official decrees of 1930 and 1934 sanctioned pay cuts, and once again employers exploited the situation to reduce wages beyond the level permitted by those decrees. Reductions in wages could in any case be achieved by the extensive manipulation of wage scales, whereby skilled workers would be given only minimum pay, and by a drastic curtailment of hours worked. In general terms, real wages in industry fell continuously between 1927 and the last years of the 1930s.[8] The cost of living fell very much less. Even in the 1930s, therefore, Italian industry tended to rely very much on the reduction of consumption in order to weather a crisis, just as it had almost always done in the years before fascism.

Wage cuts were accompanied by sackings. Unemployment in industrial areas already hit by the effects of revaluation rose sharply after 1929. In many areas the rise was massive. Local rather than national statistics (of dubious reliability) serve to indicate the extent of the increase. The figures for Brescia, for example, indicate that, of industrial workers registered in the 1927 census, 19 per cent were unemployed in December 1930, 37 per cent in December 1931, and 49 per cent in December 1932.[9] In some industries employers preferred to exploit the possibilities of shift work or a shortened working week in order to avoid overt dismissals. The picture which emerges, nonetheless, is of dramatic hardship – of total unemployment levels in certain northern provinces which hovered around 50 per cent for years rather than months.[10] As has been rightly observed, the crisis provoked by the 1927 revaluation and accentuated by the 1929 crash permitted a further redefinition of the workforce. Many of those who lost their jobs found re-employment difficult when the upturn came; their places taken by younger workers.[11] The political significance of this kind of generational change is all too obvious.

Protest against this situation was generalised and continued through 1930 and 1931 into 1932; but on the whole it was without effect. And it was protest which reflected very clearly the terms on which the working class was forced to face the recession. Prefects reported a large number of stoppages, brief strikes, and public demonstrations against conditions of great hardship. It is symptomatic of the situation, however, that protest tended to be expression of spontaneous rage and desperation and found no refuge in political organisation. Those who had jobs were careful not to put them at risk; those who had not, marched under placards which said simply 'Bread and Work', a basic demand with a ring which goes back centuries.[12] Specific anti-fascist protest appears to have had different characteristics. The number of arrests for anti-fascist statements increased notably in these years, but these were often arrests of people who began to shout 'Down with the Duce' or similar slogans, after a period in the local hostelry. This was isolated, individual, protest which found no channel beyond that of personal rebellion. It was dissent which undoubtedly reflected the resilience of workers on an individual level, but the form of that dissent is an indication of the success of fascism in breaking down more organised kinds of protest.

Some active and organised opposition to the regime did continue to exist, of course. The Communist Party, driven underground by the special legislation of 1926 and severely weakened by the emigration or imprisonment of its leaders, maintained small cells of militants in many of the major factories.[13] But the activities of these cells were limited both by changes in communist strategy in respect of fascism and by the fact that militants found it difficult to persuade fellow workers to follow them. In this last respect it is too often forgotten that the level of police surveillance under fascism was extremely high. Workers were well aware that interrogation on suspicion of 'subversive' activities at the local police station might not necessarily mean prison, but would almost certainly cost them their job.

For fascism the crisis was obviously a problem, but it was also an opportunity.[14] With dictatorship long established, the only mediators of popular discontent were either fascist or catholic organisations, and the latter had their weakest point in their contact with the industrial working class of the towns. Fascism attempted to exploit its position of strength to the fullest extent. Strongly supported in certain quarters of international opinion and presented as having a response to the crisis, fascism tried to project itself as a defence from crisis and an alternative to capitalism. In addition the regime was able to stress the fact that hardship was not confined to Italy. In practical terms, the crisis permitted fascism to extend its influence over the working class, employed and unemployed. Access to jobs, to unemployment relief, to public works programmes, and even to soup kitchens, depended on passing through one of the fascist organisations. Here it was

The working class and politics

desperation which provided the regime with the chance to assert itself among the working class in a way which had not previously been possible. The years 1930–34 do in fact see a great increase in enrolments in the various fascist welfare and leisure activities, and indeed it was during these years that the Fascist Party appears to have become very much a propaganda and welfare machine. The significance of popular involvement with fascism is very much open to question, however. Fascist welfare programmes appear to have been accepted in a very pragmatic way; it was there and it had to be taken, but the relationship ended there.

Other advantages accrued to fascism from unemployment. The crisis permitted the fascists to exploit old divisions within the working class. Tensions between established urban workers, commuters from the hinterland, and migrants from other parts of Italy were often accentuated by the intervention of the fascist unions and police. For example, non-resident unemployed workers were frequently sent back to the commune where they were officially resident, a fact which was often reported as being greeted with satisfaction by urban workers. Competition for jobs increased tensions between employed and unemployed. In the massive demonstration of the unemployed in Turin in 1930, those with jobs showed little solidarity.[15] Aspects of the fragmentation of the working class, already noted, re-emerged under the stresses of crisis.

It seems clear, therefore, that depression in Italy served to reinforce the hand of dictatorship. It was the reality of hardship rather than propaganda or rhetoric which forced workers to deal with fascist organisations. To see the greater involvement of the working class with fascist organisations during the early 1930s, and a lowering of the level of protest in 1932–33, as representing some kind of acceptance or consensus for fascism would appear to be forcing the evidence.[16] It seems, in any case, methodologically unsound to interpret, as agreement, a low level of open dissent, in a situation in which dissent is illegal. Working class attitudes to fascism during the years of the crisis would appear much more to represent resignation, the awareness of the lack of any immediate alternatives, and in some cases simple desperation.[17] By itself, the dramatically low level of political activity would seem to exclude any other conclusion.

THE WORKERS AND FASCISM

The overall picture which emerges from the years of the crisis is of a working class substantially isolated and forced to wait on events. The regime was obviously worried by the level of discontent in working class areas, but there was not the fear of insurrection which was present in Germany, with the myth of the 'stab in the back' of November 1918. There can be little doubt that fascism was convinced that it had finally defeated the 'bolshevik threat' of 1919 and 1920. It is difficult, therefore, to talk of any 'negative conditioning effect' of the Italian working class on fascism, as Tim Mason has argued for the German working class under Nazism.[18] In many ways, this simply reflects the fact that the Italian working class occupied a very much more limited position within the Italian economy, still predominantly agricultural, than that of its German counterpart. And the labour market always worked against it. Italy suffered, under normal conditions, from an excess of labour; this situation, always favourable to employers, was doubly so in a time of economic recession. Without the political levers to reinforce what was a basically weak position, most Italian workers had few bargaining points left. The fascists were well aware of this; they knew that workers had been forced back into the 'ghettos' of the working class areas of Turin, Milan, and Genoa, or the growing towns of the urban hinterlands, and that the regime possessed the means of controlling activities in these areas.

This confidence was not only a reflection of the capacity of the regime to undermine any political initiatives originating in the working class; it was also an indication of one of the demarcations of power within fascist Italy. For, if the regime established the political context in which workers operated outside the factory, industrialists were always very careful to ensure that they remained in control of the immediate treatment of the workforce. What industrialists had required, and obtained, from the fascist movement was a reduction in costs of production, a greater flexibility in the use of labour, and a guarantee of the docility of the workforce. What they very clearly did not want was government interference in factory organisation. From the moment when, in 1925, they had refused to permit the deployment of fascist *fiduciari di fabbrica* (workers' representatives) within the factories, the industrialists had been almost totally successful in retaining their autonomy of action. If this represented a considerable limitation of fascist power, it also constituted something of a guarantee to the regime. Within the factories, industrialists could be relied on to maintain discipline, even if on their own terms. It was only if industrialists were to decide to use worker discontent as a weapon with which to blackmail government that the situation risked becoming dangerous; but this possibility never became reality until the final weeks of the fascist regime.

In many important ways, however, – and of necessity – fascism presented itself to the working class, and attempted to undermine the evident hostility of that class, in terms which were not economic. International recession provided an opportunity for the regime to accentuate the more ideological aspects of fascism – those not related to economic well being. As is well known, fascism attempted to destroy identification by class and to substitute national sentiment. The destruction of the political power of the working class and the elimination of class identity – the process of disaggregation – was to be followed by a process in which workers accepted an 'aggregation' on the basis of national, rather than class, themes. The mobilisation of the masses required that the individual worker identified with the fascist state. The organisations of fascism, particularly in the areas of welfare and leisure organisation, represented efforts made by the regime to establish contact with popular opinion through channels which led the individual straight to the all-embracing control of the new Italian state.

Recent research has shown quite clearly that, while fascism may have been successful in restricting protest to an individual basis, the regime was largely unsuccessful in creating mechanisms which generated some kind of consensus for fascism, particularly among industrial workers. The organisation of leisure activities through the *Opera Nazionale Dopolavoro* (OND or fascist leisure organisation) achieved some success in terms of public attendance but none in terms of the fascistisation of the working class.[19] The *dopolavoro* remained a workers' club for recreational activities – cards, bowls, wine – but it never succeeded in the objective of imposing a fascist culture. The failure of the OND is, in fact, very instructive. Fascism had nothing to offer beyond the odd film or theatre production, generally of very low quality, which the workers dismissed immediately as 'roba dei fascisti' (more or less 'fascist rubbish'). This dismissal was based often less on ideological grounds than on the fact that the rhetorical material of fascism was, in most cases, boring and laughable. Where it was not, it was not explicitly fascist, and therefore did nothing to reinforce the image of fascism. But, apart from the poor quality of the material available to them, officials of the OND found themselves up against an insoluble problem. The creation of a fascist working class required political discussion of some kind

– and political discussion was precisely what fascism was trying to suppress. It was impossible to preside over wage reductions, a reduction in the standard of living, and unemployment, on the one hand, and, at the same time, encourage expression of political ideas, given that it was self-evident that these ideas would be antagonistic to the regime. The new 'models' of behaviour suggested by fascism were totally irrelevant to a working class which had seen nothing from the regime except repression and a lowering in its levels of consumption. The attempt of fascism to 'go to the people' says much about the confidence of the regime in attempting to break down barriers, but the reality of the situation was such that any attempts were destined to failure from the outset.[20]

Only in one respect may it be possible to say that fascism made some inroads, but even here the question needs to be qualified very heavily. By the mid 1930s a new generation was developing, which knew little of the war or the post war struggles. That this second generation of young workers was in some way attracted to themes of 'modernity', 'rationalisation', and technical efficiency, which fascism attempted to present as its discovery, is more than likely. Cars, motor cycles, aeroplanes, cinema, radio, sport – these were all clearly aspects of a new kind of society which could not but be attractive to the young people of the period.[21] There remains considerable doubt, however, about the extent to which these new phenomena were seen as being specifically products of the fascist regime, and, indeed, about the extent to which the low level of consumption of the working class permitted workers to participate in the changing life styles of the period. In any case, the appeal of modernisation could be double-edged for the regime. Some evidence suggests that, in the second half of the 30s, young people found a gulf between the novelties of industrialisation and mass communications and the very obvious political ossification of the regime which had clearly failed to proceed much beyond its victories of the early 1920s. This was a perception which led to frustration and irritation with the regime; if people did not become openly anti-fascist (by the late 1930s this choice was hardly available), they became extremely critical of the existing political situation, which failed to reflect the changes which had taken place in Italian society in the course of the *ventennio* (the 'twenty years' of fascist rule).[22]

To speak of consensus for the regime, as one historian has done,[23] would seem to claim more than the evidence can sustain. Obviously fascism drew support from those groups which it favoured, but it seems unlikely that the regime managed to express an ideological message sufficient to attract the support of those whose standard of living had suffered so much from the policies of fascism. It is true that fascism had its moments of triumph, which, because of basic nationalist sentiment, cut across class and political lines. The victory in Abyssinia in 1936 appears to have been one such moment, but so also was the Italian victory in the World Cup (football) in 1938. These were brief moments of celebration, but there is very little to suggest that they served to tip the scales in working class opinion of fascism. The Ethiopian war, in any case, produced its results soon enough in terms of shortages, rapidly rising prices, and a further reduction in living standards.

The relative silence of the working class during the 1930s invites one or two other concluding observations. It is obviously important to recognise the objective reality of the repression of the police state, but it is also worth remembering that – in historical terms – the Italian working class had known few victories. Italian workers had little to serve them as a guide, either for good or pre-war struggles of 1913–14; if they did not, their memory was of militarisation of work during the war, a brief prospect of change after the war, and thereafter a fight against unequal forces. Italian workers had nothing to serve them as a base point, either for good or ill; the distance between real experience and aspirations was greater than in many more industrialised countries. Interviews conducted in recent years with workers who were active in the 1930s suggest that there was a strong conservation of the memory of a time when things were different and better ('when we ate and drank better'), but also a clear appreciation of the fact that times had changed and that it was impossible to be other than resigned to the existing situation.[24]

The fact of resignation, rather than fear, suggests a fundamental difference between fascist Italy and Nazi Germany. Fearing the working class, the Nazis aimed at a kind of total control of the population which, if, also in theory, required by Italian fascism, the fascist government never really attempted to put into effect, precisely because it was not motivated by the same kind of fear. In Germany almost any aspect of daily life risked having political overtones; any statement risked being interpreted as a political statement, with all the well-known consequences.[25] Italian fascism worked with a net of a much larger mesh; open dissent was immediately stifled, but the everyday grumblings and curses of the working class, the general 'subversiveness' of the class, did not receive too much attention. This meant that, on the one hand, discontent was not necessarily immediately politicised in an explicit anti-fascist direction, as it was in Germany; on the other, that some kind of working class identity was free to survive up to the point at which it transformed itself into open opposition to the regime. This says a great deal about the fascist attitude to the working class. Undoubtedly frustrated by its inability to penetrate and mobilise that class, the regime appears to have recognised the position and accepted that it could do more than isolate the class and limit itself to crushing public manifestation of worker hostility.

THE SECOND WORLD WAR

The position of isolation, but controlled autonomy, of the working class suggests strong analogies with what was to become the position in Franco's Spain. Yet Mussolini's decisions to pursue a policy of rearmament from 1934 onwards, to ally with Hitler, and to attempt to 'radicalise' fascism in the later 1930s, meant that the immobilisation of the Franco regime was not to be realised.[26] The Ethiopian war and Italian intervention in the Spanish Civil War, both of which required a huge deployment of men and means, provoked shortages, inflation, and a tightening of the labour market. More fundamentally, increasing identification with Nazism and involvement in Spain heightened the levels of political tension. The Spanish struggle in particular was one which caught working class attention, inviting parallels with the working class situation in Italy. Although as yet relatively undocumented, it is beyond doubt that the final years of the 1930s saw severe internal problems for fascism. Intervention in the Second World War in May 1940 served to some extent to paper over the cracks. Faced once again with wartime legislation, the working class had little opportunity to exploit a renewed position of strength.

The war was disastrous, almost from the start, for Italy, and it was difficult to hide this fact from the home population. The extent of overseas losses could be minimised for a time, but the effect of the war on internal consumption could not. By the winter of 1942 some prefects were reporting that workers were fainting at the workbench because of lack of food. The response of workers to this situation was seen in the wave of strikes which, beginning in Turin, swept across northern factories in March and April 1943.[27] These strikes – the first mass protest against fascism seen in Italy since the 1920s – had their origins in appalling living and working conditions, on the one hand, and the awareness that the fascist government was leading Italy to disaster, on the other. The leading role of those communist cells which had remained in existence within the factories during the course of the regime is undisputed. Even if few in number, the communists played a crucial part in channelling working class exasperation into a relatively disciplined mass protest against fascism. Spontaneous rage was given an immediate political content. Many fascists – Mussolini included – rightly saw that the level of discontent and the degree of anti-fascist politicisation expressed by the strikes signified a decisive change in the fortunes of the regime. If the fall of fascism was not the direct result of working class pressures, there can be no doubt that these pressures were very present in the minds of the king and those politicians and industrialists who withdrew their support from Mussolini in July 1943.

The subsequent history of the war – the forty five days (the period between the fall of Mussolini and the armistice of 8 September), the German invasion of the peninsula, and the long struggle for liberation – could not but greatly reinforce the politicisation of the working class in an anti-fascist direction. Free trade unions were re-established immediately, as were the *commissioni interne* in the larger factories. In the face of German invasion and occupation, northern workers destroyed machinery where possible and thereafter resorted to persistent acts of sabotage. Many young workers, faced with the possibility of conscription to the army of the puppet fascist 'Republic of Salo', joined the partisan groups, the majority of which were communist led. These groups provided powerful schools of political education and re-education after the years of fascism. As was also the case with workers in the factories, young partisans often formed their political ideas in the course of a struggle which assumed the characteristics both of resistance to foreign invader and civil war.[28]

The experience of the war clearly served to bind together the Italian working class in a totally new way. The fragmentation which had been evident in the years following the First World War, and to some extent under fascism, was much less apparent in the period immediately following the fall of fascism. The common experience of the war produced a new situation in which, for the first time for twenty years, change seemed possible. The resignation, passivity, even impotence of the working class under fascism had been reflections of the fact that no alternatives existed or could be created. While the war against fascism certainly sprang from desperation,

Italy

it was also based on hopes and expectations which it had been impossible to nourish previously. Indeed, because of its sufferings under fascism, the working class made demands of the future as of right. The partisan war and the extent of popular participation in the struggle for liberation served, very importantly, to legitimise this position. This constituted a legitimation of popular aspiration which represented a fundamental turning point in the history of united Italy. If many of these aspirations were disappointed in the postwar years of the Cold War, the position of the working class as a legitimate interlocutor in the political process was never again to be seriously questioned.

NOTES AND REFERENCES

I should like to thank the British Academy for a personal research grant which permitted me to carry out research in Italy in the course of 1986.

1. On the First World War within Italy, see Giovanna Procacci, 'Popular protest and labour conflict in Italy 1915–18,' *Social History*, vol. 14, Nr. 1, 1989; A. Camarda and S. Peli, *L'Altro esercito*, (Milan, 1980); also essays in the volume edited by Giovanna Procacci, *Stato e classe operaia in Italia durante la prima guerra mondiale* (Milan, 1983).
2. See M. Clark, *Antonio Gramsci and the Revolution that Failed* (New Haven, 1977); P. Spriano, *L'Occupazione delle fabbriche* (Turin, 1964), translated *The Occupation of the Factories* (London, 1975); and G. Williams, *Proletarian Order* (London, 1975).
3. Fiat workers suffered a 10 per cent pay cut in October 1921; in April 1922 hours of work were reduced and 1300 workers sacked. See V. Castronovo, *Agnelli* (Turin, 1971), p. 344.
4. On the fascist unions and their early activities see, A. Lyttelton, *The Seizure of Power* (London, 1973), ch. 9; F. Cordova, *Le origini dei sindacati fascisti 1918–1926*, (Bari, 1974); A. Kelikian, *Town and Country under Fascism*, (Oxford, 1986) ch. 8.
5. For specific examples of this process see, D. Bigazzi, *Il Portello. Operai, tecnici, e imprenditori all'Alfa-Romeo 1906–1926* (Milan, 1988); also A. Camarda, 'Occupazione e salari nell'industria bresciana 1915–1935', *Annali della Fondazione Luigi Micheletti*, vol. 1, 1985 (Brescia, 1985), pp. 125–80.
6. On the revaluation of the lira see, R. Sarti, 'Mussolini and the Italian Industrial Leadership in the Battle of the Lira 1925–27', *Past and Present*, no. 47 (1970), pp. 97–122. For the general context see, G. Toniolo 'Ricerche recenti e problemi aperti sull'economia italiana durante la "grande crisi"', in G. Toniolo (ed.), *Industria e banca nella grande crisi 1929–1934* (Bologna, 1978), pp. 18–32.
7. A. Camarda, 'Occupazione e salari', cit. p. 159.
8. On wages see, V. Zamagni, 'La dinamica dei salari nel settore industriale', in P. Ciocca – G. Toniolo (eds), *L'economia italiana nel*

The working class and politics

periodo fascista (Bologna, 1976), pp. 329–78; A. Mortara, 'Osservazioni sulla politica dei "tagli salariali" nel decennio 1927–36', in G. Toniolo (ed.), *Industria e banca*, cit., pp. 65–71; R. De Felice, *Mussolini il Duce. Gli anni del consenso 1929–1936* (Turin 1974), p. 74; also A. Cento Bull, *Capitalismo e fascismo di fronte alla crisi* (Bergamo, 1983), pp. 144–45.

9. S. Peli, 'Elementi per una storia del proletariato bresciano (1915–1936), in *Annali della Fondazione Luigi Micheletti*, vol. 1, 1985 (Brescia, 1985), p. 113.

10. Unemployment figures remain a subject of argument, but the general picture is clear. The figures followed by De Felice show a fall in industrial employment (on a base 1926–100) to 68.7 in December 1932 and 69.9 in October 1933, (*Mussolini il Duce*, cit. p. 65). These are official figures, however, and may well underestimate the extent of the phenomenon. The three most important industrial regions in the north – Piedmont, Lombardy, and Liguria – were all very hard hit. Local statistics indicate that workers in metal and engineering, textiles, and – above all – building trades suffered most; see A. Camarda, 'Occupazione e salari', cit., pp. 176–80. Public works had very little impact on unemployment in industrial zones; it is more probable that the links which still existed for some families between industrial and agricultural work had some effect on cushioning people from the crisis, even if the crisis in agriculture was also severe.

11. S. Peli, 'Elementi per una storia', cit., p. 109.

12. *Ibid.* p. 115. Slogans which emphasised hunger dominated most public demonstrations.

13. See, for the whole period, P. Spriano, *Storia del Partito comunista italiano* (5 vols Turin, 1967–75).

14. Besides the works of De Felice, Peli, Cento Bull, and Camarda cited above, see also the essays in G. Sapelli (ed.), *La classe operaia durante il fascismo, Annali della Fondazione Giangiacomo Feltrinelli*, vol. XX (Milan, 1980); G. Sapelli, *Fascismo, grande industria, e sindacato. Il caso di Torino 1929–35*, (Milan, 1975); M. Palla, *Firenze nel regime fascista 1929–34*, (Florence, 1978); C. Gibelli, 'Il sindacato fascista a Genova negli anni della grande crisi 1929–33', *Movimento operaio e socialista*, XIX, 4, 1973.

15. G. Sapelli, *Fascismo*, cit. p. 149.

16. R. De Felice, *Mussolini il duce* cit. passim.

17. See G. Sapelli, *Fascismo*, cit., p. 189 ff; A. Cento Bull, cit., p. 164 ff.

18. T. Mason, *La politica sociale del Terzo Reich* (Bari, 1981), Italian translation of *Sozialpolitik im Dritten Reich. Arbeiterklasse und Volksgemeinschaft* (Opladen, 1977).

19. See V. de Grazia, *The Culture of Consent. Mass Organisation of Leisure in Fascist Italy* (Cambridge, 1981).

20. See P. Corner, 'Consensus and consumption: fascism and nazism compared', *The Italianist*, vol. 3, 1983, pp. 72–78.

21. See the recent work of M. Gribaudi, *Mondo operaio e mito operaio* (Turin, 1987).

22. On relations between 'second generation' students and the working class see, R. Zangrandi, *Il lungo viaggio attraverso il fascismo* (Milan, 1962).

170

23. R. De Felice, *Mussolini il Duce*, cit., ch. 7.
24. For various direct testimonies of popular opinion see the essays of Camarda and Peli, cited, and also L. Passerini, *Torino operaio* (Turin, 1984) and M. Gribaudi, cit., ch. 6.
25. This comment on nazism is taken from I. Kershaw, *Popular Opinion and Political Dissent in the Third Reich: Bavaria 1933–45* (Oxford, 1983).
26. On this period see in particular R. De Felice, *Mussolini il Duce. Lo stato totalitario 1936–1940* (Turin, 1981).
27. See, in general, P. Spriano, *Storia del PCI*, cit, vol. 5; also T. Mason, 'Gli scioperi di Torino del Marzo 1943', in *L'Italia nella seconda guerra mondiale e nella resistenza* (Milan, 1988).
28. P. Spriano, cit.; also D.J. Travis, 'Communism in Modena: the provincial origins of the Partito Comunista Italiano' in *The Historical Journal*, vol. 29, Nr. 4, 1986, pp. 875–895.

CHAPTER EIGHT
POLAND

*John Coutouvidis, Andrzej Garlicki and
Jaime Reynolds*

SOCIAL BACKGROUND:
CLASSES AND GROUPS IN INTER-WAR POLAND

The Second Polish Republic (1918–39) was a classic example of
under-development; her socio-economic situation was predominantly rural. Of a population of 35 m. in 1939, 60 per cent derived
their livelihood from the soil, a percentage similar to those who were
self-employed.[1] It is possible, in order of descending numbers, to
identify the following groups and classes in the social composition
of inter-war Poland: peasant farmers, town and village workers,
small tradesmen (members of the lower-middle class), intelligentsia
(the professional middle class) and white-collar workers, capitalists,
and great landowners. It is important to emphasize the rural aspects
of Polish society; nearly a half of all workers lived in villages.
Amongst them 3 m. agricultural workers (including families)
provided a bridge between the peasants, who in the main worked
smallholdings, and the industrial workers. The rural base of much
of the working class in Poland is of some importance in explaining
the experience of that class in the years of the depression and after.
We are in Poland dealing largely with first-generation workers with
strong ties to the villages. Thus assured of a food supply, they were
better able to endure all but the worst economic crisis. This may
explain why inter-war governments, until the mid 1930s, were less
unpopular than régimes elsewhere in Europe.[2]

An influential element of the working class was always the
workforce in heavy industry, but because of Poland's relative
backwardness this key category of workers was small in number
peaking at 800,000 at a time of greatest economic growth when

the overall number of industrial workers stood, in 1931, at 4 m. (over 9 m. with families). Miners, steelworkers, other metallurgical workers and textile workers are included in this group. The majority of them worked in small factories, workshops and mines. There were around 200 establishments employing over 1,000 workers and nearly 30,000 small factories with a labour force of up to 50, not counting 200–250,000 craft shops. Moreover, with the lack of heavy capital investment the number of large factories did not increase. The growth of the working class owed most to small units of production; between 1921 and 1938 the working class grew from 7.5 to 10.5 m. Even at the best of times these figures included many marginal workers, some of whom never had hope of permanent employment.

Workers in heavy industry were in the main better qualified and enjoyed a higher standard of living than other workers. Other well-positioned groups in the hierarchy of the working class were workers in State industries such as defence, the railways and trams, electricity and gas. Poland's heavy industry was organized into cartels and much of it was controlled by the State. In contrast most trade was characterized by its small scale of operation, most often by individual shopkeepers or entrepreneurs. Much of it was in Jewish hands as Jews did not share the dominant cultural prejudice against commerce. In 1921 the Jews numbered 2,110,000 or 7.8 per cent of the population, largely concentrated in the towns and cities. In 1931 just 270,000 of them gave Polish as their mother tongue.[3] Their concentration, coupled with different values, provoked the fervent anti-semitism common throughout eastern Europe. The destruction of Jewish society by the Germans during the Second World War evoked this response in a letter from Poland: 'The Jews have lost their dominating position especially in the economic world . . . and Polish Society will not admit that they should re-obtain the strongholds they have lost'.[4]

Jews also suffered from prejudice and discrimination as members of the intelligentsia. This group comprised a very broad membership drawn from the professions and bureaucracy. Inclusive of white-collar workers, they were the dominant urban class. With the growth of education and administration they numbered 800,000 in 1939; together with families they may have numbered altogether 2 m.[5]. They developed faster than any other social group, taking advantage of the opportunities in a nation-state which had regained its independence; most, with the exception of the Jewish intelligentsia, were civil servants. The highest social prestige and income went to lawyers, doctors, engineers, professors and senior civil servants. Other members of the bureaucracy, the white-collar workers, earned only a little more than factory workers. However, entry into this category was seen by the working class in general as socially desirable. Such advancement was sought through the education system. Yet in 1935 whereas the children of peasants made up 60 per cent in the first year of the general school system, they accounted for only 17 per cent in the year qualifying for higher education and 18 per cent in the first year of higher education. Similarly, the children of blue-collar workers constituted 15 per cent, 7 per cent and 4 per cent respectively, whereas the children of white-collar workers accounted for 2 per cent, 30 per cent and 35 per cent at the same levels of education.[6]

The constitution of 1921 which declared the right to education for all, also recognized the educational and cultural needs of the National Minorities. However, Polish xenophobia not only had a bearing on Jews but was also directed at other conspicuous minorities living within the boundaries of the new State. A distinction needs to be made between territories west and east of the Curzon Line.[7] To the west of the Curzon Line there lived a Polish majority amongst whom lived Jews and Germans. The latter group numbered 1,777,000 mostly living along Poland's western provinces of Poznania and Pomerania. Territories to the east of the Curzon Line did not have a Polish majority. According to the 1931 census these border lands (*Kresy*) contained a population of 10,768,000 of whom 37 per cent were Ukrainians, 36 per cent Poles, 9 per cent Byelorussians, 8 per cent Jews, 7 per cent Polessians; Russians, Germans and Lithuanians each made up 1 per cent.[8]

The constitution was generously endowed with articles on social rights. These matched similar provisions in the leading polities of the western world to which Poland wished to belong. As in France a liberal-democratic capitalist framework offered progressive rights to workers: the right to work and protection from the risk of unemployment as covered by such benefits as social and health insurance. The guarantee of democratic rights owed much to popular conceptions of freedom in the period that pre-dated the second republic and which were embodied in law at its birth. In a declaration of 8 February 1919, the State recognized the rights of workers to form trade unions giving them opportunities, denied under Russian occupation, to express their views as pressure groups in a free society; well over a hundred trade union periodicals sprang into being between 1918 and 1923 to publish demands and air opinions across the whole spectrum of worker interests.

This heterogeneous trade-union movement was, in those early years, a powerful social force especially as it was linked with political parties and with the Church. However, we must not exaggerate its importance to Polish workers as a whole, particularly as the early growth and development of the movement was not sustained and trade unions did not form organizations for the working class as a whole nor many of its constituent parts.

With the possible exception of the railway industry whose unions in 1923 could claim to represent 98 per cent of all employees, union membership of workers in other industries was low. In printing only 50 per cent belonged to a trade union and in the same year the figure for the mining industries was 57 per cent, the same percentage as belonged to a trade union amongst the farm labourers. In the metallurgical industries, membership of 45 per cent in 1923 dropped to 32 per cent by 1926. In general, for the period up to 1939 the trade unions represented on average never less than a fifth and not much more than a third of all workers ranged across the social spectrum to include farm labourers, blue-collar workers and white-collar workers.[9]

In considering the experience of the trade-union movement in Poland we must link this to the wider political scene; workers within and outside the trade union movement had their spokesmen in political parties represented at the *Sejm*, the Polish Parliament.

THE LEFT AND POLISH POLITICAL HISTORY TO THE DEPRESSION

The Constitution of the Second Polish Republic was modelled closely on the French system with the legislature made up of a *Sejm* or lower house and Senate. Of the two, the *Sejm* was vastly more powerful. The president, as titular head of State, had the right to appoint the government but not to dissolve parliament. The principle of universal suffrage, enshrined in the new Constitution, brought new influences into Polish politics. These were the parties of the minorities. They tended to ally themselves with parties of the left and centre. National minority parties frequently held the balance of power or had influence out of proportion to their numbers. As a result, the political system of the new Polish state was fragmented.

No party or grouping was strong enough to provide a firm basis for stable government. In the period from 1918 to 1926, when Piłsudski overthrew the parliamentary régime in favour of the *Sanacja* (see below), no fewer than fourteen governments held office. On the right, the National Democrats *Endecja* dominated. Theirs was basically a middle-class party, supported by white-collar workers and much of the intelligentsia. It was strongly nationalistic and grew increasingly anti-semitic during the 1920s. The party had, in the elections of 1919 and 1922, formed joint lists with the Christian National Party of Labour. This Catholic party gradually freed itself from dependence on the *Endecja* and in 1925 changed its name to the Christian Democratic Party. In the centre was the *Piast* Party, led by Wincenty Witos and supported, in the main, by well-to-do peasants. On the left was the Liberation Peasant Party (*Wyzwolenie*) and the Polish Socialist Party (*Polska Partia Socjalisticzna*, PPS). The Communist Party of Poland (*Komunistyczna Partia Polski*, KPP) remained politically insignificant throughout the inter-war years. Nevertheless its history during this period highlights conspicuous features of working-class political history in Poland.

The Communist Workers' Party of Poland, renamed KPP in 1925, was formed in 1918 when the Social Democratic Party of the Kingdom of Poland and Lithuania (*Socjaldemokracja Królestwa Polskiego i Litwy* – SDKPiL) merged with the Polish Socialist Party – Left Wing. The KPP existed for two decades until 1938 when the Comintern, claiming that the KPP had been overrun by 'provocateurs', disbanded the party, and much of its leadership and activists (*aktyw*) fell victim to Stalin's Great Purge. For most of its existence the KPP had little in common with the mass Communist Parties which operated in the open elsewhere in Europe. From its earliest days the KPP had been illegal. Party activists often spent more time in prison than at liberty. In 1932 when government repression was fierce, over 10,000 people were detained and nearly 7,000 were put under arrest for communist activities. Membership data bring out more vividly the narrow base of the KPP. Kowalski has estimated that the membership of the KPP in 1935 was between 7,400 and 8,200.[10] Membership in the 1920s had been less – about 3,500 in 1928–29. Of the 1935 membership total, approximately a quarter were Jewish and no more than about 1,500 were factory workers. Although the Ukrainian, White Russian and youth sections of the party supplemented its strength, these figures indicate clearly its failure to win mass support amongst the Polish population.

The other side of the party's isolation was the way in which the communists distanced themselves from the political institutions and forces of the Polish Second Republic. This sprang to a large degree from the ideological stance of the Party, its analysis of Poland's likely revolutionary development and its attitude to Polish statehood. For the most part, the KPP pursued a radical ultra-leftist line which assumed that the Polish revolution would not be generated from within, but would follow a revolution spilling across the whole of Europe from the Soviet Union or Germany. In Poland it would take a classic Bolshevik course. Armed insurrection would be followed by the dictatorship of the proletariat, exercised by a tightly disciplined, Leninist cadre party, the KPP, through councils of workers, peasants, and soldiers. Accordingly, party activity was not aimed at cultivating wide support inside Poland. Instead, it gave priority to preparation for the seizure of power. Attempts were made to arouse the working class through militant strike tactics and to agitate the national minorities through terrorist attacks on Polish authorities, while giving maximum support to the international movement. The priority given by the KPP to furthering the international revolution and, in particular, to assisting the much larger Communist Party of Germany, led it to support the demands of the German minority in Poland. This may or may not have assisted the German communists, but it was certainly highly damaging to the position of the KPP within Poland.

The party's open hostility to Polish statehood was a huge handicap in winning the support of a strongly nationalistic population which had only very recently recovered a precarious independence after more than a century of foreign domination. Nationalism was a force amongst the working class as much as any other stratum. In consequence, the influence of the communists amongst organized labour trailed behind that of the Socialists, the National and Catholic workers' movements and even the *Sanacja*. During its early years, especially, the position of the KPP was defined in the most uncompromising internationalist terms; in practice the Party's internationalism took the form of unquestioning loyalty to the Soviet Union. Though the leadership struggle in Moscow during the 1920s was reflected in the faction fights inside the KPP, this did not undermine the party's enthusiasm for the first socialist state. Hence, in the eyes of the great majority of Poles, the KPP was a foreign, subversive agent of Moscow, bent on the destruction of Poland's hard-won independence and the incorporation of Poland into the Soviet Union. Labelled a 'Soviet agency', (or the 'Jew-Commune'), it was viewed as a dangerous and fundamentally un-Polish conspiracy

177

dedicated to undermining national sovereignty and restoring, in a new guise, Russian domination.

The divergence between the KPP and the other radical movements of the left in Poland was in its origins concerned with the choice of whether or not to support the theory and practice of class warfare. This choice had demanded the taking of positions in 1905 over the impending revolution in Russia. It was faced by Józef Piłudski, leader of the PPS in Russian-occupied Poland at the turn of the century and the man who was to exert most influence in Polish affairs in much of the period covered in this essay.[11] His experience, which had much in common with a sizeable proportion of the Polish intelligentsia, is linked with the beginnings of the socialist movement in Poland and influenced its future development. Legend accords Piłsudski with the saying that he got off the Red tram at the halt called Independence. The aphorism is not consistent with the truth, because Piłsudski got off the Red tram at the start of the twentieth century and parted company then with its passengers.

The Russian uprising of 1905 was accompanied by the growth of national consciousness at a time also when rapid developments in industry gave rise to the growth of new classes, the bourgeoisie and the proletariat, in Russian-occupied Poland. The new opportunities here presented were seen and seized by the intelligentsia in shaping the life of modern Poland. There was, from the beginning of the twentieth century, a coincidence between the interests of the Polish intelligentsia, socially part of the middle class, and the history of Poland was to be challenged only when workers began separately to articulate their own demands, aims and aspirations. As a student in the 1880s and 1890s, Piłsudski flirted with Marxism and supported Socialism, as many of his generation did, as a weapon against Czardom. In common with many members of the revolutionary intelligentsia, Piłsudski believed that Socialism was important for its belief in democracy, equality, justice and freedom. Yet it is also clear that in the early history of Polish socialism many of its supporters – particularly in the right wing of the PPS – were not interested in fighting the class war but were only interested in gaining Polish independence; patriotism tended to occlude and often overwhelm the class character of the workers' movement. In the birth and development of the PPS the two tendencies, class loyalty and patriotism, rubbed together. With Piłsudski, a founder member of the Party, loyalty to the nation came first; the working class was to be the strength by which Poland would win her independence from the hated Russian oppressors.

It was this view that came into conflict with orthodox Marxism not only within the PPS but also with the SDKPiL with whose establishment the PPS lost its monopoly position in the workers' movement in Russian-occupied Poland. Increasingly impatient with the debates within and between socialist groupings, Piłsudski lost faith in the PPS as a vehicle for change. He now insisted that change would only come by direct action; workers had to be taught to support a Polish Army, believing that whilst there was an army there was a Poland. Socialism, the workers' movement, were but instruments to realize one aim – independence. And this Piłsudski believed to be in the interest of the working class. There was little else. The practicalities of politics – the workings of a liberal democracy – found scant place in his thoughts. Yet, when he took power in May 1926 he did so with the support of the workers' movements, including that of the KPP. This situation was to change, but Piłsudski's popularity remains an important factor in explaining the workers' experience during the depression. Until 1929 not only did the economy improve, aided particularly by the miners' strike in Britain, but Piłsudski's régime was respected by large sections of Polish society for its efforts to curb corruption in political life.[12] However, this respect for Piłsudski by the majority of Polish workers must be judged in the light of events in the political prelude to the years of economic crisis and beyond.

The point of departure in explaining the characteristics of the system, within which the workers' movements operated, are the changes in the political composition of the *Sejm* between 1919 and 1922.[13] After the elections of 1919 the *Sejm* numbered 364 members of whom the right claimed 35.8 per cent, the centre 33.3 per cent, the left 26.8 per cent, minority parties 3.2 per cent and non-party 1 per cent. Three years later the right could claim 24.8 per cent, the centre 53.9 per cent, the left only 16.5 per cent and minority parties 3.9 per cent. These were very significant changes. The centre grew at the expense of the left and right and a close analysis would show a marked instability amongst the political groupings in the *Sejm*.

Changes in its political composition reflected only to a certain extent changes in public opinion; in a polity lacking in parliamentary traditions and indeed political traditions election results were only an imprecise guide to political attitudes. Much depended on the qualities of candidates, above all on their ability to communicate with constituents. A party's political programme was, in a sense, of secondary importance to sections of the electorate, particularly in the conditions of illiteracy which existed widely in both town and country in independent Poland. In the elections of 1919 a significant proportion of the votes cast were directed by emotion and, because the result was only a very general measure of opinion, the passage of time would increase the distance between the political structure of parliament and that of society. Put another way, our assessment of the real strength of political parties, difficult at the best of times, is particularly so in conditions devoid of a tradition of democratic institutions as in Poland.[14]

Piłsudski may well have understood this. He was certain that there was no party or group in Poland that could claim the strength to tackle the country's problems and was at pains to make his own position clear:

> It is not a question of left or right. . .I am not of the left and
> for the left, I am for the whole (of society). . . . The Sejm will deal
> with internal problems. . . . However it comes: left or right – we shall
> see. . .Peoples' Government! I wonder whether Peoples' Governments
> or any other (governments). . .will give Poland what is needed. When
> I have an army, I shall have everything in hand.[15]

While Piłsudski's consistent emphasis on a strong army as an absolute requirement for Poland did not negate the need for political parties, their field of operation was, in his view, strictly parliamentary. This opinion was to change in time but his hopes (later to be disappointed) were that Parliament should deal with internal problems. He would be able to ignore the *Sejm* once he had established an army, one which was apolitical and independent of left or right and the fluctuation and configurations of Parliament. That was the power he sought. He hoped never to have to form a party or to come to depend on a political grouping. In this he was also disappointed as we shall see. He was, however, correct in his diagnosis of the political situation in Poland in the 1920s. Neither right nor left had sufficient support to form a stable government and this fact automatically strengthened his own position; the *Sejm* posed no threat.

Despite this, in the light of the provisions of the Constitution (see above) he sought new means of wielding political influence in a situation where so much power was accorded to the *Sejm*. He chose as his political base a grouping part military and part civilian: 'legionnaires' – veterans who remained in the army (20 per cent of its complement) and those who disbanded but who remained loyal to the Commander 'who always knew best'. The legionnaires became Piłudski's political base, independent of parliament and political party. Piłsudski was adapting himself to political games in Poland, games which are difficult to follow even to the most conscientious observers of the political scene. What is clear, however, is that a playoff between Piłsudski, the government and Parliament was in the making during the 1920s.

In Poland during the spring of 1923 it appeared that capitalism was on the edge of a precipice. Hyperinflation disrupted social life and hit hard at workers. The government could find no way out of the terrible situation. The numbers of strikes rose sharply. One diarist noted: '22 October. Outbreak of strike of rail engineers in Kraków. . .At the same time the general miners' strike continues. . .25 October. Strike in Łódź. 26 October. Postal strike in Kraków. . . .'[16] The government decided to break the strike movement by force. It decided to do so by a military call-up of railwaymen. Those refusing were to be treated as deserters. In reply to the government the PPS called a general strike.[17]

In cabinet, or rather within the narrow grouping which directed national politics, there was still no agreement about what to do; the opposition groups were even less united. Leaders of the PPS, for their part, feared a right-wing coup, distrusted the communists and suspected a take-over by Piłsudskiites. Their other conviction, that Witos, the leader of the Piast Peasant Party, intended to take power underlined their lack of faith in parliamentary democracy in Poland.[18] Piłsudski intervened to calm the situation in circumstances that threw much light on the political scene: a workers' protest movement, a weak and impotent government and Piłsudski to restore order through judicious use of the army. In this manoeuvre Piłsudski held the trust of the entire left including the KPP who at the height of the crisis on 14 May 1926, declared: 'Workers you know that our intentions go further than the Piłsudskiites. But in this fight the place of revolutionary workers is against the government. . .and against fascism.'[19] Such in fact was the view of the entire left with the exception of Witos's 'Piast' Peasants. All are agreed that in these critical days of mid-May 1926 the streets of Warsaw were on the side of the makers of the *coup d'état*. Piłsudski's personal authority saw to the rest.

The year that witnessed the beginnings of the greatest of inter-war economic crises, 1929, was also marked in Poland by equivalent political developments. Encouraged by the election results of the previous year, in which the *Sanacja* obtained one-quarter of all votes – more than any other political group or party – Marshal Piłsudski and his supporters in government now referred to as the 'Colonels' (former Legionnaires who, as senior-ranking officers, occupied high offices of State) became less willing to practise compromise in politics. This mood was clearly sensed by the parties of the left who now formed a union called *Centrolew*. Committed to counteracting the anti-democratic tendencies of the *Sanacja* the union signalled the end of support of Piłsudski from the left – support which made Piłsudski's 'revolution without revolutionary consequences' perhaps unique in Europe.[20] Poland was thus divided politically between the supporters of the *Sejm* and those who had set out on a course of circumventing its constitutional role with the ultimate result of destroying parliamentary democracy. The government, which styled itself *Sanacja* denoting the 'reform' it had in mind for parliament, pursued policies by which the latter was to occur.

DEMOCRACY, DEPRESSION AND THE WORKING-CLASS EXPERIENCE

The fate of parliamentary democracy in Poland was decided by Piłsudski on 28 November 1929. '[He] then stated that his budgetary session was the last for the present *Sejm*.' It was to be challenged after a lengthy crisis in which 'the Commander would prefer to intervene personally in March.'[21] On 12 March 1930, Prime Minister Bartel, considered a liberal within the *Sanacja* for his willingness hitherto to work with the *Sejm*, made an unexpected and vicious attack on Parliament. He told the *Sejm* that it 'had outlived its usefulness' and that it was 'unable to meet the needs required of it by a modern state'.[22] Bartel's speech attacking the *Sejm* was to have far-reaching consequences.

The reply from members of Parliament came in a vote of no confidence in the Minister for Labour and Social Welfare, Aleksander Prystor, who had incurred the wrath of the PPS in trying to remove members of the Party from membership of committees administering funds for sickness benefit (*Kas Chorych*). Under conditions then prevailing in the *Sejm* the PPS would merely have registered one more protest; Bartel's speech altered the situation: the PPS motion of no confidence gained the support of all the *Centrolew* parties as well as that of the National Democrats, (only the Piast Party abstained) and the government was forced to resign.

The crisis which Piłsudski sought had now arrived. Parliament and its members could be accused of lacking a proper sense of responsibility as the State Budget had yet to be agreed. It was, moreover, an opportune moment to distract public attention from a scandal, of great embarrassment to the régime, that was about to break. This was the so-called Czechowicz affair then being investigated by a state tribunal. It concerned the misappropriation of central funds for the benefit of the political organization set up to underpin the *Sanacja*: the non-party bloc for the support of the Government – BBWR.

Corrupt practices at the heart of Polish political life now shifted backstage to give centre stage to a farce concerning the appointment of a new Prime Minister. President Mościcki, having failed to interest Piłsudski in the job, nominated Julian Szymański. This elderly but presentable and charming man was a strange choice because he lacked political experience. Szymański accepted and sought Piłsudski's views over policy. It came to public attention that Piłsudski advised him to exclude members of the *Sejm* from the business of government, even over the budget. Furthermore Piłsudski said that it was not necessary to recall the now defunct Parliament for at least six months. This greatly angered the opposition; neither *Centrolew* nor *Endecja* (National Democrats) could accept such an erosion of parliamentary democracy. No party or grouping outside the BBWR would accept Piłsudski's now apparent perception of the *Sejm* as a mere façade behind which the *Sanacja* was to govern the country. Poland was witnessing the completion of the process, initiated by Piłsudski in May 1926, by which the *Sejm* was to be rendered politically impotent. It appeared that a clash between Government and Opposition was imminent. At its centre stood the *Sejm*.

The entire Opposition feared the loss of initiative in a crisis upon whose outcome depended their future. They could not allow their contest with the *Sanacja* to go outside the *Sejm*. All members of parliament had a vested interest in its survival at a time when most feared losing control over events in the country. Such fears were not exaggerated as the Polish economy withered in the first chill winds of the Great Depression.

Signs of recession were, in Poland, already visible in the second half of 1928 when the woollen, leather and metallurgical sectors saw a decline in orders, but it was the drop in world prices for agricultural products that hit hardest at her agrarian base.[23] The situation worsened rapidly as the uncomprehending masses of the Polish people witnessed the sudden breakdown of the system. Official statistics give some idea of the dimensions of the depression:

Index of industrial production (1928 = 100)[24]

1930	90
1931	78
1932	64
1933	70
1934	80
1935	85

Exporting industries (ranging from finished products to raw materials) were hardest hit, less so industries catering for the home market such as energy and food. The index of employment, in plants employing more than 19 workers, (1928 = 100) fell from 101 in 1929 to a low of 64 in 1933, rising to 73 in 1935.[25] The percentages of unemployed in each year between 1929 to 1935 inclusive, were (to the nearest whole number) 3, 11, 25, 41, 44, 40, 39. The depth of the Great Depression came in 1933 when 781,000 industrial workers were unemployed.[26]

In assessing the social consequences of this crisis, Landau and Tomaszewski distinguish between the periods before and after 1932.[27] The former witnessed but little change to the legal framework of welfare provisions as the government did not wish to alter the status quo and thus aggravate a situation in which social tension and unrest had become evident in a bloody confrontation between police and workers in the spring of 1930. However, as we have already shown, the *Sanacja* was keen to erode the autonomy of committees administering Sickness Benefit Funds by attacking their PPS membership. In the period after 1932 when the government sought to balance successive budgets, there were changes in the legal provisions protecting workers' interests. Hours of employment were increased by two from 46 to 48 and the so-called 'English Saturday' revoked. Sickness benefit was reduced from 60 per cent to 42 per cent of wages over a period that fell from 39 to 26 weeks after the termination of employment due to illness or disability. Annual leave was cut by 1 – 2 days reducing the total (depending on length of service) to 3 – 12 days. Also, in response to the financial crisis, the State recognized as valid fewer applications for welfare benefit; for example, it honoured only half of applications for sickness allowance. The quality of life of the Polish working class slumped even after the economic indices began to climb out of the trough of 1932–33.

The tragedy of unemployment haunted the working class as it had to accept an average cut of hourly rates from 1.02 złotys to 0.80 zł. in 1933 and further to 0.73 zł. in 1935. Measured against purchasing power, particularly of food, such figures meant the pauperization of the working class: the average weekly pay of a Polish industrial worker in 1933 was 24 zł; 23 per cent of workers earned less than 10 zł and another 30 per cent between 10 and 20 zł. Only 10 per cent earned over 50 zł. per week. This salary of 200 zł. per month compares to the average pay within the civil service of 304 zł. per month in the same year. The monthly living expenses per individual within a family of four in Warsaw were 128 zł.[28] Standards of living in this stratum ranged from the abysmally low to the bearable, with poverty the norm.

The response of the workers was, at first, rather muted; fears over job security did much to control feelings. The early years of the crisis witnessed fewer strikes with employers responding to workers' demands by a 'take it or leave it' attitude as entries in order books diminished. Numbers of workers on strike for each year between 1929 to 1935 show the overall impact of the crisis upon working-class militancy[29]:

1929	217,000
1930	48,000
1931	107,000
1932	314,000
1933	343,000
1934	369,000
1935	446,000

After the debilitating shock of the Depression in its first phase the workers' response was to take political and industrial action. With respect to the latter, 1931 saw the first example in Poland of the sit-in strike. In comparison with 1930 the number of strikes in 1935 had increased by 373 per cent and an increase in the number of workers on strike by 929 per cent. Plants and factories affected by withdrawal of labour increased by 890 per cent and days lost due to this action by 704 per cent. More importantly the number of strikes involving more than one group of workers had dipped dramatically before 1930–31.[30] Thereafter strikes became more general and took on a greater political role as the growing number of successful strikes gave the opposition parties the hope of making political capital out of the economic crisis: and the depression did indeed make a good argument in the political battle, but that was all. Neither *Centrolew* nor any party within it had a workable programme with which to combat the crisis. For its part the Government faced up to its responsibilities by engaging in the 'politics of burying its head in the sand'.[31] Its attention was fixed upon the future of parliament.

The core of BBWR, known as the 'Colonels group', proposed constitutional changes long advocated by Piłsudski, particularly the strengthening of the executive at the expense of the legislature. These proposals provoked violent reactions culminating in a huge rally in Kraków on 29 June 1930. The crowds called for the resignation of the president, Ignacy Mościcki, who was a close friend of Piłudski. The Marshal himself was pilloried as an enemy of democracy. However, the opposition parties seemed unable to exploit this mood; the political initiative remained with Piłsudski. In August 1930, intent on holding elections for a new *Sejm* and Senate, he decided to disolve Parliament and become Prime Minister. He then ordered the arrest of his political opponents, variously members of the PPS, the *Wyzwolenie*, the National Workers' Party, the *Piast* (including its leader Wincenty Witos), National Democrats and several Ukrainian nationalists. As intended, the arrests ensured Piłsudski's victory in the election of November 1930; the *Sanacja* won a majority in both houses of parliament.[32] Piłsudski had out-manoeuvred the *Centrolew* which had fallen victim to its belief that 'electoral confrontation would prove decisive', and had 'refused to resort to illegal measures in its struggle against the Government'.[33]

Disillusionment with the outcome of the election led to the disintegration of the *Centrolew*. Of its constituent parties the PPS suffered the greatest defeat. This was explained at its twenty-third congress in 1934 as 'the willingness of Socialists to acquiesce in half measures in the cause of national unity'.[34] It now advocated the distancing of the working class from the State and, in concert with the rest of the opposition, boycotted elections in 1935. However, this outburst of defiance did not prevent the operation of the new constitution.[35] It greatly extended the power of the president, who could now appoint and dismiss the prime minister, appoint one-third of the members of the Senate, dissolve the *Sejm* and appoint his successor in time of war. The provisions were tailor-made for Piłsudski. However, he died on 12 May 1935.

After Piłsudski's death and until the outbreak of war,

the 'Colonels group' ruled, led by Mościcki, Śmigły-Rydz
(inspector-general of Polish forces) and Beck. Attempts were
made to revive popular support for the *Sanacja*, but these
failed and instead there was an increased tendency towards
authoritarian rule by the oligarchy. A cycle of protest and
repression came to characterize the régime. In Polonsky's words
the 'political standing of the government was finally undermined
by a serious outbreak of labour unrest in the Spring of 1936. By this
time, the seemingly unending economic crisis. . .had thoroughly
exasperated the working class, which was increasingly prepared to
turn to newer and more violent methods of struggle.'[36] A number
of workers died and many more were wounded in clashes with
police. Bloodier still was the outcome of the peasant strike called
on 15 August 1937. This was the largest manifestation of social
unrest during the Second Republic.[37] The strike, organized by
the new leader of the Peasant Party, Stanisław Mikołajczyk,
who was in 1943 to succeed General Sikorski as Prime Minister of
the 'London' government, was brutally put down. In circumstances
which witnessed barricades going up in Polish villages for the first
time in the history of Poland between the wars, forty-four died
at the hands of the militia. What could have been the makings
of a political upheaval came to nothing; the régime's repressive
measures proved too effective and the opposition's new-found
radicalism too half-hearted for the strikes to have threatened the
State from within.

The threat which did come was from without, from Hitler's
Germany; and it was recognized too late by Beck and his circle. Their
underestimate of the dynamic and aggressive character of Nazism in
relation to Poland, and their associated neglect of informed opinion
to the contrary marked Polish foreign policy until the beginning
of 1939 and were symptomatic of the deep malaise in the Polish
Government. The Colonels' disdain for the democratic process in
the tradition of the departed but no less revered Piłsudski thus
contributed greatly to Poland's collapse.[38] When, sixteen days after
the German invasion of 1 September 1939, the Red Army crossed
Poland's eastern frontier, the Polish Government and High
Command left their country.

The possible social and political consequences of their defeat,
of relevance here, were first commented on by Lewis Namier:

> . . .A marked radicalization of the Polish masses *may* easily be
> the consequences of the defeat and emigration – they will not
> necessarily distinguish between those who had been responsible for

the mismanagement of the Polish State and the defeat of the Polish Army, and those who had no share in the Government. There had been a government of 'gentlemen' in black coats and white collars. The Polish masses had suffered considerable hardship under that government, had been muzzled, had been put down...They will now say – it is the 'gentlemen' who ruined Poland, who were responsible for the defeat, and who left the country after it had occurred. However unfair such reasoning may be to thousands among the refugees, it is likely to catch on with the masses of those left behind; the more so in proportion as these Poles suffer under the Nazis and fight them.[39]

It remained to be seen how far defeat and occupation were to influence the politics of Polish society in general and of workers in particular.

THE EXPERIENCE OF OCCUPATION

Between 1939 and 1945 Poland underwent a series of territorial changes. After their victory in 1939, the Germans created the 'Government General for the Occupied Polish Territories' in Central Poland (population 10.6 m). The other occupied territories in the west and north (population also 10.6 m.) were incorporated directly into the *Reich*, and those in the east occupied by the Red Army (population 13.2 m.) were incorporated into the Soviet Union between 1939–41. With the German invasion of Russia in 1941, part of the eastern territory was added to the 'General Government', the predominantly Polish Białystok region became separately administered by the Germans and the remaining areas were placed under the jurisdiction of Alfred Rosenberg, Reich Minister for the Occupied Eastern Regions. In 1945, as a result of the agreements at Yalta and Potsdam, Poland was shifted geographically to the west. She lost about 70,000 square miles in the east to the Soviet Union. To the 80,000 square miles remaining from her pre-war territory, she added some 40,000 square miles in the north and west, which had been part of Germany.

A number of points should be stressed in assessing the impact of the German occupation on Polish society and, in particular, the working class. First, the Germans did not rule the Polish territories through a collaborationist régime as in Vichy France and elsewhere. This was a matter of policy, though it is also true that hardly any collaborationists were available in Poland.[40] Partly because of this, the occupation in Poland was harsher than almost anywhere else in the Nazi empire. In the areas incorporated into the *Reich*, Nazi racial policies aimed at the suppression of Polish national identity through deportations and colonization. The Germans exploited the General Government as a reservoir of labour and materials for their war effort. Enormous quantities of raw materials, foodstuffs and more than a million people were removed to service the German war industry. The *łapanka* (round up) was commonly used by the Germans to press-gang Poles into forced labour in the *Reich*. The local population was left with inadequate food and other necessities and the townspeople in particular suffered great hardship. The severity of Nazi rule increased as the war continued. From 1942 the extermination of the Jewish population began in earnest.[41] By the end of the war Poland's population was 24 m. compared with 35 m. in 1938. Some 3 m. Jews, including nearly all of the pre-war Polish Jewish working class, had been killed.

The effects of this régime on the urban working class can be illustrated by the experience of the population of Warsaw. Wage rates were fixed by the German authorities and increased only marginally during the war. At the same time, one estimate suggests that the cost of feeding a family of four increased by 1700 per cent in Warsaw between 1939 and 1944. The comparable figure for Paris was 600 per cent, considerable but of an altogether smaller order. As Szarota has pointed out, on these figures the workers would have starved to death if Polish employers had not found ways to supplement workers' incomes. Encouraged by the underground authorities, many employers paid higher wage rates or bonuses, and frequently provided food in canteens. In fact payments in kind were often more important to an employee than his cash earnings. Workers also fended off starvation by stealing material from their work-places. In one Warsaw textile factory in 1941 it was estimated that about 10 per cent of the daily production was being stolen by the workers. It was reported that 'Almost the whole factory steals. It's easy to know who does not steal because they drop from hunger.'[42]

The Polish resistance movement was very highly developed. This was a response to the severity of the threat to Polish nationhood, but also reflected the strong tradition of underground political and military activity in Polish history. By 1944 a very extensive and broadly based Polish underground State had developed, loyal to the Government-in-Exile in London. It had its own army – the Home Army (*Armia Krajowa*–AK) which at its peak claimed to have 380,000 soldiers.[43] This movement was greatly weakened both by the failure of the Warsaw Uprising in mid-1944 and by the divisions within the 'London' underground over relations with the Soviet Union and the communists. Nevertheless, it retained the loyalties of very wide sections of Polish society and of pretty well all of the mainstream political groups up until the end of the war. Although it is probably true to say that the intelligentsia in the towns and the peasants in the rural areas gave the AK its broad social character, the working class also played an important part in the movement, as even the communists recognized.[44]

The main form of working-class resistance to the Germans was through economic sabotage and low productivity. We have seen already that stealing was endemic. So was absenteeism–the Germans estimated in 1943 that an average 30 per cent of the Warsaw workforce was absent. The symbol of passive resistance in the factories was the tortoise, drawings of which appeared everywhere. The precise fall in productivity during the war is impossible to estimate, but it was certainly considerable, particularly in the larger factories producing goods for the German military. There were also a number of short-lived strikes by Polish workers during the war. Most were brutally crushed by the Germans, but in some cases they conceded improved conditions–for example following a wave of strikes in Warsaw in spring 1943.[45]

Finally, the violent shocks Poland experienced between 1939–45 and afterwards meant that the working class was a fluid element in Polish society during these years. Amidst the general turmoil, dislocation and hardship, pre-war social and occupational barriers broke down. There was a general levelling of society in the common struggle for survival. Of course, some of the pre-war working class communities in the big cities, Warsaw, Łódź, Katowice, remained intact, but this 'old' working class was deluged by the 'new' working class formed during the war and the industrialization of Communist Poland in the 1940s and 1950s.

WORKING-CLASS POLITICS 1942–45

It is probably true to say that most wartime working-class social and political activity took place within the mainstream underground movement or in the Catholic Church and its agencies, rather than through political parties. Nevertheless, the parties were active. The largest working-class party was the Polish Socialist Party – Freedom,

Equality and Independence (PPS – WRN), which was supported by most of those members of the pre-war Socialist Party who remained active. It is estimated that in mid-1944 its underground organization had about 4,000 cadres. Its main leaders in Poland, Pużak and Zaremba, and in London, Arciszewski, Kwapiński and Ciołkosz were all strongly opposed to compromise with the Soviet Union and the communists. For this reason, WRN withdrew from the political leadership of the 'London' underground between 1941–42, when the Prime Minister of the Government-in-Exile, Sikorski, attempted to reach an understanding with the Russians. For the rest of the war they represented the socialist movement in the underground leadership. However, the socialists' political influence was certainly less than other elements in the resistance, the military, or the Peasant Party, in particular.

Not all socialists joined the WRN. Some, such as Żuławski, one of the leading figures in the PPS and trade unions in the 1930s, remained out of politics until 1945. Some spent much of the war in German concentration camps – for example Cyrankiewicz, Rusinek and Kuryłowicz, all of whom were prominent in the post-war PPS. A few, notably Drobner, were in the Soviet Union. There were also some smaller socialist groups to the left of the WRN. Próchnik's Polish Socialists (PS) replaced WRN in the underground political representative body in 1941–42. PS later split into various sections, one of which became the Workers' Party of Polish Socialists (RPPS) which existed from 1943–45, with less than 2,000 members. This revolutionary socialist party opposed both the London Government and the Communists, but in 1944 a splinter from it led by Osóbka-Morawski and Szwalbe allied itself with the Communists. This group formed the embryo for the postwar PPS, which by 1947 had over 700,000 members.

Following Stalin's dissolution of the Communist Party of Poland (KPP) in 1938, the Communists had no party organization until the Polish Workers' Party (PPR) was established in 1942. The PPR was intended to be a fresh start for Polish Communism. It attempted to distance itself from the KPP's sectarianism and anti-Polish reputation. In 1942–43 it sought to become a partner in the mainstream underground, but was rebuffed by the 'London' parties. In 1943–44 it changed tactics, attempting to mount a rival underground movement and win over centre-left elements from the 'London' camp. These manoeuvres were an almost complete failure. By the eve of liberation in mid-1944 the PPR's membership was only about 20,000 with most of its activists drawn from the old

KPP network. It was isolated – the tiny RPPS group was virtually all it had to show for its efforts to mount a national front. This failure led to serious disputes within the leadership over tactics and strategy in summer 1944. Communists were also active in the Polish emigration to the Soviet Union where they formed the political leadership of the Polish Army which fought alongside the Russians. Although they were only a few hundred strong, with the support of the Soviet authorities they were able to pursue national-front tactics much more successfully than the underground PPR in Poland. In 1944–45, the organization established by the Polish Communists in the Soviet Union was a vital source of cadres for the party, military, police and media apparatuses set up as the Red Army advanced westwards across Poland. The Red Army, together with several Polish divisions trained in the Soviet Union, liberated Poland in two offensives – one in the spring and summer of 1944, the second starting in January 1945. During the first the communist-controlled Committee of National Liberation (PKWN) was established in Lublin under Soviet sponsorship to administer the portion of the country – roughly one-third – then freed from Nazi occupation. This government continued until mid-1945, recognized by neither the United States of America or the United Kingdom nor the bulk of the Polish underground movement, which as before regarded the Government-in-Exile in London as the only legitimate authority.

In June 1945 this confusion was largely resolved when Stanisław Mikołajczyk, leader of the Peasant Party, the most important of the 'London' parties, returned to Warsaw with various other émigré politicians to become deputy Prime Minister in a coalition Provisional Government of National Unity, accepted by all the Allied Powers. The Prime Minister was a left-wing socialist Osóbka Morawski and the other deputy premier was Władysław Gomułka, leader of the Communist Polish Workers' Party (PPR). There followed – until the rigged elections of January 1947 – an intense and violent struggle for power between Mikołajczyk's Peasants and the Communists, supported hesitantly by the Socialist Party (PPS).

POLAND IN 1945

The military operations of 1944–45 added to the economic destruction of the German occupation. National income in

1945 was estimated to have fallen to just 38 per cent of its 1938 level; 65 per cent of industrial plants had been destroyed, with the greatest destruction in heavy industry and the Western and Northern territories.[46] There was in fact an almost complete economic breakdown in the final months of the war with three rapidly depreciating currencies in circulation. Transport and raw materials were lacking. The labour force was dispersed in many cases and pre-war factory owners had long since disappeared. In April 1945 industrial production was just 19 per cent of its 1938 level. The authorities concentrated their efforts on the immediate task of feeding the millions of Red Army and Polish troops fighting the Germans. Warsaw was in ruins as a result of the fighting during the failed Uprising in August and September 1944 and the systematic demolition by the Germans of what remained. In December 1943 Warsaw had 965,000 inhabitants; by January 1945 it had just 162,000, with 85 per cent of them in Praga, the suburb on the eastern bank of the Vistula which the Red Army had captured in their 1944 offensive.[47]

In this chaotic situation, the industrial workers who remained attempted to resume production in the mines and factories. Factory councils representing the manual workers were formed to run the factories and in the winter and spring of 1944–45 the Communist authorities gave these committees a major role in management. This often led to disputes between the committees, on the one hand, and factory directors and non-manual staff, on the other. By May 1945, the Government decided that this experiment in workers' control had gone too far. In the interests of 'efficiency', the powers of the factory councils were reduced to a consultative and social-welfare role, while the real levers of management were returned to the factory directors.[48]

Economic recovery in 1945–46 was rapid once military operations had ceased. By December 1945 industrial production had returned to 60 per cent of its 1938 level.[49] During 1946 employment in industry overtook the level of 1937, with employment in coalmining, and the steel and textile industries growing most rapidly.[50] Comparison of industrial earnings is perilous because of the effects of price inflation during the war and the fact that the wartime practice of payment in kind rather than cash continued after 1945. Nevertheless, one estimate suggests that total real income in 1945 averaged about 13 per cent of the 1938 level. In 1946 this average rose to 40 per cent.[51] Wartime low productivity also continued. Short strikes and stoppages were commonplace during 1945–47. It is difficult to say how far such industrial action was an expression of political as distinct from economic protest. Anti-communist opposition groups such as the illegal WRN were certainly active in some factories in 1945, and the Communists saw their hand behind much of the unrest. Even Mikołajczyk's legal Polish Peasant Party (PSL) had some success in recruiting industrial workers. But the Communists' main competitor for the support of the working class was its ally, the Polish Socialist Party (PPS), which in many industrial areas had more members than the PPR.[52]

The Polish communists had less success in securing a mass popular base than many of their counterparts elsewhere in Europe. In December 1945 the PPR had 235,000 members, of whom 143,000 (61 per cent) were classified as manual workers. This total represented about 1 per cent of the population. By comparison, Communist Party membership at this time was about 8 per cent of the population in Czechoslovakia, 6 per cent in Hungary and about 4 per cent in Italy. The party organization was weakest in the rural areas of east and central Poland where the opposition was most active. But popular support for the Communists was also thin in some industrialized towns too. This was revealed in the referendum held in 1946 which developed into a vote for or against the Communists. There were 80 per cent votes against the party in industrial Stalowa Wola and Rzeszów. The result was the same in Kraków. There was also talk of a fiasco for the Communists in the textile city Łódź, but the true results there were suppressed.[53] Nationalism, anti-Russian feeling and loyalty to the Catholic Church were powerful constraints on communist influence amongst the working class, as they were within Polish society generally.

To sum up, the working-class movement remained a secondary force in wartime Poland. In contrast to other countries such as Yugoslavia, Italy, France or Czechoslovakia the Polish Communists and left-wing parties were able neither to impress their stamp on the mainstream anti-Nazi resistance, nor to mount a major movement of their own. Moreover, the huge change in Polish society which occurred between 1939–45 did not result in a general radicalization of the working class and other social groups of the kind which assisted the left in many other parts of Europe. There is no evidence of a spontaneous shift of opinion towards the Communists at the end of the war. The key to their success in consolidating power in 1945–47, apart from the Soviet factor, lay in the effectiveness of their control over the State and local bureaucracy, the army and the security forces. Their grassroots support was sufficient to provide the manpower to achieve this, but fell far short of the mass base achieved by other European Communist parties in the period. If mass radicalization of the working class was absent in Poland, the war certainly had a huge impact on the political outlook of all sectors of society. The territorial and social transformation and the vast human and material losses seem to have produced a general mood of political weariness, a yearning for stability and reconstruction. This mood made it more difficult to sustain opposition to the Communists. In Poland in 1945, political fatigue, not mass radicalization, was probably the prevailing factor amongst the working class and society generally. But it was a factor working in the Communists' favour. The story of the Communist consolidation of power after 1945 is not dealt with here. However, it is important to conclude that for the Polish working class, 1945 was a political and social watershed. Until then, the working-class political movement had been largely excluded from power. After 1945, the working-class movement – as embodied by the Communist Party – became all-powerful within the Polish state.[54]

NOTES AND REFERENCES

1. Janusz Żarnowski, 'Społeczeństwo i Kultura II Rzeczypospolitej', p. 290 in *Z Dziejów II Rzeczypospolitej* (hereafter referred to as *Z Dziejów. . .*) ed. A. Garlicki, Warsaw, 1986.
2. A. Garlicki, in discussion with J. Coutouvidis, Warsaw, May 1987.
3. Andrzej Chojnowski, 'Problem Narodowościowy Na Ziemiach Polskich w Początkach XX w. oraz w II Rzeczypospolitej', p. 186, in *Z Dziejów. . .*ed. A. Garlicki, Warsaw, 1986.
4. 'A letter from Poland', PRO, F0371, 26723/C/287, quoted in J. Coutouvidis and J. Reynolds, *Poland 1939–1947*, Leicester, 1986, p. 9.
5. Janusz Żarnowski, op. cit. p. 295.
6. Ibid. p. 296.
7. Poland's eastern frontier was not settled by the Treaty of Versailles, see L. Kirkien, *Russia, Poland and the Curzon Line*, 2nd edn, (1945), 5.
8. L. Kirkien, op. cit., p. 47.
9. Ludwik Hass, 'Ruch Związkowy w II Rzeczypospolitej,' pp. 258–64, *Z Dziejów. . .*, ed. A. Garlicki, Warsaw, 1986.
10. J. Kowalski, *Kommunistyczna Partia Polski, 1935–1938*, Warsaw, 1975, pp. 69–70.
11. For details see A. Garlicki, *U Źródeł Obozu Belwederskiego*, Warsaw, 1983, (hereafter referred to as *U Źródeł. . .*).

12. A. Garlicki, in conversation with J. Coutouvidis, Warsaw, May 1987.
13. This line of argument follows the thesis developed in A. Garlicki, *Przewrót Majowy*, Warsaw, 1987.
14. A. Garlicki, *U Źródeł*... p. 64.
15. A. Garlicki, *Przewrót Majowy*, footnote on p. 12.
16. Ibid. pp. 89–90.
17. Ibid. p. 91.
18. Ibid. p. 100.
19. Ibid. p. 230.
20. A. Garlicki, *U Źródeł*... p. 13.
21. Record of a meeting between Piłsudski, Sławek and Świtalski, minuted by Świtalski and quoted in A. Garlicki, *Od Brzescia do Maja*, Warsaw, 1986, p. 6.
22. Ibid.
23. Z. Landau, J. Tomaszewski, *Zarys Historii Gospodarzej Polski, 1918–1939*, 5th edn, Warsaw, 1986, p. 180.
24. M. M. Drozdowski, 'Życie Gospodarcze Polski w Latach 1918–1939' in *Z Dziejow*..., ed. A. Garlicki, Warsaw, 1986, p. 165.
25. Ibid.
26. Taken from Z. Landau and J. Tomaszewski, *Gospodarka Polski Międzywojennej*, Vol. III, 1930–1935, Warsaw, 1982, p. 122. Their study is one of 4 vols. and is the standard work on the economic history of Poland 1918–1939.
27. Ibid.
28. I. Kostrowicka, Z. Landau, J. Tomaszewski, *Historia Gospodarcezaj XIX i XX Wieku*, 4th edn, revised, Warsaw, 1984, pp. 327–8.
29. Z. Landau and J. Tomaszewski, op. cit.
30. Ibid.
31. A phrase by Landau and Tomaszewski quoted in A. Garlicki, *Od Brześcia do Maja*, Warsaw 1986 p. 23 and see note 13.
32. See A. Garlicki, *Od Brześcia do Maja*, Warsaw 1986, pp. 47–55.
33. A. Polonsky, *Politics in Independent Poland 1921–1939. The Crisis of Constitutional Government*, Oxford, 1972, p. 318.
34. Ibid. p. 364.
35. Ibid. pp. 386–99.
36. Ibid. p. 408.
37. See A. Zakrewski's article, 'Dlaczego Wówcas Chłopski Bunt?' in *Polityka*, Warsaw, 6.VI. 1987.
38. Of particular interest and importance in this regard is the evidence amassed by the Winiarski Commission, called into being to enquire into the September defeat, whose files held at the Polish Institute and Sikorski Museum in London are currently being researched by Professor A. Garlicki. Refer also to E. Duraczyński, *Kontrowersje i Konflikty 1939–44*, Warsaw, 1979, pp. 57–9.
39. Namier to Butler, 28 November 1939, PRO, F0371, C/19304. See J. Coutouvidis, 'Lewis Namier and the Polish Government-in-Exile, 1939–40', *Slavonic and East European Review*, vol. 62, no. 3 (July 1984), pp. 421–8.
40. For details on the handful of Polish collaborationists, see S. Korboński, *Polskie Państwo Podziemne* Paris, 1975, pp. 145–8.

41. H. Roos, *A History of Modern Poland*, London, 1966 pp. 171–3, 187–8.
42. T. Szarota, *Okupowanej Warzawy Dzień Powszedni*, Warsaw, 1978, pp. 150–81.
43. *Polskie Siły Zbrojne W Drugiej Wojnie Światowej*, Vol. III *Armia Krajowa*, London, 1950, p. 119.
44. E. Duraczyński, *Wojna i Okupacja*. *Wrzesień 1939–Kwiecień 1943*, Warsaw, 1974, p. 460.
45. Szarota, op. cit.
46. F. Ryszka (ed.). *Polska Ludowa 1944–1950*. *Przemiany Społeczne*, Wrocław, 1974, pp. 279, 285.
47. Ibid. p. 302.
48. See further, J. Reynolds, 'Communists, Socialists and Workers: Poland 1944–48'. *Soviet Studies*, vol. XXX no. 4 October, 1978, pp. 516–39.
49. Ryszka op. cit., p. 302.
50. Ibid. p. 354.
51. Ibid. pp. 358–9.
52. J. Coutouvidis and J. Reynolds op. cit. pp. 238–9.
53. Ibid. pp. 253–4.
54. See further J. Coutouvidis and J. Reynolds, *Poland 1939–1947*, Leicester, 1986.

CHAPTER NINE
SPAIN

Martin Blinkhorn

INTRODUCTION

When George Orwell arrived in Barcelona in late December 1936, en route for the Spanish Civil War battlefront, he found a city in the throes of social revolution. The working class, he recorded with pleasure, was 'in the saddle'.[1] The situation may have been destined to endure for only a few months more, but the excitement of an upper-middle-class English socialist such as Orwell is easy to understand, especially against the European background of the 1930s. As Orwell inhaled the revolutionary air of Barcelona, fascism or semi-fascist authoritarianism was in control of Italy, Germany, Austria, Portugal and much of eastern Europe; in France the Popular Front was in serious difficulties; and in Britain a conservative-dominated National Government utterly commanded the political stage. In Republican Spain, in contrast, it seemed that the working class was standing up for itself: resisting fascism and participating in the most exciting and far-reaching revolutionary experiment since the early stages of the Russian Revolution.

However ingenuous they may appear to have been in retrospect, Orwell's observations do serve to illustrate how the political experience of the Spanish working class was out of phase with that of much of Europe in the period between the Wall St Crash and the end of the Second World War: assertive in the early 1930s, and again in 1936, when its comrades elsewhere were suppressed or passive; involved between 1936 and 1939 in a civil war with no parallel elsewhere in Europe; largely cut off by Spain's neutrality from the direct impact of the Second World War; and still, in 1945, as the light began to dawn abroad, subjected to a repression from which no escape was in prospect. As the only European country in which the organized working class offered prolonged resistance to fascism in the 1930s, and the only major country in which, in 1945, the working class found itself still crushed by right-wing dictatorship, Spain, as Franco's tourist publicity was later to proclaim, was 'different'.

The principal factor conditioning subsequent working-class politics in Spain was the country's transition, between 1929 and 1931, from dictatorship to democracy. In January 1930 the dictatorship of General Miguel Primo de Rivera, who had ruled Spain since killing off her corrupt and oligarchic parliamentary system in 1923, finally collapsed; just over a year later in April 1931 the monarchy of King Alfonso XIII also fell, giving way to the democratic Second Republic. Democracy thus arrived in Spain at a time when it was well and truly in retreat throughout much of Europe, offering the Spanish urban and rural working class overdue emancipatory opportunities of which its foreign counterparts were simultaneously being deprived. The moment was hardly propitious, however, for along with democracy there arrived the first shock-waves of an economic depression that was to make agonizingly difficult the task of a would-be reforming régime.

SPAIN 1929–1936: BACKWARDNESS AND DEPRESSION

The Spain bequeathed by Primo de Rivera to his successors, despite having shared in the general European boom of the mid–1920s, remained an industrializing, rather than an industrialized, nation. Her industry, and hence her industrial working class, was concentrated in a few regions, mostly situated on the Spanish periphery: Catalonia, where Spain's textile industries were centred; the Basque region, home of most of her metallurgical, shipbuilding, armaments and paper industries; the coalmining region of Asturias; and other, isolated, mining communities scattered across the southern half of the country. Elsewhere, urban workers were mainly involved in the construction industry, which had expanded enormously during the 1920s; transport and docks; a disproportionately large service sector; and white-collar activities. Madrid, with almost a million inhabitants, may have been rather more than a city of 'bricklayers, clerks and maids' but, with as yet little large-scale manufacturing industry, she remained a vastly inflated reflection of many Spanish provincial capitals.[2] The situation was not, however, static; the

The working class and politics

construction bonanzas of the war years and the 1920s had sucked
into Madrid, Barcelona, Seville, Zaragoza and other large cities a
new, unskilled immigrant working class whose members were to be
a volatile factor during the 1930s.[3]

Immigrants into Spain's expanding cities more often than not
sought escape from desperate rural poverty. However inadequate
wages and conditions in the factories of Spain, it was in the
countryside, especially in the south, that the workers' lot was
harshest. In 1930 agriculture, despite the significant recent
shift into non-agricultural occupations, remained overwhelmingly
Spain's biggest single 'industry', involving 46 per cent of her active
population and employing some 1.9 m. out of her 4 m. wage-
earners; this compared with some 430,000 construction workers,
340,000 metal-workers, 300,000 textile workers, 219,000 transport
workers and 176,000 miners.[4] Unlike in some countries, moreover,
Spain's agricultural workers constituted a true proletariat. The
classic Spanish agricultural unit was the *latifundio* of Andalusia,
Extremadura, La Mancha and Salamanca. *Latifundios* were vast
private estates typified by absentee ownership, under-investment,
wasteful land use, and the seasonal employment of armies of ill-paid,
ill-used labourers (*braceros* or *jornaleros*). Agricultural labourers in
other regions were more dispersed and relatively better-off than the
southern *braceros*, but their condition too was frequently abject.[5]

During the half-century before 1923 three rival trade-union
strands had grown up in Spain. The Socialist UGT (*Unión General
de Trabajadores*: General Union of Workers) was founded in 1888
and by 1930 boasted a membership of just under a quarter of a
million; a union of craft, skilled and white-collar workers, it had
a tradition of moderation and reformism and was strongest in
Madrid, Asturias and the Basque country. Its chief rival was
the anarcho-syndicalist CNT (*Confederación Nacional del Trabajo*:
National Confederation of Labour), founded in 1910 but built
on a tradition going back to the 1860s. With its stress on loose
organization, rejection of state involvement in labour relations, and
belief in revolution through general strikes, the CNT, with a million
affiliates by 1917, was strongest among urban workers in Catalonia,
Zaragoza, Valencia and other provincial cities, and among the
rural poor of Andalusia. The third strand, numerically much the
weakest, was that of Catholic unionism. Most Catholic unions were
originally founded in the early twentieth century as sincerely meant
alternatives to 'Godless' socialism and anarchism, recruited mainly
artisans, shop-and service-workers and white-collar workers, and,

like the *sindicatos libres* in the early 1920s, tended to evolve into employers' or 'yellow' unions.[6]

In both industry and agriculture, labour relations in the years immediately preceding Primo de Rivera's coup had been bitter. The narrow and insecure profit margins of many Spanish industries – textiles and coalmining particularly – engendered in employers an intense hostility to workers' demands and organizations. In the countryside the interests of the landowner were guaranteed by a mixture of surplus labour and coercion by armed private retainers and Civil Guard. As this last point illustrates, in the old régime which was temporarily saved in 1923 and appeared to have collapsed in 1931, the Spanish state was to a considerable extent both the preserve and the guarantor of privilege.

Class conflict reached a climax between 1917 and 1923, chiefly in urban Catalonia and rural Andalusia, and constituted one of several factors contributing to the collapse of parliamentarism in 1923. Primo de Rivera, an amiable paternalist, sought to impose social harmony within a semi-fascist, corporativist political system. Having driven the CNT underground, he attempted, successfully for a time, to integrate the more moderate UGT into his régime. Primo's most enduring positive contribution to Spanish labour relations was the introduction into industry of worker–employer *comités paritarios* ('parity committees') for the negotiation of wages and working conditions.[7]

Before examining the relationship of the Spanish working class with the Second Republic, it would be wise to consider briefly the impact upon Spain of the 1930s Depression. It is usual for economic historians to suggest that Spain was less affected by the Depression than other, more developed, countries.[8] In terms of crude unemployment statistics, this is true enough. At its highest point in early 1936 – that is, shortly before the outbreak of the Civil War – unemployment reached around 800,000 in a population of 23 m.: perhaps 18 per cent of insured workers. This was a lower figure than in, for example, the United Kingdom, the United States and, of course, Germany. The social and political historian must, however, look beyond statistics, and in this instance recognize the exacerbatory impact of the Depression on an economy which already provided insufficient work and income for much of its population, and the influence which this in turn was bound to exercise upon social relations and political developments.

The Depression was slowest to harm those areas of the economy least affected by the contraction of international trade.

Although traditionally sluggish, Spain's domestic market was boosted between 1931 and 1933 by rising wages resulting from Republican legislation; the most notable beneficiaries were the Catalan textile industries and the emerging consumer-goods industries. Hardest hit were those areas geared to exports or boosted by the shortlived prosperity of the 1920s. The iron-ore extracting and metallurgical industries of the Basque country suffered a halving of production between 1929 and 1935 and a corresponding rise in unemployment and short-time working, the result both of declining exports (that of iron ore fell by almost two-thirds between 1928 and 1935) and of reduced demand due to contraction in the building and railroad-construction industries. Depression in the Basque country infected nearby Asturias, whose ramshackle mining industry, already contracting during the 1920s following an artificial wartime boom, depended for survival upon the appetite of Basque industry. Every city and provincial capital of Spain, from Madrid and Barcelona downwards, was hit by the collapse in 1930 of the construction boom, which increased urban unemployment and drove thousands of unskilled immigrant labourers back into an unwelcoming countryside.[9]

The biggest single component of general unemployment was to be found in agriculture. With Spanish foreign trade as a whole declining by over 70 per cent between 1928 and 1935, and exports by 73 per cent, agricultural exports fell disastrously. Foreign earnings from the wine trade fell by 95 per cent between 1928 and 1935; from the export of oranges by 60 per cent; from that of rice by 90 per cent; and from that of olive oil by 80.5 per cent. From 1931 down to the Civil War, agricultural labourers, whose lives were wretched enough even when work was available, made up between 58 and 67 per cent of all unemployed.

The effects of industrial and agricultural depression have to be viewed in relation to an already low-wage economy in important sectors of which – mainly agriculture and construction – seasonal unemployment was structural and chronic; in which unemployment insurance was minimal; in which overseas emigration outlets were now closed, and former emigrants returning in their tens of thousands; and in which employer attitudes were often crudely exploitative. In sharply reversing the recently improving situation of some sections of the working class, notably in construction, and aggravating the already desperate conditions in mining and agriculture, the Depression unquestionably exerted an important influence upon events in Spain between 1930 and 1936.

THE POLITICS OF REFORMISM, 1930–33

If the economic climate of the early 1930s was hardly favourable to the Spanish working class, the political climate, for a time at least, was more favourable than at any time in Spanish history. The uncertain liberalization which followed the fall of Primo de Rivera permitted a dramatic upsurge in working-class organization and activism which played a major part in bringing about the destruction of the monarchy. The CNT, re-legalized in April 1930, quickly confounded the expectations of its Socialist rivals by re-emerging as a major syndical force. While King Alfonso XIII and Primo de Rivera's ministerial successors vainly sought a political formula which might save the monarchy amid a deteriorating economic situation, the CNT launched a new wave of labour militancy. During 1930 a Republican campaign to overturn the monarchy rapidly gathered momentum. Socialist leaders were divided as to what attitude to adopt; in the end, rank-and-file pressure within the UGT helped push the union's cautious leadership and that of the Socialist party, the PSOE, into lending their support and assisting the monarchy's eventual collapse in April 1931.[10]

Given the limitations and deficiencies of Spain's pre-1923 parliamentarism, the Second Republic which was born on 14 April 1931 represented her first experience of truly mass politics and her first genuine essay at democracy. For two years, moreover, she was ruled by forces broadly sympathetic to working-class interests and aspirations. Between April 1931 and September 1933, for most of that time under the premiership of the Republican Manuel Azaña, Spain was governed by alliances of middle-class Republicans and Socialists committed to a far-reaching programme of reform. The Socialists, who emerged as the largest single party in the Constituent Cortes elected in June 1931, were not unanimous in wishing to participate actively in the affairs of a 'bourgeois democracy'. Some Socialists, misinterpreting the coming of the Republic as a bourgeois revolution, argued that the Spanish bourgeoisie should be left to fulfil its own historic role; others insisted that with or without Socialist participation, reformism within a capitalist system was bound to be frustrated.[11] The great majority of Socialists, however, were for the moment eager to use the Republic's machinery to advance the cause of the working class, and in particular to achieve the transformation through land reform of the desperate lot of the southern rural proletariat. Although bourgeois Republicans like Azaña were more concerned with educational and institutional reform, consciousness of their own lack of mass support counselled generalized support for the Socialists' goals. Between 1931 and 1933 the PSOE occupied three ministries, most notably the ministry of Labour which was taken by Francisco Largo Caballero, a former plasterer and leading UGT official.

Largo Caballero's most consistent characteristics were his dedication to the UGT and sensitivity to shifts of rank-and-file opinion. In this spirit he had first collaborated with Primo de Rivera, had later switched to opposing him, and after months of hesitation had belatedly come round to supporting the Republican cause.[12] The results of Largo Caballero's tenure of the Labour ministry were significant in a number of respects. Socialist control of the ministry and through it the 'mixed juries' – a development of Primo de Rivera's *comités paritarios* – tilted the balance in determining wages and conditions in labour's favour, pushing up wages at a time when, left to market forces, they would probably have fallen. Significant in urban Spain, this was still more so in the countryside. Here, where Primo de Rivera's paternalistic reforms had never penetrated, the mixed juries appeared as a major threat to the dominance of landowners and employers. As if this were not enough, the eight-hour day was introduced into agriculture, where hitherto a sixteen-hour day had been customary; a decree on 'municipal boundaries' curbed employers' ability to control the local labour market by importing cheap outside labour; and a further decree on 'obligatory working' (*laboreo forzoso*) effectively banned agricultural lock-outs. The effect was to force up agricultural wages dramatically and, on paper at least, to shift the balance of power in rural Spain away from the wealthy and powerful. In many districts the new assertiveness of the Spanish working class was backed up by sympathetic left-wing local councils elected in April-May 1931.[13]

The influence and patronage at the disposal of the Labour ministry also had the effect, as Largo Caballero intended, of greatly strengthening the UGT. Its membership figures, which had shown little benefit from its privileged position under Primo de Rivera, increased from 277,011 in December 1930 to over 950,000 a year later and more than a million by June 1932. Growth was particularly marked in the UGT's newly founded agricultural workers union, the FNTT (*Federación Nacional de Trabajadores de la Tierra*: National Landworkers Federation). From a membership of 27,340 at its birth in April 1930, the FNTT expanded explosively; by June 1932 its paid-up membership stood at 392,953 and a year later it was 451,337. With close on 40 per cent of the UGT's membership now consisting of impoverished rural labourers, the entire character of what until now had been mainly a moderate union of craft workers and labour aristocrats was transformed, and in a potentially radical direction. For the present the FNTT leadership, like that of most of the UGT's component unions, was politically moderate and capable of restraining any restlessness among the rank and file. How long this state of affairs would continue was quite another matter.[14]

The position of labour during the early years of the Second Republic was complicated by the fact that approximately half of Spain's unionized workers belonged to organizations affiliated not to the Socialist, and therefore *de facto* pro-Republican, UGT but to the apolitical CNT. Although the CNT's unbureaucratic character makes it difficult to obtain precise membership statistics, a figure of around a million by 1933 represents a reasonable estimate. Where the UGT expanded disproportionately in the countryside during this period, it seems to have been in the cities, especially among unskilled construction workers and in the service sector, that the CNT's new growth was most marked. It is important to stress that an individual worker's membership of a CNT union did not necessarily indicate anarchist conviction. Many Spanish workers joined one union or another out of insouciance, lack of choice, or at most a relative preference for confrontation or negotiation, rather than considered belief. Consequently, by no means all so-called 'anarchist' workers were either opposed *ab initio* to the Republic or hostile towards rank-and-file members of the UGT. Nor, to begin with, were CNT leaders necessarily as antagonistic towards the new régime as their beliefs might suggest. The anarchist zealots of the FAI (*Federación Anarquista Ibérica*: Iberian Anarchist Federation) certainly were, but others were more inclined to judge the Republic on its achievements.[15]

It nevertheless remains true that the contrasting syndical and political cultures of the CNT and UGT made problems likely. Where the traditionally moderate, reformist UGT looked to the machinery of the state, in this case the Republican state, to mediate labour relations and improve the workers' condition, the CNT rejected bodies such as the mixed juries in favour of direct dealings and often confrontation with employers. Mistrust between *cenetistas* and both bourgeois Republicans and Socialists was mutual, and within a few months the CNT had moved into a position of ever-increasing militancy and opposition to the Republican authorities. Whilst ingrained suspicion of any state authority undoubtedly contributed to what may have been an inevitable development, CNT attitudes were also strongly influenced by the evident wish of Republican ministers and provincial Civil Governors to demonstrate toughness on public-order issues, often loosely defined to embrace CNT-led strikes, and by the Socialists' determination to use their new political and bureaucratic power to weaken and if possible destroy the rival union. As early as July 1931 a Republican government containing Socialist ministers was using Civil Guard and artillery against CNT workers. Later in 1931 the CNT came under extremist control and in January 1932 there occurred the first of three anarchist risings which were to take place before the end of 1933.

If within the CNT dissatisfaction with the Republic arose early and derived from a combination of conviction and experience, within the UGT it developed more gradually and was almost entirely due to the latter. As the months passed it became increasingly clear that in the Spain of the Second Republic the mere existence of reforming decrees and legislation did not guarantee their observance. The change of régime in 1931 having been unaccompanied by any social revolution, Spain's wealthy classes remained powerful, especially where still cushioned within stubbornly unchanging local power structures. The government lacked both the financial means and the qualified personnel necessary to enforce the law; hence employers and landowners, in particular where not pressed by left-wing local authorities, were often able to flout labour legislation. Unions were refused recognition and their members victimized; in many areas employers successfully delayed the elaboration and/or operation of *bases de trabajo* (agreed working conditions), the creation of labour exchanges, and the implementation of arbitrated wage settlements. Decrees on rent control and non-eviction of agricultural tenants were frequently ignored with impunity.[16] In the Asturian mines the Depression-hit owners attempted to cut wages and resisted demands for improved working conditions and insurance coverage.[17] Meanwhile the political representatives of the landowners, chiefly organized in the centre-right Radical party and the Catholic right-wing organization *Acción Popular*, were successfully delaying passage of the touchstone of reforming Republicanism, the Agrarian Reform bill. Eventually passed in September 1932, the Agrarian Reform quickly proved to be an emasculated, contradictory and unproductive piece of legislation which, by the time the political climate changed in autumn 1933, had done next to nothing to improve the plight of Spain's landless rural labourers.[18]

By early 1933 the frustration provoked by the limitations of Republican legislation, the continued power and renewed aggressiveness of employers and landowners, and the political resurgence of the right, was generating a growth in working-class militancy apparent within not only the CNT but also, politically more significant, the UGT. The Casas Viejas episode of January 1933, when several Andalusian villagers were massacred by Civil and Assault Guards during an anarchist rising, was a symbolic turning point, incensing the UGT rank and file and profoundly embarrassing the Socialists politically.[19] The UGT's moderate leaders, particularly those of the FNTT, continued to demand discipline and loyalty to the Republican–Socialist government from their increasingly restless members, but found their position more difficult with every passing week. It is clear that this new mood, marked by a sharp increase in strike activity during 1933, was a response to the political climate and what were essentially chronic employer/landowner attitudes rather than to simple economic cirumstances which, of themselves, would have been more likely to dampen than inflame working-class activism.

The mood of the UGT grass roots had an important influence upon the trajectory of the PSOE.[20] Just as in 1930 it had been grass-roots pressure that had pushed the party in the direction of co-operation with Republicans to overthrow the monarchy, so now rank-and-file dissatisfaction with the fruits of Socialist participation in government, combined with the leadership's fear of losing support to the CNT and the emergent Communists, propelled the party towards a parliamentary and electoral break with Republicanism. The rupture came during the summer of 1933, and produced a fatal break in the left-of-centre ranks at the general election of November. The result was a victory for the parties of property: the Radicals and the new umbrella-party of the Catholic Right, the CEDA (*Confederación Española de Derechas Autónomas*: Spanish Confederation of autonomous right-wing groups).

THE POLITICS OF CLASS CONFLICT, 1933–36

Between 1930 and 1933 large sections of the Spanish working class had become unionized, formed concrete expectations, and developed a sharper political consciousness: all this against the background of a contracting economy, an inadequately funded government, and an intransigent employer/landowner class. The apparently favourable political climate of the early Republic had nevertheless proved less helpful to working-class interests than had at first seemed likely. From September 1933 until February 1936 the situation, from a working-class point of view, became immeasurably worse. In September 1933 Azaña fell from office and the period of left-of-centre government came to an end. Power now passed into the hands of the increasingly right-of-centre Radical party under its crafty leader Alejandro Lerroux; following the November 1933 general election, cabinets were Radical-dominated but dependent for survival upon the parliamentary support of the rightist CEDA. Under the leadership of José María Gil Robles, the CEDA withheld its total commitment from the Republic and, not without reason, was regarded on the left as at the very least semi-fascist.[21]

From the moment that government fell into Radical hands, but even more so after the election threw Lerroux on the CEDA's mercy, the employer/landowner counter-offensive which had been gathering momentum throughout the previous year was freed of serious restraint. It was not so much that the reforming legislation of 1931–33 was immediately repealed or reversed, as that laws and regulations protecting the interests of labour and tenants were suspended or a blind official eye turned on their infraction. The mixed juries now fell under employer/landowner control, the fixing of rural wages was effectively removed from the juries' competence and handed over to the landowners, the Agrarian Reform Law was modified, and in May 1934 the Municipal Boundaries law was actually repealed by the Cortes. At the Ministry of the Interior the obsessively anti-leftist Radical, Salazar Alonso, used his extensive powers to order wholesale sackings of Socialist mayors and councillors, thereby depriving workers and poor peasants in many districts of what little protection remained to them. By the spring of 1934 conditions throughout much of rural southern Spain were desperate, and the atmosphere of class conflict palpable.[22]

The immediate and predictable consequence of the shift in the political wind was a still sharper rise in working-class militancy. December 1933 witnessed the most extensive of the three anarchist risings to occur during the Second Republic. In the election of November the anarchists had solidly abstained. Their expectation was that this would assist the victory of the right and the installation of an unambiguously 'bourgeois' government which would expose the 'true' nature of the Republican régime and thereby persuade

Socialist workers to join in the rising which was planned to follow the election. In the event the rising, strongest in CNT bastions such as Catalonia and Aragon/Rioja, attracted no Socialist support and was crushed militarily.[23] The vigour and resilience of Aragonese anarchism were nevertheless still evident in the spring of 1934 when the city of Zaragoza was paralysed for several weeks by a general strike.[24]

Within several sections of the UGT, too, rank-and-file militancy was on the increase in the wake of an electoral defeat widely regarded on the left as fraudulent. The most significant example was the FNTT, whose moderate leadership was overturned by militants in January 1934, but a similar trend was also apparent among metalworkers, construction workers and miners.[25] The mood was paralleled by a growth in verbal revolutionism within the PSOE itself; strongest within the Socialist Youth, the vogue for revolutionary rhetoric also seized many of their elders. For some, like Largo Caballero, now the standard-bearer of the Socialist left, the experience of 1931–33 had exposed the limitations of reformism and convinced them that power-sharing with Republicans was futile; in a confused way, they began to look forward to a Socialist assumption of power. Largo Caballero's revolutionism was, and was to remain, purely verbal, probably intended to assuage the impatience of the rank and file, deflect the possibility of the CEDA's entering the government, and hasten new elections which might produce a Socialist victory; certainly it was bereft of any revolutionary plans. The Socialist left's fear of the CEDA was shared by otherwise more moderate Socialists such as Indalecio Prieto, who also began to threaten revolution in order to prevent the CEDA's being admitted to the government.[26]

The expected crisis came between June and October 1934. In June the FNTT, after attempting every legal recourse against the anti-labour campaign of the landowners, declared a landworkers' strike. Despite the revolutionary language of the union's new leaders, their goals in this instance were strictly reformist. The strike, which failed to receive the support of the rest of the UGT, was a catastrophic failure; all the resources of the state were employed to crush it, and the FNTT emerged almost fatally weakened.[27] The FNTT's overnight collapse placed the Socialist left in a difficult position when an even more serious crisis broke a few months later. When, in October 1934, the CEDA was finally given three ministries in a reshuffled cabinet, the PSOE's response was confused and half-hearted; the nationwide revolutionary general strike which had once seemed a possibility failed to materialize. Only in Asturias, where there occurred an extensive workers' revolt lasting a fortnight and requiring a massive military response to defeat it, was talk effectively translated into action.

The Asturias commune, which was accompanied by smaller-scale revolutionary activity in the Basque country, conveyed a number of important lessons. First, where the Socialists were concerned it was essentially a rank-and-file movement, strongest where the PSOE party bureaucracy was weakest and carried on independently of the cautious leadership of the UGT miners' union. Second, it took place in one of the few parts of Spain where solidarity among Socialist, anarchist and Communist workers was a reality. Third, although defeated it offered a serious warning to the Right of what the organized working class nationwide might be capable of in the event of an attempted rightist *putsch*; though the issue is hotly debated, it is more than possible that Gil Robles' failure to engineer a coup during 1935 owed something to the lesson of Asturias.[28]

The fact remained that in the immediate aftermath of Asturias the labour movement, and the political left, were subjected to even greater repression than in the months before. Perhaps 30,000 left-wingers were imprisoned, among them for a time Largo Caballero and the entire executive of the UGT; other Socialists, like Prieto, went into exile; left-wing and trade-union meeting places were closed and their press suspended; union activity became virtually impossible, union membership rapidly fell, and the conduct of many employers and landowners became even more discriminatory and vengeful than before. As a result, 1935 became the most 'peaceful' year for labour relations in the five-year history of the Republic.

As long as the Radical–CEDA partnership remained in power and retained its cohesion and confidence the Spanish labour movement seemed likely to remain on the defensive. As 1935 wore on, however, two developments occurred which together made possible the reintegration of the working class into Spanish politics. The first was the rapid disintegration of the governing coalition due to policy disagreements and a succession of financial scandals; the second was the gradual recovery of the Left and the formation of a Popular Front to fight the election which the coalition's collapse made necessary.[29] The Popular Front, chiefly embracing left-Republicans, Socialists and Communists, was the fruit of two processes: the desire of Socialist moderates and left-Republicans to re-forge the alliance of 1931–33, and a growing closeness between the self-consciously 'bolshevizing' Socialist left and an increasingly influential Communist Party bound, from 1935, to Moscow's policy of Popular Front against fascism. The Communist union organization, the CGTU, dissolved itself in December 1935 and its members joined the UGT.

Rank-and-file working-class opinion was important both in the formation of the Popular Front and in bringing it victory at the election of 16 February 1936. During late 1935 pressure from the UGT base in favour of a Popular Front was yet again decisive in pushing Largo Caballero in a direction he was not keen to go. At the polls, the electoral participation of anarchists, principally in order to return a government that would free their thousands of prisoners, helped tip the balance just as their abstention had done, in the opposite direction, in 1933.

WORKERS AND THE REPUBLIC, FEBRUARY 1936– MARCH 1939

Whilst the Left's electoral victory may not have made a civil war inevitable, it ensured that the Right, deprived of the power to transform the Republic into an authoritarian, corporatist régime, would attempt a *coup d'état* unless forestalled. Whether or not this meant civil war depended upon the Left's response. Meanwhile, between the February election and July 1936 Spain was ruled by a government of Republicans headed first by Azaña and then, after Azaña became President in May, by the ineffectual Casares Quiroga. Under Largo Caballero's influence the PSOE chose to remain outside the cabinet.

As was to be expected following the events of 1935, the return of a left-of-centre government was accompanied by a dramatic recovery of union membership and resurgence of working-class militancy. During the late spring of 1936 large-scale urban strikes were accompanied in the southern countryside by the spontaneous occupation of large estates as the government set about tackling land reform with a resolution lacking in 1931–33. The atmosphere of class conflict was more intense than ever before, as workers attempted to force often intransigent employers to take back workers sacked after Asturias. In Madrid, where the CNT had made significant strides among unskilled

211

construction and service workers, working-class assertiveness and class antagonism had replaced the atmosphere of 'popular fiesta' of 1931. In Catalonia, shielded from the worst of the Depression in 1931–33, unemployment had been rising since 1933 owing to the effects upon the domestic market of wage cuts elsewhere in Spain; now, the Catalonian economy sank into a trough marked by rising unemployment, wage-cutting and lock-outs. Throughout many parts of both urban and rural Spain, the mixed-jury system, in which labour once more held a nominal advantage, was breaking down; employers and landowners, accustomed to a free hand between September 1933 and the end of 1935, were unwilling to give ground to a workforce bent upon reversing the punitive measures of the previous two years and ensuring that the tide never turned again.[30]

Intense as the working-class militancy of spring 1936 was, it did not necessarily amount to the revolutionary situation of which right-wing propagandists untiringly spoke. Most of the demands underlying it were essentially reformist and conformed with government policies, if not always with the pace at which those policies were being carried out. The CNT, experiencing another of its periods of sudden recovery and growth, was certainly in explicitly revolutionary mood, but this was neither new nor uncontainable by those in power. The Socialist leadership was bitterly divided between moderates like Prieto who wished to reinforce Republican democracy and the 'bolshevizing' left: yet few even of the latter, and certainly not the so-called 'Spanish Lenin', Largo Caballero, saw in the present situation an imminent revolution or sought to give it leadership. Amid all the effervescence, UGT – even FNTT – leaders sought to restrain their members from going too far. The Communists, a small but rapidly growing force, were openly anti-revolutionary, in line with Stalin's current policy.[31]

Militancy, even if, as some would suggest, beginning to subside, nevertheless remained at a high level as rightist conspiracy finally bore fruit in the rising of 17–18 July 1936. It is this which helps explain the events which followed in what became the Republican zone in the Civil War. In those parts of Spain – notably Catalonia, the Valencian region, southern Aragon, eastern Andalusia and Madrid – where the military rising, backed up by right-wing civilians, failed to achieve quick success, organized labour played a vital role in two closely linked respects. First, the UGT and CNT demanded and eventually received arms with which to resist 'fascism', enabling the union militias to make a major contribution to, for example, defeating the rising in Barcelona and later resisting the assault upon Madrid. Secondly, where the authority of the Republican state temporarily disintegrated amid the confusion surrounding the rising, the unions played a major part in replacing it with what, clearly, were revolutionary alternatives: anti-fascist militia committees, village collectives, etc.[32]

In relation to the revolution within Republican Spain, a number of points need to be stressed. The first is that without the political oscillations of the previous few years, and more particularly the militant mood of spring 1936, few elements of the Spanish working class would have been psychologically or organizationally prepared to mount any such revolution. The second, notwithstanding the first, is that without the situation created by the July rising the very revolution that the latter's authors had been predicting might never have taken place. Thirdly, the revolution itself, involving the assumption of local and regional power by bodies independent of the Republican government, and the pursuit by these bodies of such unambiguously revolutionary policies as the collectivization of land and workers' control of industry, was a complex mixture of conviction and pragmatism. Obviously the organizations most involved – the CNT, the anti-Stalinist communists of the POUM (*Partido Obrero de Unificación Marxista*: Workers' Party of Marxist Unification), and leftist elements within the UGT – were all in their different ways committed to a revolutionary future; nevertheless the details of the revolution itself were often governed more by practical needs than by ideology.

It is important not to sentimentalize the Spanish revolution of 1936–37. It was based upon, or at least accompanied by, a process of bloodletting which was largely but not entirely spontaneous, and which extended well beyond the most selfish economic exploiters and most fanatical rightists of the pre-war period. Its economic accomplishments were mixed; the war made revolution possible but also, by establishing the framework within which it was pursued and the criteria by which it was bound to be judged, dictated and distorted the revolutionary process. Nor was working-class participation in revolutionary change as total, wholehearted and selfless as militants desired and foreign idealists such as Orwell liked to believe; many workers, it appears, behaved no more and no less disinterestedly or farsightedly now that they, or more properly their organizations, held power than they had done under capitalism.[33] The revolution was also, it must be acknowledged, fundamentally shaky at the foundations, in that it occurred in the context of a war that probably could not be won, either by the adoption of a 'revolutionary' strategy or by any other. And yet, for all the revolution's excesses and shortcomings, it is difficult not to share something of Orwell's excitement in the presence of an episode which brought large numbers of Spanish workers and peasants a brief taste of the power of which they were accustomed to being the victims.

The revolution enjoyed its heyday between July 1936 and May 1937. In September 1936 Largo Caballero became prime minister of a Popular Front government in the hope that he might be able to harness and discipline the revolutionary process. By late 1936, however, the chief influence upon Republican Spain's internal development, thanks to the vital role of the Soviet Union as the Republic's only significant provider of military supplies, was the previously marginal Communist Party. Paradoxically, in view of the right's use of the 'Bolshevik' bogey, the Communists were hostile to the revolution. Revolution before victory ran counter to the Popular Front policy of a Soviet Union anxious to woo the western democracies, a line relatively easy for the Spanish Communists to swallow owing to the limited support which they enjoyed among workers in the Republican zone. As the Communist grip strengthened, the power of the Republican state was reasserted and the revolution forced into retreat. The climax of this process was reached between May and August 1937. In May there erupted in Barcelona the 'civil war within a civil war' so graphically described by Orwell, resulting in the crushing of the anti-Stalinist POUM and the irreversible weakening of the CNT; shortly afterwards, at Communist instigation, the insufficiently co-operative Largo Caballero was replaced as premier by the more pliant Juan Negrín; and in summer the Communists achieved the physical and legal destruction of the last major focus of anarchist power, the CNT-dominated Council of Aragon.[34]

Whether or not Communist analyses of the war's needs were correct, there can be little dispute that some of the effects of their application between 1937 and 1939 were negative. The most notable features of the working-class experience within the Republican zone from late 1937 down to the end of the Civil War were disillusionment and plummeting morale. There would seem to have been three main reasons for this: the rolling back of the social revolution or, at best, its domestication by Communists and 'bourgeois' leaders; the intolerance of the Communists themselves towards anything resembling opposition; and the deteriorating everyday conditions within a shrinking Republican zone which was unable adequately to feed its urban population. If working-class leaders and activists looked forward to the increasingly likely Nationalist victory with understandable trepidation, for many rank-and-file workers life in the Republic was coming to seem little preferable to a future life under 'fascism'.

THE WORKING CLASS IN THE SPAIN OF FRANCO, 1936–45

While the working class within the Republican zone was actively participating in the experience of social revolution and anti-fascist struggle, workers who found themselves in insurgent territory faced a very different, essentially passive, and in thousands of cases tragic, fate. Although most of Spain's largest cities and industrial areas were initially held by the Republic, there were important exceptions. Two strongholds of working-class militancy, Seville and Zaragoza, fell unexpectedly to the rebels in the first days of the rising, to be quickly followed by other important cities such as Córdoba, Granada and La Coruña. Many lesser urban centres and several provincial capitals, especially in northern Spain, also came under rebel control from the outset. During the next year, as the rebels advanced, other industrial regions fell into their hands, notably the Basque country and Asturias. From early in the Civil War rebel-held territory also embraced regions where there existed a large rural working class: western Andalusia, Extremadura and Salamanca particularly; indeed, by spring 1937, for all the revolutionary activity in Republican Spain, a majority of pre-war agricultural labourers were to be found in the enemy zone.

The most immediate and painful experience for workers in Nationalist Spain was the repression which followed in the wake of rebel conquests.[35] Since well before the rising, local right-wingers had been compiling lists of left-wing leaders, union militants, and even mere union members, any or all of whom were now liable to suffer execution at the hands of Civil Guard or rightist militia. During the first nine months of the war, political executions were often summary; thereafter, as Franco's grip tightened, the process became 'regularized' and courts martial became the usual route to the firing squad or the *garote vil*. Such repression was harshest in those southern provinces which had been the scene of the bitterest

215

The working class and politics

class conflict before the war; the massacre in the Badajoz bullring, in which several hundred leftists perished, is the most notorious but far from the only example. Even in less front-line regions, however, no chances were taken, as the calculated elimination of between 1,000 and 3,000 working-class activists in Navarre indicates.[36] As well as expressing the vengefulness and class hatred of landowners, employers, and the right-wing zealots who fought their battles, wartime repression was deliberately designed by the Nationalist authorities to smash working-class organizations and destroy their former members' will to resist: goals which were amply fulfilled. Although a relatively small number of former militants took to mountainous districts of Nationalist Spain to wage a guerrilla struggle which, on and off, persisted until the end of the 1940s,[37] most of those who survived the actual repression were obliged either to fight in the nationalist army or continue to labour on terms imposed by their victorious masters.

Before the war, right-wing spokesmen, publicly at least, had been careful to stress that their quarrel was with the leaders and militants of the Left and not with ordinary workers. In conformity with this argument, they had embraced a variety of paternalistic and corporativist ideas, some of Catholic and some of fascist provenance, concerning how in a future authoritarian régime the working class should be organized and, in theory at least, its interests protected. All the rightist parties – the CEDA, the fascist *Falange* and the Carlist and Alfonsine monarchist parties – had sponsored or created workers' organizations, but without conspicuous success.[38] Now, even as working-class militants were being eliminated, attempts were under way to replace their organizations with safe alternatives, and to persuade 'ordinary' workers that the Right had something to offer them in place of the UGT and CNT, declared illegal within the insurgent zone in September 1936. In Seville, the brutal (former Republican) military commander, General Queipo de Llano, went out of his way to woo with paternalist measures a working class whose leaders had mostly been executed;[39] the ultra-Catholic Carlists inaugurated an ambitious scheme, the *Obra Nacional Corporativa* (National Corporative Enterprise), which on paper at least absorbed much of the pre-war Catholic union structure and sought to create the infrastructure of a Catholic corporate state;[40] and the *Falange* opened its ranks to any workers willing to join.[41] Many did, out of a combination of self-preservation and awareness that of all the right-wing parties the *Falange* was the most ostentatiously plebeian.

216

During 1937–38 the outlines of what was to be the Franco dictatorship became clear. In April 1937 Franco put an end to open political divisions within Nationalist Spain when he created a single party, the FET y de las JONS (*Falange Española Tradicionalista y de las Juntas de Ofensiva Nacional-Sindicalismo*). The principal components of this awkward creation were the ultra-Catholic Carlists and the fascist *Falange*. Although the FET, later to be more generally known as the *Movimiento*, was never to play within Franco's Spain the active role of the Nazi party in Germany, or even the Italian Fascist party, it nevertheless did provide carefully selected channels for Falangist activism. The most important of these was the organization of labour. From the start of 1938 there slowly took shape a fascist-style syndical structure which, with only minor modifications, was to endure throughout the life of the Franco régime. The ideological basis of worker organization was the *Fuero del Trabajo* of March 1938, a document intended to play a similar role to the Italian Fascist Labour Charter and representing (after much manoeuvring and redrafting) a compromise between fascist and social-Catholic positions. Affirming a middle way between liberal capitalism and 'Marxist materialism', the *Fuero* defended private property and enterprise while promising to cushion the worker with a superficially comprehensive array of provisions on, for example, a minimum wage, working hours and conditions, holidays, family assistance and social insurance, and labour courts to arbitrate in disputes. In the new 'National-Syndicalist' order, the principal agencies of the state's economic policy would be 'vertical syndicates' of employers, technicians and workers; within each syndicate the three elements would co-operate on an equal basis, thereby bringing class conflict to an end. The responsibility for operating 'national syndicalism' lay with a new ministry, also founded early in 1938, the Ministry of Syndical Action and Organization. From the outset the ministry, and the entire syndical apparatus, became the Falangist preserve it was always to remain; however, it was not until after the end of the Civil War that significant strides began to be made in actually constructing a nationwide syndical organization.[42]

After several months of near stalemate, the end of the Civil War came swiftly between midsummer 1938 and 1 April 1939. The Nationalist victory brought a measure of relief to the undernourished and war-weary working population of those central and eastern regions of Republican Spain which had held out longest, but at the same time confronted working-class activists with similar punitive measures to those earlier meted out to comrades in other areas. As the Nationalist armies advanced, some chose suicide rather than fall into Falangist hands; tens of thousands more fled the country, the majority – especially of working-class refugees, who could afford to go no further – to France. There, a few years later, many Spaniards were able to resume the anti-fascist struggle by joining – and playing a major role in – the French Resistance.[43] Those who stayed behind faced a continuation of wartime repression. Many thousands of left-wing militants were executed in the immediate aftermath of the war, while thousands more died in jail or remained incarcerated for many years. Conservative estimates put the total number of fatal victims, wartime and post-war, of Nationalist repression at over 70,000[44]; even if other claims, of over 200,000, are probably inflated, a true figure of over 100,000 would not be surprising; we shall probably never know the truth.

Most of those executed or imprisoned were, of course, activists, though in the light of the events of the war and the revolution 'activism' had become a very loose concept. Nevertheless even right-wing dictatorships need workers and must accordingly draw the line at wholesale class extermination. With post-war Spain in a state of economic dislocation, the new régime saw it as essential that labour be organized and disciplined for the task of recovery. In the immediate aftermath of the war, forced labour was employed on a major scale and a new impetus given to the construction of national-syndicalism. Differences nevertheless existed within the régime about how much autonomy and initiative the syndical system should possess. Radical Falangists in particular favoured the greatest possible degree of autonomy. Between 1939 and July 1941, the heyday of radical Falangism, the leadership of the syndical system was in the hands of one of its leading figures, the ex-Socialist Salvador Merino. Like fascist labour leaders elsewhere, Merino attempted to build up the syndical organization as a vigorous, autonomous element within the régime. The attempt, which provoked the disapproval of régime conservatives, proved unsuccessful and in July 1941 Merino was removed.[45] The syndical system which took shape during the years of Spain's neutrality consequently proved to be hierarchical and bureaucratic, completely subordinated to the state and limited in its role and influence by the separate ministry of Labour. Within the syndicates the original commitment to 'verticality' quickly gave way to the separate organization of workers and employers, with the latter effectively independent and dominant and the workers

Spain

all but impotent: a situation very similar to that created in Fascist
Italy by the late 1920s. Only at the very lowest level of the system
did a limited degree of worker representation operate – though in
the long run, i.e. from the late 1950s onward, this was to prove
important in the emergence of an 'alternative' trade unionism.[46]
For the time being, however, Spanish workers displayed little
interest in a syndical system constructed on the ashes of free trade
unionism.[47] Nor was the Spanish working class in any position, as
the Second World War drew to a close, to offer significant resistance
to the Franco régime. Demoralized by defeat, shamed by mutual
antagonisms, bereft of their leaders, cowed by repression, and
weakened by low living standards, its members could do little more
than hope that, with the end of the war, the victorious Allies would
overturn Franco. They were, of course, sadly disappointed.

NOTES AND REFERENCES

1. George Orwell, *Homage to Catalonia* (Harmondsworth, 1966 edn) p. 8.
2. Santos Juliá, 'Economic crisis, social conflict and the Popular Front:
   Madrid 1931–6', in Paul Preston (ed.) *Revolution and War in Spain
   1931–1939* (London, 1984) p. 140.
3. On Madrid, see ibid., pp. 139–40 and Santos Juliá, *Madrid 1931–1934.
   De la fiesta popular a la lucha de clases* (Madrid, 1984) pp. 41–92; on
   Barcelona, see Nicholas Rider, 'Urbanization, anarcho-syndicalism and
   social conflict in Barcelona, 1900–1932' (University of Lancaster Ph.D.
   thesis, 1988).
4. Manuel Tuñón de Lara, *La II República* (2 vols., Madrid 1976),
   I, pp. 1–9.
5. Edward Malefakis, *Agrarian Reform and Peasant Revolution in Spain* (New
   Haven and London, 1970), pp. 35–92 (on latifundism), pp. 93–132 (on
   the rural working class). On latifundism see also Pascual Carrión, *Los
   latifundios en España* (Madrid, 1932).
6. The classic partisan history of the UGT is Amaro del Rosal, *Historia de
   la U.G.T. de Espana 1901–1939* (2 vols., Barcelona, 1977); the CNT
   lacks an equivalent, but see Murray Bookchin, *The Spanish Anarchists.
   The Heroic Years, 1868–1936* (New York, Hagerstown, San Francisco
   and London, 1977). On the *sindicatos libres*, see Colin M. Winston,
   Workers and the Right in Spain, 1900–1936 (Princeton, 1985), pp. 108–70
   and 'The Proletarian Carlist Road to Fascism: Sindicalismo Libre',
   Journal of Contemporary History, 17, 4, October 1982, pp. 557–86.
7. Shlomo Ben-Ami, *Fascism from Above. The Dictatorship of Primo de
   Rivera in Spain* (Oxford, 1983), pp. 282–312.
8. Joseph Harrison, *An Economic History of Modern Spain* (Manchester,
   1978), pp. 125–48.
9. Santos Juliá, *Madrid, 1931–1934*, pp. 93–144.

The working class and politics

10. Rosal, op. cit., I, pp. 294–315; Paul Preston, *The Coming of the Spanish Civil War* (London, 1978), pp. 16–25.
11. G. Mario de Coca, *Anti-Caballero. Una crítica marxista de la bolchevización del partido socialista obrero español* (Madrid, 1975 edn), pp. 38–9; on leftist scepticism towards the Republic, see Javier Bueno, *El estado socialista: nueva interpretación del comunismo* (Madrid, 1931) and Gabriel Morón, *La Ruta del socialismo en España* (Madrid, 1932).
12. On Largo Caballero's ideological and tactical gyrations, see Santos Juliá, 'Socialismo y revolución en el pensamiento y la acción política de Francisco Largo Caballero', introduction to Francisco Largo Caballero, *Notas históricas de la Guerra en España (1917–1940)*, ix–lxvi; the best discussion in English is to be found in Preston, *The Coming of the Spanish Civil War, passim*.
13. Malefakis, op. cit., pp. 162–85; Santos Juliá, 'Objetivos políticos de la legislación laboral' and Julio Aróstegui, 'Largo Caballero, ministro de Trabajo', both in J. L. Garcia Delgado (ed.), *La II República española. El primer bienio* (Madrid, 1987), pp. 27–48 and 59–74 respectively.
14. Paul Preston, 'The agrarian war in the south', in Preston (ed.), *Revolution and War in Spain 1931–1939*, pp. 165–6; Malefakis, op. cit., pp 290–4.
15. Manuel Tuñón de Lara, *El movimiento obrero en la historia de España* (2 vols., Madrid, 1985 edn), II, pp. 321–5.
16. Mércedes Cabrera, *La patronal ante la II República* (Madrid, 1983), pp. 152–68, 196–217; Preston, op. cit., pp. 167–9.
17. Adrian Shubert, 'The epic failure: the Asturian revolution of October 1934', in Preston (ed.), *Revolution and War in Spain 1931–1939*, pp. 118–20.
18. The best and fullest discussion of the Agrarian Reform in English remains Malefakis, *Agrarian Reform and Peasant Revolution in Spain*, especially pp. 205–57; see also Pascual Carrión, *La reforma agraria de la 2a República y la situación actual de la agricultura española* (Barcelona, 1973); Manuel Tuñón de Lara, *Tres claves de la Segunda República* (Madrid, 1985), pp. 21–215; and, more briefly, Jacques Maurice, *La reforma agraria en España en el siglo XX (1900–1936)* (Madrid, 1975), pp. 2–67.
19. The bibliography on Casas Viejas is extensive: see Jerome R. Mintz, *The Anarchists of Casas Viejas* (Chicago, 1982).
20. On the changing mood within the UGT and PSOE between 1931 and 1933, see especially Santos Juliá, 'República, revolución y luchas internas', in the collective volume produced by the Fundación Pablo Iglesias, *El socialismo en España. Desde la fundación del PSOE hasta 1975* (Madrid, 1986), pp. 231–45; also Preston, *The Coming of the Spanish Civil War*, pp. 51–91.
21. The fascism or non-fascism of the CEDA is the subject of intense debate: see R. A. H. Robinson, *The Origins of Franco's Spain. The Right, the Republic and Revolution 1931–1936, passim*, especially pp. 134–5; Paul Preston, 'Spain', in Stuart Woolf (ed.), *Fascism in Europe* (London, 1981), pp. 329–52; Martin Blinkhorn, 'Conservatives, Traditionalists and Fascists in pre-Civil War Spain', in Martin Blinkhorn (ed.), *Fascists and Conservatives* (forthcoming).

22. Preston, *The Coming of the Spanish Civil War*, pp. 92–113; Rafael Salazar Alonso, *Bajo el signo de la revolución* (Madrid, 1935), *passim*.
23. Enrique Pradas Martínez *et al.*, *8 de diciembre de 1933. Insurrección anarquista en La Rioja*; Graham Kelsey, 'Anarchism in Aragon during the Second Republic: the emergence of a mass movement', in Martin Blinkhorn (ed.), *Spain in Conflict 1931–1939. Democracy and its Enemies* (London, 1986), pp. 70–1.
24. Kelsey, op. cit., p. 72.
25. Preston, *The Coming of the Spanish Civil War*, p. 94.
26. Juliá, 'Socialismo y revolución en el pensamiento y la acción política de Francisco Largo Caballero' and 'República, revolución y luchas internas' (see above, notes 12 and 20).
27. Fernando Pascual Cevallos, *Luchas agrarias en Sevilla durante la segunda república* (Seville, 1983), pp. 91–3; José Manuel Macarro Vera, *La utopia revolucionaria. Sevilla en la Segunda República* (Seville, 1985), pp. 388–93; Manuel Pérez Yruela, *La conflictividad campesina en la provincia de Córdoba 1931–1936* (Madrid, 1979), pp. 183–95; Luis Garrido González, *Colectividades agrarias en Andalucía: Jaén (1931–1939)* (Madrid, 1979), pp. 17–20; Malefakis, op. cit., pp. 335–40.
28. An up-to-date compendium of research and analysis on Asturias is Gabriel Jackson *et al.*, *Octubre 1934. Cincuenta años para la reflexión* (Madrid, 1985); for an English-language account, see Shubert, 'The epic failure: the Asturian revolution of October 1934', in Preston (ed.), *Revolution and War in Spain*, pp. 113–36.
29. Santos Juliá, *Orígenes del Frente Popular en España (1934–1936)* (Madrid, 1979) and 'The origins and nature of the Spanish Popular Front', in Martin Alexander and Helen Graham (eds.), *The French and Spanish Popular Fronts: Comparative Perspectives* (Cambridge, 1988); see also the chapters by the editors and by Adrian Shubert in Helen Graham and Paul Preston (eds.), *The Popular Front in Europe* (London, 1987).
30. Juliá, 'Economic crisis, social conflict and the Popular Front: Madrid 1931–6', in Preston (ed.), *Revolution and War in Spain 1931–1939*, pp. 151–5; Alberto Balcells, *Crisis económica y agitación social en Cataluña (1930–1936)* (Barcelona, 1971), pp. 228–37, 243–91; Malefakis, op. cit., pp. 364–87; Preston, *The Coming of the Spanish Civil War*, pp. 177–201.
31. On the 'bolshevization' of the Socialist left, see Santos Juliá, *La izquierda del PSOE (1935–1936)* (Madrid, 1977) and Andrés de Blas Guerrero, *El socialismo radical en la II República* (Madrid, 1978). The Communists under the Republic are dealt with in Rafael Cruz, *El Partido Comunista de España en la II República* (Madrid, 1987); see 217ff. on the Popular Front policy.
32. The historiography of the Spanish revolution is vast and rapidly expanding. The contemporary atmosphere is caught by Orwell, op. cit. and by Franz Borkenau, *The Spanish Cockpit* (London, 1937). Ronald Fraser, *Blood of Spain. The Experience of Civil War 1936–1939* (London, 1979) provides vivid oral recollections; see also his 'The popular experience of war and revolution' in Preston (ed.), *Revolution and War in Spain*. For a recent scholarly analysis of the rural collectives, see Julián Casanova, *Anarquismo y revolución en*

la sociedad rural aragonesa 1936–1938 (Madrid, 1985) and 'Anarchism and revolution in the Spanish Civil War: the case of Aragon', *European History Quarterly*, 17, 4, October 1987.

33. Michael Seidman, 'Towards a history of workers' resistance to work: Paris and Barcelona during the French Popular Front and the Spanish Revolution, 1936–1938', *Journal of Contemporary History*, April 1988, pp. 191–220.

34. Burnett Bolloten, *The Spanish Revolution. The Left and the Struggle for power during the Civil War* (Chapel Hill, 1979) is the authoritative analysis of the Communist role between July 1936 and May 1937, and Orwell's a classic first-hand account; for a Communist recollection see Santiago Carrillo, *Dialogue on Spain* (London, 1976), pp. 46–68. On the destruction of the Council of Aragon see Casanova, *Anarquismo y revolución*, pp. 264–97.

35. Stanley G. Payne, *The Franco Regime 1936–1975* (Madison, 1987), pp. 209–28 provides a thorough and balanced analysis of the Nationalist repression. See also Alberto Reig Tapia, *Ideología e historia: sobre la represión franquista y la guerra civil* (Madrid, 1984).

36. Repression in Navarre is discussed in Ramón Salas Larrazábal, *Los fusilados en Navarra en la guerra de 1936* (Madrid, 1983); Colectivo Afán, !NO, General! Fueron más de tres mil los asesinados (Pamplona, 1983); and Colectivo Afán, *Navarra 1936. "De la esperanza al terror"* (2 vols., Pamplona, 1986).

37. Hartmut Heine, *La oposición política al franquismo de 1939 a 1952* (Barcelona, 1983).

38. José R. Montero, *La CEDA. El Catolicismo social y político en la II República* (2 vols., Madrid, 1977), I, pp. 747–80; Martin Blinkhorn, *Carlism and Crisis in Spain 1931–1939* (Cambridge, 1975), pp. 116–17, 171–5; Javier Jiménez Campo, *El fascismo en la crisis de la II República* (Madrid, 1979), pp. 241–55, 288–96.

39. J. de Ramón-Laca, *Bajo la férula de Queipo. Como fue gobernada Andalucía* (Seville, 1939), p. 32 and *passim*; see also Antonio Bahamonde y Sánchez de Castro, *Un año con Queipo* (Barcelona, 1938).

40. Blinkhorn, op. cit., pp. 274–5.

41. Ricardo Chueca, *El Fascismo en los comienzos del régimen de Franco. Un estudio sobre FET–JONS* (Madrid, 1983), pp. 138–46; Stanley Payne, *Falange. A History of Spanish Fascism* (London, 1962), pp. 128–9.

42. Sheelagh Ellwood, *Prietas las Filas. Historia de Falange Española. 1933–1983* (Barcelona, 1984), pp. 117–23; Chueca, op. cit., pp. 341–99.

43. Heine, op. cit.; Alberto E. Fernández, *La España de los maquis* (Mexico D.F., 1973) and *Emigración republicana española 1939–1945* (Madrid, 1972); David Wingeate Pike, !*Vae Victis! Los republicanos españoles refugiados en Francia 1939–44* (Paris, 1969).

44. Payne, *The Franco Regime*, p. 217.

45. Ellwood, op. cit., pp. 123–5.

46. Ibid., pp. 125–54.

47. Sheelagh Ellwood, 'The Working Class under the Franco Régime' in Paul Preston (ed.), *Spain in Crisis. The Evolution and Decline of the Franco Régime* (London, 1976), p. 161.

CHAPTER TEN

The Soviet Union

Hiroaki Kuromiya

INTRODUCTION

The Soviet working class experienced the turbulent decade and a half from 1929 to 1945 in a political environment significantly different from that in other European countries. The country was governed by the Communist Party in the name of the proletariat, the first 'proletarian dictatorship' in world history. Historians disagree sharply over whether these years, so intimately associated with Stalin's dictatorship, indeed fulfilled the October Revolution or on the contrary betrayed it.[1] This disagreement notwithstanding, it is clear that, in contrast with Western countries enduring the agonies of mass unemployment, the Soviet Union eliminated mass urban unemployment through vast economic transformations: the size of the working class grew almost continuously, trebling from 6.8 m. in 1928 to 20 m. in 1940.[2] This growth was hailed as a great achievement in the country of proletarian dictatorship, which in 1928 was still an overwhelmingly agrarian society, with over 80 per cent of the population of 150 m. engaged in the agricultural sector. Not only did Stalin's rapid industrialization swell the ranks of workers, but it also provided them with an unprecedented degree of upward mobility.[3] Like its other European counterparts during the Depression, however, the Soviet working class was economically severely squeezed by the state: its living standards almost halved between 1928 and 1932, and were to recover to the level of 1928 only during the 1950s.[4] Administrative controls over labour were continuously tightened.[5] One might well argue that the Soviet working class had already been placed under a quasi-war régime before the war began. Whatever the case, the Soviet working class that fought the actual war in 1941–45 was one that had at once enjoyed the security of full employment and endured enormous material hardships.

In exploring factors that shaped the political behaviour of the Soviet working class, historians encounter special problems. First, one-party dictatorship had changed the concept of politics itself. Parliamentary politics, multi-candidate elections, public-opinion polls, and other forms of Western democracy had virtually disappeared since 1917. The trade unions, deprived of political autonomy, came under the firm control of the party, and by the mid-1930s been transformed into social-service organs.[6] These changes have made the study of Soviet working-class politics notoriously difficult. More generally, Stalinist politics appeared to many Western observers as 'a puzzle': 'When we discuss democracy the central question is the people, because they make the government. But in a dictatorship the government makes the people. The dictator who is deified until he seems to be more like a god than a man, tries to recreate the people in his own image'.[7] The study of the Soviet people has actually tended to examine state control, indoctrination, and mobilization rather than the people themselves.

Secondly, the vast economic transformations made the society so mobile that the whole question of class affiliation and identity became extremely tricky. The ranks of workers were flooded with millions of former 'petit-bourgeois' elements such as peasants and artisans as well as smaller numbers of former 'exploiters' such as *kulaks* (rich peasants) and private traders who had managed to escape the worse fate of execution, internment, or deportation; and millions of workers moved into different social positions from lower white-collar jobs to administrative positions of responsibility.

Yet it is also these complicating factors that had shaped the political behaviour of Soviet workers: one-party dictatorship gave them no alternative but to endure the acute economic hardships; and the vast social transformations created full employment, which helped the population endure the hardships.

THE DEPRESSION AND INDUSTRIALIZATION

The economic crisis, which in the autumn of 1929 assaulted the Western capitalist world, had little direct impact on the Soviet working class. The Depression was hailed with great fanfare in the Soviet Union 'as a vindication of the Marxist diagnosis of the moral sickness of capitalism and a harbinger of the promised revolt of the proletariat'.[8] The First Five-Year Plan (1928/29–1932/33), launching a rapid industrialization programme, painted a rosy picture of a new Soviet society, in sharp contrast to the depressed West. The setting up of central economic planning was supported by the belief that the national economy and the working class should not be left at the mercy of market forces.

The plan, succeeded by the Second and Third Five-Year Plans, *did* bring about great industrial development in the Soviet Union. Western estimates of Soviet gross industrial production in 1937 vary from 249 per cent to 370 per cent of 1928, or an annual average increase of 10 to 16 per cent.[9] This increase, spectacular by any standard, continued, albeit at a somewhat abated rate, until it was interrupted by the Second World War.[10]

One feature of Soviet central economic planning undoubtedly enhanced its prestige in the eyes of Western as well as Soviet workers: it fundamentally transformed the labour market and eliminated mass unemployment, thereby making at long last the country of proletarian dictatorship a land of full employment. When the First Five-Year Plan was launched, the number of unemployed was very high, approximately 1.5 m., or some 13 to 14 per cent of the employed population in the entire national economy.[11] By 1931, however, industrial expansion had rapidly absorbed unemployment: in the autumn of 1930 unemployment was declared to have disappeared, and unemployment benefits terminated.[12] The Soviet government presented this transformation (which had not been envisaged by the First Five-Year Plan)[13] as a resounding political victory over the West in the grip of mass unemployment. The Soviet press of the 1930s was filled with articles and photographs sharply contrasting the misery of unemployed Western workers with the benefits of full employment in the Soviet Union. In early 1934 Stalin triumphantly declared: 'Unemployment, the scourge of the working class, has disappeared. In the bourgeois countries millions of unemployed suffer want and privation owing to lack of work, whereas in our country there are no longer any workers who have no work and no earnings'.[14]

The elimination of unemployment opened the door of opportunity to millions of urban unemployed and particularly village youth who saw 'no hope' in the countryside.[15] For instance, Ivan Gudov, a future worker hero (Stakhanovite), left his native village in the 1920s to 'find a new life' but owing to mass unemployment, was not able to find a secure industrial job. Work as a *Komsomol* teacher at an orphan colony did not satisfy him, because he felt as if 'all the grandiose events [of industrialization] had passed him by'. In 1934 he left to find an industrial job. 'He was now much more confident in himself than when he had left the countryside, because unemployment had long disappeared and so, he thought, he would not starve in any event'.[16]

Moreover, the transformation of the labour market from a buyers' to a sellers' market greatly increased workers' bargaining power. The government responded in 1930 by attempting to organize planned distribution of labour on a nation-wide scale. Clearly, the workers gained the upper hand; and the failure of this experiment in planning left the Soviet labour market largely 'free' – with the important difference from a capitalist free-labour market that the price of labour, i.e. wages, was not freely established but was regulated by the central authorities.[17] In the 1930s, the whole society was thus 'on the move'; 'a great migration of people went on'; indeed, they were so mobile that a 'fierce battle' had to be waged against them.[18]

Like workers in other European countries during the war, Soviet workers in the 1930s were able to take full advantage of their enhanced market strength, changing jobs almost as they pleased. This chaotic state of affairs invited progressively harsher labour legislation and administrative controls. Industrial labour turnover, measured by the rate of workers leaving jobs to the annual average number of employed workers, was thus reduced from the high of 152.4 per cent in 1930 to 86.1 per cent in 1935.[19] Yet these reduced rates do not seem to have satisfied the political leadership. As the threat of war became increasingly real, the government introduced work books in 1938 in an attempt further to restrict workers' freedom of movement, and in 1940 ended free labour relations by prohibiting workers and employees from quitting jobs of their own accord.[20] Simultaneously, the political leadership came to rely heavily on convict labour to make up the workforce on remote and inhospitable construction sites and in other unpopular areas and industries such as timber-cutting.[21]

If Soviet workers had escaped the direct impact of the Depression, they had to suffer from its indirect effect – a decline in their standard of living. The Depression turned the terms of foreign trade against the Soviet Union. To expand import capacity, grain and other raw materials were exported despite acute domestic shortages. Soviet export prices, however, dropped much more rapidly than import prices in the depressed world market. Reduced foreign-currency reserves were spent largely on the import of ferrous metals, tractors, and other capital goods at the expense of consumer goods.[22] The Depression thus adversely affected the consumption of Soviet workers.

It would be misleading, however, to attribute the main cause of the decline in the standard of living to the Depression. The Depression only aggravated a pre-existing problem. The massive diversion of resources to investment inevitably squeezed national consumption. Workers' real wages fell rapidly between 1928 and 1933, when the pace of this diversion was slowed down. The modest rise of the mid-1930s, however, was not maintained in the late 1930s, when the huge increase in defence expenditure again depressed national consumption.[23] The per-capita norm of urban living space also declined as a result of the low investment priority accorded to housing construction and of the rapid migration into the cities.[24] A whole range of services deteriorated precipitously or disappeared altogether as private businesses were forced to shut down. High labour turnover in the 1930s thus reflected not only the transformation of the labour market but also unbearably harsh living and working conditions, which forced workers to search for a better life elsewhere.

Some factors cushioned the impact of the decline in real wages. Large numbers of women were forced to seek employment in order to supplement family income[25]: the proportion of female labour in large-scale industry thus increased from 28.8 per cent in 1929 to 40.1 per cent in 1936.[26] Consequently, the number of dependants per wage earner in a worker family declined from 2.05 in 1930 to 1.59 in 1935 and at least the nominal household income per head increased accordingly.[27] Other changes, particularly large increases in 'socialized wages', also counteracted the depreciation of real wages. ('Socialized wages' referred to a variety of benefits such as social insurance, health care, education, housing, and other welfare services that were provided free or heavily subsidized by the government).[28] The Soviet government made every effort to depict such 'socialized wages' as something that the capitalist countries would not offer to workers.

Nevertheless, these years are remembered in the Soviet Union as a time of hunger and privation. Workers responded in a variety of ways. Some spoke of the difficulties 'with pain in their hearts', others 'with hatred and malicious pleasure': 'They demand a lot from us, but as to providing us they provide nothing . . . See how the bosses live, but how about us?'[29] Strikes did take place here and there,[30] but organized action had become almost impossible in the 1930s as the trade unions came under the firm grip of the party. Rather, workers resorted to safer methods of protest and resistance. Changing places of work was one such method, defiance of managerial authority another. The rapid industrial expansion increased the bargaining power of workers, who no longer feared 'the scourge of unemployment'. This shift in the balance of power between labour and management complicated shop-floor politics. On the one hand, it gave rise to managerial indulgence: for fear of losing workers, managers often overlooked their lack of discipline in work, made considerable concessions in determining their output quota, and thus inflated their wages.[31] On the other hand, the shift led to managerial despotism: managers, at other times, found themselves powerless and resorted to massive repression. These contradictory kinds of treatment were often found amalgamated in one and the same manager.[32] Workers often had good reason for welcoming police intervention.[33]

STALINISM

Unlike the image presented by the so-called totalitarian model of Soviet politics, the control of the Stalinist régime over the population was actually far from total. Yet the régime managed to mobilize vast human and material resources for the rapid industrialization drive. What is it that politically sustained the régime in this relentless drive?

One important factor was the ideology of class war, part and parcel of Marxism and Leninism, which pitted workers and Communists against the perceived class enemies: foreign capitalists, former Russian factory owners who were alleged to conspire for their comeback from abroad, survivors of the former exploiting classes such as *kulaks* and private entrepreneurs and traders, and those deemed as inheritors of bourgeois ideology and values such as 'bourgeois' (i.e. old) experts. The savage attack on these and other formerly privileged elements proved to be a powerful mobilizing force, particularly during the First Five-Year Plan.[34] The attack was also used skilfully to remind workers that it was they who were the masters of a new society.[35]

The 1930s are thus chronicled in the memory of the nation as years not only of hunger and privation but also of enthusiasm, heroism, and romantic self-sacrifice. Young workers were the embodiment of the spirit of the time. 'There were all sorts of events – happy events, tragic events, lively events, infinitely difficult events', according to a contemporary observer, but 'we least of all thought about ease, comfort, and profit. What we were doing seemed to us as the most fascinating, the most interesting thing on earth'.[36]

The establishment of full employment doubtless helped workers to endure the harsh living and working conditions. Despite the hardships in the town, industrial labour appeared to many to be far more attractive than agricultural labour: in the 1930s, according to Soviet statistics, collective farmers' money wages amounted to a mere one-sixth to one-seventh of those of industrial workers.[37] Hence, fearless of unemployment and starvation, millions of former peasants permanently settled in the cities and acquired the celebrated status of worker.

If even the least skilled and therefore the lowest-paid new arrivals from the countryside found industrial labour to be something of a boon, skilled workers and the norm-busting labour heroes (like shock workers and Stakhanovites) were lavishly rewarded by the application of widely differentiated wage scales (which, Leon Trotsky and others contended, betrayed the revolution). Some of these came to feel that their enhanced material well-being had made them 'bourgeois'.[38]

Moreover, as recent works on social mobility under Stalin have shown, workers (more precisely, former workers) made up considerable portions of the new ruling élite. In 1930–33 alone, a total of 1.5 m. workers moved up into white-collar employment: 'Most of these jobs were clerical or low-level administrative, but a comparatively large number were in the élite category then called "leading cadres and specialists".' Many of these, trained as engineers in an attempt to overcome the dichotomy between 'Red' and 'expert', indeed provided the core of the new generation of administrative and political leaders.[39]

All this suggests that Stalin's rule had created a political base for its survival. Among the workers on the shop floor, there also existed resistance and protest, which, however, were not allowed to articulate themselves into a political force. Under one-party dictatorship, supported by a pervasive secret police, the workers had no political alternative but to conform.

THE THREAT OF WAR

The above generalization is perhaps valid, with necessary corrections, for the political behaviour of Soviet workers in relation to world affairs. If one-party dictatorship allowed the Soviet Union to dispense with the complication of domestic politics that accompanied the Depression in the Western countries, the Soviet Union was not so fortunate in international politics. The rise of openly anti-Versailles and anti-Soviet régimes dramatically increased the threat of war both from the west and from the east. The outbreak of civil war in Spain and the involvement therein of Italy, Germany, the Soviet Union, and other powers made the threat all the more real.

Stalin and the Comintern, whose policy zigzagged from hostility to 'Social Fascism' to united (later popular) fronts, are often held responsible for having irreparably damaged the international anti-fascist movement. Yet the confusion, dismay, and shock that the Western working class had to suffer from these abrupt changes of course affected the Soviet working class to a much smaller degree, because there were no domestic forces competing with the ruling party for political alternatives. The population as a whole had been politically socialized to a remarkable degree.

The 1930s were a period not only of hunger and heroism but also of constant war threat. It was in terms of this threat that Stalin sought to justify the breakneck speed of industrialization. In February 1931 he declared:

> One feature of the history of old Russia was the continual beatings she suffered because of her backwardness. She was beaten by the Mongol khans. She was beaten by the Turkish beys. She was beaten by the Swedish feudal lords. She was beaten by the Polish and Lithuanian gentry. She was beaten by the British and French capitalists. She was beaten by the Japanese barons. All beat her because of her backwardness, because of her military backwardness, cultural backwardness, political backwardness, industrial backwardness, agricultural backwardness. . . . Do you want our socialist fatherland to be beaten and to lose its independence? If you don't want this, you must put an end to its backwardness in the shortest possible time and develop a genuine Bolshevik tempo in building up its socialist economy. There is no other way. . . . We are fifty to one hundred years behind the advanced capitalist countries. We must cover this distance in ten years. Either we do this, or they'll crush us.[40]

Ten years later, in 1941, the Soviet Union was almost crushed by the Nazi attack. This fact, however, should not obscure the vast effort the Soviet Union had made to prepare for war in the 1930s.

As Stalin's speech suggests, during the 1930s the rhetoric of war threat came to lose its previous emphasis on the class war of international capitalists against the country of proletarian dictatorship. Rather, future war came to be presented as a war of foreign fascists against 'Mother Russia'.[41] This change in rhetoric and the Comintern's strategic shifts took place in tandem with a reappraisal of Soviet domestic politics: the shift in emphasis from proletarian dictatorship to 'socialist' democracy, a democracy for all people.[42] Accordingly, the political leadership came to imply that the main enemy was not so much the class enemy as the 'enemy of the people'. These shifts were accompanied by increasingly explicit appeals to Russian patriotism.

It was against the background of an hysterical outburst of political xenophobia that the so-called Great Purges took place in 1936–38: large numbers of people, estimated in millions, were killed or interned in labour camps by the political police. This extraordinarily complex phenomenon has yet to be comprehensively analysed.[43] As far as the most publicized event, the execution of former oppositionists and leading political and military leaders, was concerned, the main accusation was that they were foreign spies, agents of Nazi Germany and Fascist Japan. In the West this accusation is almost universally dismissed as a pure fabrication. What seems to be overlooked in the West, however, is that the indictments had an enormous potential for mass mobilization. In fact, there is considerable evidence that many workers, particularly Stakhanovite labour heroes, sincerely believed in the criminal charges.[44] Aleksei Stakhanov, for example, wrote in April 1937 about the 'despicable traitors of the motherland and the betrayers of the working class'. 'All these fascist spies and saboteurs, Pyatakovs, Rataichaks, Loginovs and other dregs got what they deserved'.[45] Stakhanovites and the like were firmly integrated into the régime.

Certainly, not all workers believed such accusations: those whose families were affected by the state terror maintain that their belief in justice had been broken. Even so, they state that their belief in the régime itself had not been shattered by the terror.[46]

Soviet workers' reaction to the Nazi–Soviet pact of August 1939, which took the whole world by surprise, was characteristic. According to John Scott, an American worker who left the United States as a consequence of the Depression and worked in the Soviet

Union in the 1930s, his Soviet colleague, Syemichkin, responded to a question about the pact by shrugging his shoulders and saying that 'Stalin did it'. Russians believed, maintains Scott, that Stalin 'knows what he is doing':

> He [Syemichkin] was a Soviet engineer, and had become a very good technician and administrator. He knew his business. He made his mistakes sometimes, but by and large he knew how to run a coke by-products plant. Stalin had worked his way to the top of the complicated Soviet state apparatus. He had done well in steering the Soviet Ship of State through the stormy seas of recent European politics. He might make mistakes sometimes, but by and large he knew his business.
> This typified the attitude of the Soviet people.
> I went to a workers' meeting in a large Moscow factory in 1940. I saw workers get up and criticize the plant director, make suggestions as to how to increase production, improve quality, and lower costs. They were exercising their rights of freedom of speech as Soviet citizens. Then the question of the new Soviet–German trade pact came up. The workers unanimously passed a previously prepared resolution approving the Soviet foreign policy. There was no discussion. The Soviet workers had learned what was their business and what was not.[47]

After the pact, anti-German propaganda was ended and anti-fascist posters removed. The whole nation appeared to be suspended between peace and war. It is said that people knew, or at least felt, that the country 'married the Germans out of expediency, not love'.[48] In fact, the preparations for war did not slacken, but intensified as Germany fought against France and then Britain, while the Soviet Union invaded Finland and annexed the Baltic states, Bessarabia, and North Bukovina. According to a Western estimate, the country's military expenditure increased rapidly from 4.8 billion (in 1937 US dollars) in 1938 to 11.8 billion in 1940; and consumption was accordingly pushed down from 14.6 billion to 10.5 billion in the same period.[49] Draconian labour laws were enacted in anticipation of war; and criminal charges were brought against managers for non-fulfilment of plans. According to John Scott, in 1940 there was 'no talk or at least very little talk of Fascist spies, insidious murderers of great literary figures, and the like, as there had been in the purges. The defendants [managers] were accused of not producing as much as the country needed to defend itself'.[50] The size of the armed forces shot up from 1.3 m. in 1935–36 to over 5 m. by June 1941,[51] and the military training of civilians was strengthened by the trade unions and other voluntary organizations.[52]

232

WAR

In spite of all these preparations, the German invasion of June 1941 came as a surprise: 'It seemed that everybody had been expecting the war for a long time and yet, at the last moment, it came like a bolt from the blue'.[53] The Stakhanovite Ivan Gudov recalls his reaction on the day of the invasion: 'We've known that the war was inevitable. We've prepared for it, but how could it have happened today, on 22 June, so unexpectedly, so suddenly? . . . bewilderment, indignation, rage – all got messed up in my head'.[54] The tremendous suffering that ensued beggars description. The available estimates of the Soviet casualties show 20 m. dead and 10 m. wounded, in a country with a pre-war population of 200 m.[55]

The whole nation literally endured utter destitution. Between 1940 and 1945, the average real wages of workers and white-collar employees plummeted by 60 per cent.[56] The average per-capita consumption of food and other consumer goods declined by 35–40 per cent in the same period.[57] Food consumption was forced to become 'vegetarian': the average worker family's consumption of meat and meat products declined 40 per cent, that of potatoes more than doubled.[58] These are official data, and real life was almost certainly much worse. Leningrad was particularly hard hit by the German blockade. Many could not survive the hardships. According to the diary of a party official at the famous Kirov (formerly Putilov) factory, in the winter of 1941–42:

> People are swelling from malnutrition. There is almost no food . . . . In the streets are often observed people carrying corpses on the sledge. It is a terrible scene never seen before in the city . . . . In the rolling mill workshop 4 died of hunger from 1 to 10 December, 20 from 11 to 20 December, yet another 20 from 21 to 25 December . . . . [59]

Another observer has recorded that workers 'died everywhere' in Leningrad; some fell dead while walking in the streets, others in the canteen, in the cloak-room, in the work place, etc. The most fortunate ones 'went along with a swollen face, swollen legs, and parched lips'.[60] The blockade starved 800,000 Leningraders to death out of the pre-war population of 2.5 m.[61]

Many workers are said to have fought, worked, and 'died without uttering a single word, without moaning and complaining'.[62] They had few other choices. At the beginning of the war, one-third of the workforce had either volunteered or had been conscripted into the Soviet military. (As in other countries at war, labour was rapidly 'feminized' to replace them.) Certainly, there was genuine patriotic heroism among the workers, and there is no shortage of memoirs and historical accounts attesting to this fact. Yet the Stakhanovite Gudov still criticizes Soviet historians for underestimating the psychological factors of war-time labour heroism. Without taking full account of these factors, he contends, it would be impossible to understand why the starved workers did the impossible to support the war efforts of the country.[63] In occupied territory, some workers became partisan fighters, others resisted Nazi conscription by leaving the factories for their villages.[64]

Far from all workers, however, heroically accepted the war-time economic hardships. Labour turnover, for instance, remained high, despite the draconian measures taken to control this. In the midst of war, in 1943, 11.2 per cent of the iron and steel workforce dared leave their jobs *of their own accord*, a criminal offence punishable by imprisonment.[65] The allegedly totalitarian Stalinist régime could not totally control labour even under war conditions.

At the beginning of the war, the advancing German troops were greeted by a considerable portion of the population in the western part of the country.[66] (During the early stage of the war, the Germans managed to occupy large areas of Soviet territory with a pre-war population of 85 m., or 45 per cent of the total Soviet population.[67]) If Ivan Gudov quickly recovered from the confusion he had felt initially, many others did not: 'How could all this be? each of us wondered. For twenty-five years we prepared for foreign attack, twenty-five years we economized, worked day and night, got almost nothing in return, suffered privations, went around in poor clothes and torn shoes – and believed that everything we earned went for defence. Now it seems that we had been living on lies'.[68] As inhabitants of occupied territory, prisoners of war, or *Ostarbeiter* in the *Reich*, they were given political alternatives. During the war, 1 m. or more Soviet POWs served in the *Wehrmacht* or joined the anti-Soviet Vlasov army. After the war, of several million displaced Soviet citizens, an estimated 500,000 remained in the West[69]; the remainder were repatriated irrespective of their wishes. Among those who chose to remain in the West were large numbers of former workers.[70] A post-war study of Soviet refugees shows that 'despite their anti-Soviet bias, [they] reported virtually no disloyal *behavior* on their own part during their life under the Soviet régime' and that 'Many persons who would otherwise have had conscious doubts about the Soviet order repressed or suppressed those doubts because they saw no viable alternative except to live within the Soviet system on its own terms'. Only under the conditions of war did they become actively disloyal.[71]

The majority of workers, however, were not given any political alternative but to 'live within the Soviet system on its own terms' and to endure whatever ordeals they happened to face. The present was sacrificed for the future, as one worker noted: 'We worked for the future'.[72] Or, as a Soviet poet put it in 1944: 'After the victory we shall call a halt, drink a cup, and rest to our heart's desire'.[73]

CONCLUSION

It is often said that the victory over Nazi Germany politically justified the Stalin régime. Indeed, even former die-hard opponents of Stalin's rapid industrialization came to maintain during the war: 'What would we have done without our *pyatiletki* [Five-Year Plans] against a Germany that is fighting us with all the industry of western Europe?'[74] As James R. Millar notes, no other nation or state in modern times 'has withstood such terrible costs in war and survived intact as a political and economic system'.[75] Justification or not, the Soviet working class played an important role in the survival of the régime.

In the late 1920s it was probably the only social class that lent some measure of support to Stalin's rapid industrialization drive. Along with the members of the party and the *Komsomol*, workers proved to be the main beneficiaries of the drive. Not only were many promoted into the élite ranks, but millions of former peasants (who formed the bulk of the working class in the 1930s) acquired education and skill and climbed up the social ladder. Implicit resistance and protest were also evident. Workers had virtually no other political alternative but to conform and to endure the harsh economic hardships. Yet, in their endurance, they were assisted by some distinct features of Soviet society. Even the indignant and the discontented fully enjoyed the benefit and security of full employment: taking advantage of a sellers' labour market, they gained a considerable bargaining power with management. To mitigate the privations and retain the work force, the factories were developed into what one Western observer called 'a complete world of its own, provided with every possible ministration to individual and community needs'.[76] Extensive social-welfare benefits and job security won almost universal support even among the Soviet war refugees openly hostile to the Stalinist régime.[77]

The war against Germany was followed by the Cold War. Hopes of 'resting to our heart's desire' were dashed:

> It wasn't 'time to live up' after all – but to gear up for another great war whose strong possibility was lodged, Stalin said on February 9, 1946, in the nature of 'imperialism'. Hence, three or four more five-year plans ('five-year plan' symbolized sacrifice) would be needed to guarantee against 'all contingencies'. A Russian in whose apartment I was sitting when Stalin's speech came over the radio, lay his head on his folded arms when he heard those words. All over Russia, I believe, people did the same. It was the end of expectations for a post-war life free of the tensions and privation experienced throughout the 1930s.[78]

The working class, like the rest of the population, had to wait for Stalin's death in 1953. Yet it neither would nor could have endured the tensions and privation had it not enjoyed the protection of full employment and social security. The Soviet working class was forced to 'trade off' its political conformity for this protection.

NOTES AND REFERENCES

1. For the 'fulfilment' view, see Adam B. Ulam, *The New Face of Soviet Totalitarianism* (Harvard University Press, 1963), and Sheila Fitzpatrick, *The Russian Revolution* (Oxford University Press, 1982); for the 'betrayal' view, see Leon Trotsky, *The Revolution Betrayed* (London, 1937).
2. A. V. Mitrofanova, *Rabochii klass SSSR v gody Velikoi Otechestvennoi voiny* (Moscow, 1971), p. 36. The number of industrial workers grew from 3.1 m. to 8.3 m. in the same period. For a standard Soviet work in English on the Soviet working class in this period, see V. G. Troukhanovsky, 'The Working Class of the U.S.S.R. 1929–1939', in *Mouvements Ouvriers et Dépression Économique de 1929 à 1939* (Assen, 1966).
3. Sheila Fitzpatrick, *Education and Social Mobility in the USSR, 1921–1934* (Cambridge University Press, 1979); id., 'The Russian Revolution and Social Mobility: A Re-examination of the Question of Social Support for the Soviet Regime in the 1920s and 1930s', *Politics & Society*, 13:2 (1984).
4. John Barber, 'The Standard of Living of Soviet Industrial Workers, 1928–1941', in Charles Bettelheim (ed.), *L'industrialisation de l'URSS dans les anées trente* (Paris, 1982), and Janet Chapman, *Real Wages in Soviet Russia since 1928* (Harvard University Press, 1963).
5. See Donald Filtzer, *Soviet Workers and Stalinist Industrialization: The Formation of Modern Soviet Production Relations, 1928–1941* (Armonk, New York, 1986).
6. Hiroaki Kuromiya, *Stalin's Industrial Revolution: Politics and Workers, 1928–1932* (Cambridge University Press, 1988), Ch. 11.

7. Louis Fischer (ed.), *Thirteen Who Fled* (New York, 1949), p. 4.

8. E. H. Carr, *The Twilight of Comintern, 1930–1935* (New York, 1982), p. 3.

9. S. G. Wheatcroft, R. W. Davies and J. M. Cooper, 'Soviet Industrialization Reconsidered: Some Preliminary Conclusions about Economic Development between 1926 and 1941', *The Economic History Review*, second series, 39:2 (May 1986), p. 277. The official Soviet data indicate an annual average increase of 18 per cent.

10. According to official Soviet data, gross industrial output increased 45 per cent from 1937 to 1940. Eugene Zaleski, *Stalinist Planning for Economic Growth, 1933–1952*, tr. from the French and ed. by Marie-Christine MacAndrew and John H. Moore (University of North Carolina Press, 1980), pp. 524–5.

11. R. W. Davies, 'The Ending of Mass Unemployment in the USSR', in David Lane (ed.), *Labour and Employment in the USSR* (Sussex, 1986), p. 23, and R. W. Davies and S. G. Wheatcroft, 'A Note on the Sources of Unemployment Statistics', ibid., p. 43.

12. Kuromiya, op. cit., Ch. 8. This declaration was somewhat premature because at that time some 0.33 m. unemployed were still registered at labour exchanges, but evidently mass unemployment was being replaced by acute labour shortages.

13. The plan projected 500,000 unemployed for 1933 on the grounds that a sharp rise in labour productivity would make it impossible to absorb unemployment wholly. The actual elimination of unemployment reflected not only the rapid industrial expansion but also the failure in achieving the projected labour productivity: the failure necessitated the employment of a far greater number of workers than planned. This, in turn, raised the cost of production and made the accumulation of capital for investment difficult without squeezing national consumption. Full employment was thus coupled with the shortage of consumer goods.

14. I. V. Stalin, *Sochineniia*, vol. 13 (Moscow, 1951), p. 334.

15. Kuromiya, op. cit., p. 306. A. Busygin, *Zhizn' moia i moikh druzei* (Moscow, 1939) and id., *Sversheniia* (Moscow, 1972).

16. Kuromiya, op. cit., p. 307; Ivan Gudov, *Put' stakhanovtsa. Rassakaz o moei zhizni* (Moscow, 1938), pp. 3–19, and id., *Sud'ba rabochego* (Moscow, 1970), pp. 3–4 and 111.

17. Kuromiya, op. cit., p 307.

18. Iurii Zhukov, *Krutye stupeni* (Moscow, 1983), p. 83. Moshe Lewin called this state 'a society in flux', 'a society unhinged and temporarily amorphous'. Moshe Lewin, 'Society and the Stalinist state in the period of the Five Year Plans', *Social History*, 1976, no. 2, pp. 139–40.

19. *Sotsialisticheskoe stroitel'stvo SSSR. Statisticheskii ezhegodnik* (Moscow, 1936), p. 531.

20. Solomon M. Schwarz, *Labor in the Soviet Union* (New York, 1950), pp. 100–8.

21. See, for example, Peter H. Solomon, Jr., 'Soviet Penal Policy, 1917–1934: A Reconsideration', *Slavic Review*, 39:2 (June 1980).

22. Michael R. Dohan, 'The Economic Origins of Soviet Autarky 1927/28–1934', *Slavic Review*, 1976, no. 4.

23. See note 49.

24. Barber, op. cit., pp. 113–14.
25. Gail Warshovsky Lapidus, *Women in Soviet Society. Equality, Development, and Social Change* (University of California Press, 1978), p. 102.
26. A. I. Vdovin and V. Z. Drobizhev, *Rost rabochego klassa SSSR, 1917–1940 gg.* (Moscow, 1976), p. 131. See also Lapidus, op. cit., p. 99.
27. *Trud v SSSR. Statisticheskii spravochnik* (Moscow, 1936), p. 342.
28. See Schwarz, op. cit., pp. 238–50.
29. Busygin, *Sversheniia*, pp. 11–12. See also Kuromiya, op. cit., pp. 302–3.
30. See, for example, Filtzer, op. cit., pp. 83–6; Kuromiya, op. cit., p. 305; and Roy Medvedev, *All Stalin's Men* (New York, 1984), p. 120.
31. Filtzer, op. cit.; Lewis H. Siegelbaum, 'Soviet Norm Determination in Theory and Practice, 1917–1941', *Soviet Studies*, 36:1 (January 1984), and Vladimir Andrle, 'How Backward Workers Became Soviet: Industrialization of Labour and the Politics of Efficiency under the Second Five-Year Plan, 1933–1937', *Social History*, 10:2 (May, 1985).
32. Hiroaki Kuromiya, '*Edinonachalie* and the Soviet Industrial Manager, 1928–1937', *Soviet Studies*, 1984, no. 2, p. 197.
33. For police intervention, see Kuromiya, *Stalin's Industrial Revolution*, Ch. 7. Merle Fainsod, *Smolensk under Soviet Rule* (Harvard University Press, 1958), Ch. 16, vividly describes police surveilance of workers, drawing on Soviet archival material.
34. Kuromiya, *Stalin's Industrial Revolution*. See also Sheila Fitzpatrick, 'Cultural Revolution as Class War', in *Cultural Revolution in Russia, 1928–1931*, ed. Sheila Fitzpatrick (Indiana University Press, 1978), and Lynne Viola, *The Best Sons of the Fatherland. Workers in the Vanguard of Soviet Collectivization* (Oxford University Press, 1987). For the belligerent mood of workers in the 1920s, see William J. Chase, *Workers, Society, and the Soviet State: Labor and Life in Moscow, 1918–1929* (University of Illinois Press, 1987).
35. Rationing of food and other scarce consumer goods, for instance, which had lasted from 1928 to the mid-1930s, explicitly discriminated in favour of industrial workers. Kuromiya, *Stalin's Industrial Revolution*, p. 86.
36. Zhukov, op. cit., p. 21.
37. L. A. Gordon, 'Sotsial'naia politika v sfere oplaty truda (vchera i segodnia)', *Sotsiologicheskie issledovaniia*, 1987, no. 4 (July–August), pp. 10, 12.
38. See the case of a Donbas coal miner, I. Zhukov, in *Vsegda vosemnadtsat'* (Donetsk, 1968), p. 76. Se also Kuromiya, *Stalin's Industrial Revolution*, p. 309.
39. Fitzpatrick, 'The Russian Revolution and Social Mobility', pp. 133–4.
40. Stalin, op. cit., pp. 38–9.
41. This rhetoric is employed as the title of Maurice Hindus's book on Soviet war efforts: *Mother Russia* (New York, 1943).
42. See Stalin's speech on the new 1936 constitution in *Sochineniia*, ed. by Robert H. McNeal, vol. 1(14), (Stanford, 1967), pp. 136–83.
43. For the Great Purges, see J. Arch Getty, *Origins of the Great Purges. The Soviet Communist Party Reconsidered, 1933–1938* (Cambridge University Press, 1985), and Robert Conquest, *The Great Terror. Stalin's Purges of the Thirties* (London, 1968).

44. This is analyzed in Hiroaki Kuromiya, 'Soviet Memoirs as a Historical Source', *Russian History/Histoire Russe*, 12:2–4 (Summer-Fall-Winter, 1985).
45. A. Stakhanov, *Rasskaz o moei zhizni* (Moscow, 1938), p. 179. Pyatakov, Rataichak and others were tried and shot as foreign agents.
46. See the recently published important sociological study, V. A. Bykov, '. . . i postupaiut cherty pokolenii', *Ekonomika i organizatsiia promyshlennogo proizvodstva*, 1987, no. 10, p. 66. This observation is consistent with the findings of the post-war study of Soviet war refugees. See Alex Inkeles and Raymond A. Bauer, *The Soviet Citizen. Daily Life in a Totalitarian Society* (Harvard University Press, 1959), Ch. XII.
47. John Scott, *Behind the Urals. An American Worker in Russia's City of Steel* (Cambridge, Mass., 1942), p. 264. For a similar interpretation, see Alexander Werth, *Russia at War, 1941–1945* (New York, 1984), pp. 47, 83–4. While Werth reports Russians' deep perplexity at what happened, he says that there also was 'widespread chuckling among many Russians about the punishment meted out to England and France "after all their dirty tricks" '. (Ibid, p. 47.)
48. See a Soviet soldier's memoirs in Fischer, op. cit., p. 36. See also Werth, op. cit., pp. 83–4.
49. Study by Wassily Leontieff in *The Impact of World War II on the Soviet Union*, ed. Susan J. Linz (Totowa, New Jersey, 1985), pp. 41, 45.
50. Scott, op. cit., p. 255.
51. John Ericson, *The Soviet High Command. A Military–Political History, 1918–1941* (London, 1962), p. 763, and *Velikaia Otechestvennaia voina. 1941–1945. Entsiklopediia* (Moscow, 1985), p. 174.
52. See, for example, *Profsoiuzy Moskvy* (Moscow, 1975), pp. 250–2. For the Society of Friends of Defense and Aviation-Chemical Construction, which played an important role in the training, see William E. Odom, *The Soviet Volunteers: Modernization and Bureaucracy in a Public Mass Organization* (Princeton University Press, 1973).
53. Werth, op. cit., p. 119, citing the hero of K. Simonov's novel.
54. Gudov, *Sud'ba rabochego*, p. 256. See also Aleksei Stakhanov, *Zhizn' shakhterskaia* (Kiev, 1975), p. 159.
55. James R. Millar, *The ABC of Soviet Socialism* (University of Illinois Press, 1981), p. 42.
56. A. N. Malafeev, *Istoriia tsenoobrazovaniia v SSSR (1917–1963 gg.)* (Moscow, 1964), p. 235.
57. I. M. Volkov, M. A. Vyltsan and I. E. Zelenin, 'Voprosy prodovol'stvennogo obespecheniia naseleniia SSSR (1917–1982 gg.)', *Istoriia SSSR*, 1983, no. 2, p. 13.
58. *Istoriia Velikoi Otechestvennoi voiny Sovetskogo Soiuza, 1941–1945 gg.*, vol. 6 (Moscow, 1965), p. 77.
59. *Oborona Leningrada. 1941–1944. Vospominaniia i dnevniki uchastnikov* (Leningrad, 1968), pp. 514–15. All in all, the factory had in the first nine months of the blockade lost 13,454 people: 4,104 died, mainly of hunger; 3,282 were transferred or evacuated elsewhere; 3,318 disappeared for unknown reasons; and 1,162 were invalided out. K. Govorushin, *Za Narvskoi zastavoi* (Moscow, 1975), p. 186.

60. *Oborona Leningrada*, p. 563.
61. See V. M. Koval'chuk and G. L. Sobolev, 'Leningradskii "rekviem": o zhertvakh naseleniia v Leningrade v gody voiny i blokady', *Voprosy istorii*, 1965, no. 12.
62. *Oborona Leningrada*, p. 519.
63. Gudov, *Sud'ba rabochego*, p. 272.
64. Ibid., p. 376. See also Stakhanov, *Zhizn' shakhterskaia*, p. 172.
65. *Sovetskaia ekonomika v period Velikoi Otechestvennoi voiny, 1941–1945 gg.* (Moscow, 1970), p. 196.
66. Alexander Dallin, *German Rule in Russia, 1941–1945. A Study of Occupation Policies*, 2nd rev. edn (Boulder, Colorado, 1981), pp. 64–5. For a more cautious view of the response of Ukrainians, see Bohdan Krawchenko, *Social Change and National Consciousness in Twentieth-Century Ukraine* (New York, 1985), p. 155.
67. V. B. Tel'pukhovskii, 'Obespechenie promyshlennosti rabochimi kadrami v pervyi period Velikoi Otechestvennoi voiny', *Voprosy istorii*, 1958, no. 11, p. 25.
68. Fischer, op. cit., p. 149 (a student's memoirs).
69. Sheila Fitzpatrick, 'Postwar Soviet Society: The "Return to Normalcy", 1945–1953', in Susan J. Linz, ed., op. cit., p. 135.
70. One case study shows that 28 per cent were former workers, a rate close to the pre-war occupational structure in which 32 per cent were classified as workers. Inkeles and Bauer, op. cit., pp. 28, 73.
71. Ibid., pp. 284, 285. (Italics in the original.) It is also shown that ordinary workers expressed much stronger hostility toward the Soviet régime than did skilled workers (p. 260).
72. S. A. Antonov, *Svet ne v okne* (Moscow, 1977), p. 114.
73. Quoted in Adam B. Ulam, *Stalin. Man and His Era* (London, 1973), p. 615.
74. Quoted in Hindus, *Mother Russia*, p. 165.
75. Millar, op. cit., p 43.
76. Maurice Hindus, *Russia Fights On* (London, 1942), p. 153.
77. Inkeles and Bauer, op. cit., p. 238. According to Raymond A. Bauer, Alex Inkeles and Clyde Kluckhorn, *How the Soviet System Works* (Harvard University Press, 1959), p. 188, worker refugees, unhappy though they were with harsh living and working conditions, questioned 'hardly a single major aspect of the general organization of the Soviet factory system'.
78. Robert C. Tucker, 'V-E Day, Moscow: Time to Live!' *New York Times*, 11 May 1985. The author was an American diplomat stationed in Moscow.

CHAPTER ELEVEN
The United States of America

Patrick Renshaw

INTRODUCTION

Between 1929 and 1945 the United States faced the challenge of economic depression, dictatorship and war. The nation emerged triumphant, with power and influence immeasurably increased. Much the same was true of American labour, which faced all three challenges and played a vital part in helping the country overcome them. By 1945 the world seemed on the brink of the American Century, and also the Century of the Common Man, who in America enjoyed the highest standard of living in the world. Few would have predicted this in 1929, when capitalism started to collapse, nor in the dark days of 1932, when Franklin Roosevelt was elected President on the promise of 'a New Deal'. For though historians may call the 1930s the decade of the New Deal, to contemporaries it was the decade of the Great Depression. For no group was this more true than industrial wage workers. Yet for organized labour this was also a decade of astonishing progress. Unions began the 1930s in weakness and defeat but ended in strength and victory. In 1933, after a decade of corporate hegemony, class collaboration and trade union retreat, the American Federation of Labor (AFL) had a falling membership of fewer than 3 m. By 1940, after a period of class consciousness, violent conflict and radicalism, union membership had tripled and was rising. The open shop had been eroded and manufacturing industry substantially organized, while labour formed the core of the Democratic Party's new coalition of liberal and increasingly urban reform.

This was a real and decisive shift in economic and political power, greatly enhanced by labour's gains during the Second

World War. Yet New Left historians argue that more could have been done: that independent, class-conscious unions of the kind rank-and-file activists wanted might have appeared. Instead, after the initial eruption, American labour leaders rapidly restored their chronic conservatism. Soon employers could co-opt them into management, with the vital task of disciplining the workforce, so that they became, as Mark Hanna (a Republican party manager at the turn of the century) had hoped, 'labour lieutenants of the captains of industry'. In this revisionist account the great enemy is the union contract, ending independence and binding labour to the employer. Yet despite a certain plausibility, such criticism is seriously misplaced. Fundamentally, it misinterprets the mood of the time. For most workers in the 1930s, engaged in desperate battle with the largest and most ruthless corporations in the world, the contract was not a sell-out but the supreme prize.[1] Equally important, this whole debate neglects the fact that unions helped solve the riddle of unemployment and replaced privation with prosperity.

THE WORKING CLASS: EARLY DAYS OF THE UNIONS

In 1933, few anticipated the spectacular growth in union strength which occurred in the next decade or so. With 15 m., or one in four of the total working population, jobless in 1933, output halved in less than four years, and agriculture, banking and business at the point of collapse, there could be no doubting the danger to capitalism. Yet the system was saved and unemployment ended partly by the creation of powerful unions which raised wages. These unions sought their members amongst the American working class which, though more affluent and less class conscious than in other nations, was similar in most respects. It consisted mainly of wage-earning manual workers – skilled, semi-skilled and unskilled – usually hourly-paid and lacking much job security. It worked in basic industries, such as mining, iron and steel, or the huge lumber trade, and in manufacturing, transport and construction. Part of the working class was white-collared; part uniformed, like railwaymen. This non-agricultural labour force, as historians usually call it, numbered some 30 m. in 1930, larger than the still vast agricultural sector, and about half the total workforce.

The greatest number worked on the railways, in basic extractive or manufacturing industries, and in construction. Yet with the transition of the American economy from a capital-goods to a consumer-goods phase in the 1920s, increasing numbers were found in motor manufacturing, the electrical industry, radio, rubber, chemicals, textiles and clothing. The major industrial states of New England, New York and the Great Lakes area from Pennsylvania to Wisconsin, where the nation's industrial and business heartland had developed in the 19th century, still contained the great bulk of the working class. Yet by 1920 a majority of Americans were living in urban areas, and every town and city had its working class. Rail and transport workers, of course, worked all over America, and mining often occurred in remote areas; but in many sectors of the economy, big industrial centres stood out like islands in a rural sea, and the South was still mostly without major industry or unions.

The continental size of the United States, and its agricultural background, had long presented obstacles to the emergence of united working-class organizations. But other things complicated the picture. Though immigration had been severely restricted in the 1920s, the American working class on the eve of the Depression was still ethnically very diverse. Successive waves of immigrants since the 1820s had established an elaborate ethnic hierarchy, within which the position of individual groups of workers was largely determined by the date when their ethnic group had first arrived. Thus, the British stood at the top, followed by the descendants of Dutch, German and Scandinavian immigrants. The Irish arrived in strength during the potato famine of the 1840s. Disadvantaged by desperate poverty, their Roman Catholic religion and the prejudices these aroused, their sheer numbers, command of English and the political experience they had gained in the cause of Irish nationalism gave them strength. Moreover, they arrived in America as industrialization and urbanization were really getting underway, and so became a powerful new element in the working class. By the 1870s, they were prominent in early unions and running the politics of such cities as New York, Philadelphia and St. Louis. By 1910, white Anglo-Saxon Protestants exercised effective economic power and Germans provided a solid middle class, but Irish urban and union influence helped them organize later immigrants from eastern and southern Europe.

Black workers were almost totally excluded from unionization, though by 1930 they formed an increasingly important part of the American working class. Freedom from slavery after the Civil War had been followed by steady relegation to second-class citizenship and the most vicious racist exclusion. Nine-tenths of the black population of the United States still lived in the South as late as 1900, four-fifths of them in rural areas. The great shift in the black working population came after 1914, as the First World War both cut off supplies of immigrants from Europe and boosted the order books of American companies as industry sought to fulfil Allied war orders. This labour shortage was filled not least by black workers, and between 1915 and 1918 about 500,000 blacks moved from the rural South to the urban North, especially to cities such as Chicago, Cleveland, Detroit and New York. This was the beginning of a steady migration of blacks, so that by 1930 more than 2 m. had left the South; and by 1940, nearly a quarter of the black population lived in the North and West.

Blacks who moved to the North improved their lot. While denied the vote in the South, they could now participate in politics; and, on the economic front, pay, job choice and employment opportunities were better. But they still fell victim to white racism (which fuelled several bloody race riots), were crowded into evil city ghettoes and trampled on by recent immigrants – such as Italians, Slavs and Poles – in the struggle for jobs, housing, schools and welfare. In this conflict blacks received virtually no support from unions, which generally reflected the prejudices of their white members, prevented blacks from joining and used their power to exclude blacks from traditionally white trades. A few black unions, such as the Brotherhood of Sleeping Car Porters, provided union leverage. Segregated, excluded, exploited, black workers made little headway during the prosperous 1920s, and were hardest hit of all by the economic collapse after 1929. 'The reason the Depression did not have the impact on the Negro that it had on the whites', explained a black intellectual, 'was that the Negroes had been in the Depression all the time.'[2]

Like blacks, women also played an important part in the workforce but were generally excluded from unions and faced barriers of prejudice. Young women, prominent in certain industries such as textiles, clothing manufacture and the service sector, on marriage commonly dropped out of the labour market to devote themselves to child rearing and homemaking. During the labour shortage of the First World War they had, like blacks, taken on an invaluable role in war industries, but were rapidly replaced when men returned from the fighting forces on peacetime economic conversion. In any case, they were (again like blacks) nearly always poorly organized and lacking influential leaders. They had finally won the vote in

1918, and the more fortunate benefited from wider educational opportunities, greater social emancipation and the spread of electricity and consumer durables to lighten household drudgery. Yet these same gadgets were reducing jobs in domestic service for the less advantaged.

Such ethnic, racial, sexual and social divisions clearly weakened the American labour movement. Moreover, the prosperous 1920s, when employers launched aggressive campaigns to spread the open shop and welfare capitalism, proved a disastrous decade for unions. Total membership, which had peaked at about 5 m. members, or about 20 per cent of the non-agricultural labour force in 1920, had fallen below 3 m., or about 11 per cent of an expanded working population, in the early 1930s.[3] Political activity was equally divided and ineffective. The white, skilled craftsmen of British, German and Irish descent, who led the AFL, looked to unions to defend their trades rather than advance the wider interests of labour as a whole. They had fought off the efforts of Socialists and the Industrial Workers of the World to influence the labour movement during the Progressive period before 1914. Then the war divided the Left and the IWW and stimulated the Red Scare. The Bolshevik revolution in 1917 led to further factionalism and created the American Communist Party which outflanked the Socialists on the left. Finally, the apparent success of capitalism in the 1920s made the Socialist alternative seem increasingly irrelevant and contributed to its irreversible decline.

Hostile to Socialists and Communists, with their talk of revolution and millenial promises, labour leaders accepted the capitalist system and sought only to sell their labour at the highest price. Fearful that government intervention would reduce rather than advance their freedom, they followed a policy in politics of 'rewarding friends and punishing enemies', voting Democratic, Republican or Progressive as seemed best according to time, place and candidate. But, beneath the surface, a quiet revolution was taking place in the voting habits of the American working class. Easy Republican victories at the polls after 1916 masked the fact that the Democrats were actually winning a steadily increasing share of the urban vote. In 1928, the Democratic candidate for President, Al Smith, won a small but significant majority in America's dozen major cities. What this meant is now clear: after 1928 the sons and daughters of the last great wave of newcomers to American shores between 1900 and 1914 were seeking their first job and casting their first vote as the Republican politics of prosperity were crumbling to dust.

So, all the ingredients for a massive realignment of the American working class – ethnic, racial, sexual, regional, occupational – were in place as the decade of the Depression and New Deal began. One final influence acted as a catalyst in this upsurge, not just of organized labour but of semi-skilled and unskilled workers, blacks and women in mass-production. This catalyst was provided by the ideas of the British economist J. M. Keynes. Keynes was one of the few struggling to seek a solution to the riddle of unemployment. He believed that the crisis of the Depression had been caused by under-consumption, not over-production; that ending under-consumption would end unemployment; but also, that if the cure were to be permanent, due weight must be given to the role of reflation, sustained public spending and above all raised aggregate demand to revive and control the economy.

Keynes, whose first attempts to influence the New Deal met little success, adopted the idea of the multiplier effect and elaborated this in his seminal *General Theory of Employment, Interest and Money*, publication of which in 1936 coincided with efforts to strengthen labour and raise demand through Senator Robert Wagner's National Labor Relations Act. Such events were part of the emerging pattern of the 1930s, but the situation had been very different in 1933. The prevailing attitude of government, employers and labour leaders then was orthodox. Witness after witness before the Senate Finance Committee in February 1933 gave the same glum advice about the need to balance the Federal budget – precisely the opposite of what was needed.[4]

Heretics proclaiming the prophet Keynes – the economist William T. Foster, the Philadelphia newspaper publisher J. David Stern, the head of General Electric, Gerard Swope, and an unknown banker from Utah named Marriner Eccles, were voices crying in the wilderness. At this stage, such advocates lacked weight. More authoritative proponents of high-wage capitalism in the 1920s, such as Bernard Baruch and Henry Ford (and indeed President Herbert Hoover himself) still existed. But in the depths of the Great Depression they did not see how high wages, or indeed any wages, could be paid. Labour leaders, naturally committed to higher pay, might have used Keynesianism to justify this aim. Yet they were equally baffled.

FRANKLIN D. ROOSEVELT AND THE FIRST NEW DEAL

Roosevelt's Secretary of Labour, Frances Perkins, told the President

in March 1933 that 'We are beginning to appreciate today the close
connection between the commerce of the nation and the number
of persons employed . . . *The working classes are the great reservoir
of purchasing power*'.[5] Some labour lobbyists urged that 'recovery
depends upon the securing of mass purchasing power', adding
that, 'the sure and direct way of accomplishing this is the complete
unionization of labor'.[6]

Yet in the depths of the Depression they were in poor shape
to do this. Seduced by prosperity in the 1920s, they had in those
years seen union membership fall, while the open shop, company
unions and welfare capitalism flourished. Then came catastrophe
after 1929. Yet most of them – William Green, president of the AFL,
'Big Bill' Hutcheson, 'king' of the carpenters, Dan Tobin, 'tsar' of the
teamsters – still accepted the system as slavishly as their employers.
Only two important labour leaders – John L. Lewis of the coalminers
and Sidney Hillman of the clothing workers – challenged this view.
Lewis, a Republican in the 1920s, was a massive man and powerful
orator who had bulldozed the United Mineworkers together and
then seen the UMW fall apart again. Though he had voted for
Hoover in 1932, and so had no friends at FDR's court, he believed
the time had come to cast aside old concepts like 'laissez-faire',
'competition' and 'rugged individualism'. Balanced Budgets would
not end poverty, and the planning he had long advocated for his
own ailing industry should be extended to industry as a whole.[7]

Hillman, a man of quite different background and type,
faced similar problems in the cut-throat garment trade and
had reached similar conclusions. A Russian Jew jailed for his
small part in the Revolution of 1905, he had fled to Chicago,
quickly became a labour activist and established the Amalgamated
Clothing Workers. He helped ACW members benefit from the
war-time boom and defended their gains in the 1920s. Though
primarily an intellectual, Hillman knew how to take care of himself
and kept eclectic company: afternoons with Lepke Buchalter, of
Murder Incorporated, evenings with Felix Frankfurter, of Harvard
Law School.[8] 'Cut-throat competition makes the unscrupulous
employer the leader in each industry', Hillman observed, 'and
the rest willingly or otherwise follow'.[9] The businessman who cut
wages had the further satisfaction of knowing he was following the
injunction of orthodox economics that the effort to maintain low
wage rates increased employment.

'Really to control unemployment', Hillman concluded, 'we
must think and act in terms of economic planning'; and 'vol-

The working class and politics

untary ... planning is not enough'.[10] Roosevelt's close advisers, like Adolph Berle, Raymond Moley and Rex Tugwell, all believed in varieties of the kind of planning Hillman deplored. And current experience of this was not encouraging. The National Recovery Administration (NRA) was trying to put a ceiling on hours and a floor on wages without really raising demand. NRA Public Works provisions were being enacted with painful slowness. In agriculture, the Agricultural Adjustment Administration, in Richard Hofstadter's mordant phrase, solved the paradox of hunger in the midst of plenty only by doing away with the plenty. Though Lewis was melodramatic and Hillman low-keyed, they had much in common. Both came from industries ruined by vicious competition. Both led industrial unions – the UMW and the ACW – often outside or at odds with the AFL. Both were masters of the mundane side of union bargaining yet retained a keen sense of labour's wider mission. And when action came in 1933 and 1934 it came in their two industries.

Encouraged by the new and more favourable legal and political climate of the New Deal, rank-and-file insurgents breathed life into moribund Locals in clothing and coal. The Norris–La Guardia Act of 1932 had already outlawed 'yellow-dog' contracts (which forbade workers to join unions) and also restricted injunctions against strikes. The NRA Codes had been planned rather to regulate industry as a whole than give labour new powers. Yet Section 7(a) did reinforce the right to organize. This, plus the upturn in the economy which followed the first Hundred Days of the New Deal, gave rise to an eruption of purely rank-and-file radicalism. In addition to mining, the garment trades and textiles, other activists filled hastily chartered AFL Federal Locals in the car, electrical and rubber industries, created an independent grass-roots movement in the totally unorganized steel industry, captured company unions or joined unemployed protests for protection and relief. Finally, general strikes in Minneapolis, Toledo and San Francisco showed that radicalism could break the mood of apathy and demoralization which typified labour during the early New Deal.

Yet these NRA boards actually diluted union demands in 1933 and 1934, while steelworker insurgency collapsed when NRA officials and the President forced them to postpone and then cancel a strike over recognition. The South had long been stony ground for unions, and here police and local officials quickly re-established the open shop in textiles. As Johnson put it, 'greasy little human buzzards' used 'the whip of starvation to lash the bent back of emaciated women and under-nourished children for no more wages than will keep body and soul in speaking distance'.[11] Yet although the dawn of labour activism during the early New Deal proved false, it did have some positive results. The rank and file's crucial weakness had been inability to organize on a national level. Labour leaders were now fully persuaded of the over-riding need for this. Moreover, militancy frightened left-wing New Dealers into fighting for the Wagner Act which could help union organization at a national level.

THE WAGNER ACT

Still, Senator Robert Wagner was only able to pilot his Bill through Congress because, as the *New York Times* declared, 'The President and his New Deal . . . won the most overwhelming victory in the history of American politics'[12] in the mid-term elections of 1934. They gave the Democrats a staggering majority of 45 in the Senate and 219 in the House. More interestingly, Wagner presented the Bill in a wholly Keynesian context.

Industrial concentration, Wagner argued, which had destroyed the worker's bargaining power, left him with an inadequate share of the nation's wealth. Yet economic recovery and stability could only be achieved through wider distribution of that wealth. In the 1920s, when labour had been weak, the gains of productivity had gone into plant, profits and speculation rather than into boosting demand, and depression had resulted. The only way to secure 'that fair distribution of purchasing power upon which permanent prosperity must rest', Wagner concluded, was by strengthening collective bargaining and so raising those on the bottom.[13]

Removing such inequalities within the wage structure would benefit society as a whole by creating mass purchasing power to fill the troughs in the business cycle. This economic philosophy was combined with a constitutional foundation, vital because the Supreme Court was already striking down much New Deal legislation. Wagner's constitutional argument was that deterrents to mass purchasing power were detrimental to interstate commerce, and that strikes caused by bad labour law and labour relations further obstructed it. The Act would remove disagreement over the right to associate as a prime cause of strikes and establish collective bargaining to eliminate other causes.[14]

Equally important, the Wagner Act established an effective enforcement agency, outside the Department of Labor, in the National Labor Relations Board. The NLRB's new powers – to order elections to see who should represent workers, to define and prohibit unfair labour practices, such as employer-dominated company unions, unfair dismissal or refusal to bargain, and firmly enforce its decisions – would have a dramatic impact on labour relations.[15] This reduced anti-union litigation substantially and transformed the NLRB, whose three members were to be selected with union agreement, into a kind of 'Supreme Court' of labour. Not surprisingly, employers fought the Bill tooth and nail.

Initially the Administration was cool, if not hostile to Wagner's proposals. The President – never sure-footed on labour affairs – felt a continuing loyalty to the NRA, its administrator Hugh Johnson and Section 7(a). Then in May 1935 the Supreme Court, in a 9–0 decision, tore the heart out of the first New Deal by striking down the whole of Title 1 of the NRA, including the pro-labour provisions of Section 7(a). After fifteen months silence, an angry Roosevelt finally endorsed the Wagner Bill and signed it when it passed reasonably rapidly, without damaging amendment, on 5 July 1935.

The Wagner Act marked the high-point of New Deal reformism. It could not have passed at any other time. Fearful of the demagogic appeal of the Southern populist Huey Long with his 'tax the rich and share the wealth' campaign, and backed by huge majorities in Congress, Roosevelt saw social security, public housing and wealth tax laws enacted in the legislative flurry of the second New Deal. The Wagner Act was clearly the longest stride of all on the road not just to new power for labour but to a Keynesian economy. Automobile and steel industries vowed they would ignore it. Yet it was in steel and cars that the Wagner Act passed its first great test.

For years Lewis had been urging AFL president William Green to do something about organizing steel. For years Green had been promising millions of new members. But at the end of 1935 the nation's largest basic industry remained unorganized. Fears of craft-union leaders like Hutcheson and Tobin that the new law would stimulate industrial unions among ethnic groups Tobin dismissed as 'rubbish' reached a violent climax at the AFL convention in October 1935 when Lewis floored Hutcheson in a fist fight. Blocked by the conservative leadership, industrial union activists like Lewis and Hillman moved immediately to set up the Congress of Industrial Organizations (CIO) to reach the unorganized in steel and elsewhere. Lewis, whose miners were economically linked to the steel industry, which in addition wholly owned the so-called 'captive mines', took the lead. In February 1936 he pledged 350 paid organizers, an annual budget of $500,000 and his best lieutenant Philip Murray to establish the Steel Workers Organizing Committee. SWOC marked the start of the CIO's offensive in mass production.

True, the first open pitched battle came with the sit-down strike by United Autoworkers to establish a union shop at General Motors and the industry as a whole. As SWOC's legal counsel Lee Pressman put it 'The success or failure of the Autoworkers strike meant the success or failure of the budding CIO. The loss of the strike might have been the end of the CIO.'[16] Yet, while the UAW was capturing headlines by its dramatic occupation of part of the GM empire in Michigan, SWOC had been engaged in a stealthy campaign of infiltrating US Steel, whose 220,000 workers produced more steel than Germany.

The leader of SWOC was Philip Murray who, like Hillman, was a member of the rising generation of younger labour leaders. A Scots immigrant of Irish-Catholic stock, he kept a copy of Leo XIII's encyclical on the Condition of Labour on his desk. Jews like Hillman were prominent in union leadership, but much of the American working class was Catholic – descendants of the great 19th- and early 20th-century influx of Irish, Italian and Polish immigrants. Frances Perkins and others had long recognized his outstanding abilities; but Murray had worked in Lewis's giant shadow. Free at last to play an independent and decisive role, his strategy fell into three parts. First he planned to work with the ethnic groups who were so important in the steel workforce – Poles, Czechs, Slavs and blacks. Then he chose to exploit the Federal government, reviving the phrase 'The President Wants You To Join the Union', used so effectively by Lewis in NRA days, which had more force following the Wagner Act. Finally, and most successfully, Murray cleverly infiltrated and then captured the company unions hastily set up by US Steel in 1933 to make some pretence of complying with NRA Codes.[17]

If aggregate demand were to be raised it was vital that mass-production workers be organized. The whole process was helped by Roosevelt's landslide re-election in November 1936. He had emphasized the importance of purchasing power in his campaign. 'Employment and weekly pay envelopes', he said in a Labor Day address, 'have increased steadily during the past three years, stimulated by the spending of the Federal government in useful ways. This increased buying power of wage earners and farmers has resulted in increased sales for merchants, more orders for factories and rising profits for investors.'[18] Lewis and the CIO provided funds and tens of thousands of political organizers who made a massive contribution to Roosevelt's re-election in November 1936. More important than FDR's personal victory was the fact that it swept many liberal Democrats to power in industrial States such as Illinois, Ohio and Pennsylvania. In Michigan, Governor Frank Murphy's refusal to evict sit-down strikers from GM property speeded the company's decision to capitulate and sign a contract recognizing the UAW in February 1937. The following month, to general incredulity, US Steel did the same with SWOC with Lewis playing the crucial part, since neither of the agreements offered by GM or US Steel could have been enforced under the Wagner Act.[19]

Many were misled into thinking that SWOC's agreement with US Steel made the CIO triumph complete. But 1937 and 1938 were exceptions to the rule that where US Steel led the rest of the industry followed. The real trouble for SWOC came in the so-called 'Little Steel' companies like Bethlehem, Republic, or Youngstown Sheet and Tube, who fought a bitter and bloody rearguard action. Clashes between pickets, company guards and police in Chicago on Memorial Day in May 1937 saw ten strikers killed. As the 'Little Steel' struggle dragged on to defeat it revealed sharply the limitations of presidential support. The La Follette Civil Liberties Committee Investigation showed clearly where blame should be put. Steel executives found it hard to explain to the Senate why they spied on their own workforce, hired goon squads to attack them, stored guns, grenades and explosives, and practised sabotage.[20] Yet the President's view was 'a plague on both your houses'.

In the concerted CIO drives, not only in cars and steel but in chemicals, rubber and textiles FDR played no part. Though he had spoken movingly in his second inaugural of 'one-third of a nation, ill-housed, ill-clad, ill-nourished' he neglected their plight while pursuing his political battle to reform the Supreme Court. True the Court had struck down the NRA and much of the first New Deal. Moreover, there was sound reason for fearing it might do the same to the Wagner Act and the second New Deal. In fact the Court upheld the Wagner Act and left the other acts alone. The Court changed partly because it was scared by FDR's plan to 'pack' it, partly because it became more attuned to public opinion on social questions, partly because some judges – notably Owen Roberts – changed their views. Finally, retirement of older and more reactionary judges enabled the President by 1940 to appoint his own Court, which included Frank Murphy, friend of the UAW, and Felix Frankfurter, a key recruiter of staff for the New Deal and convinced Keynesian. Moreover, though the President had been cool towards organized labour he was a political opportunist who knew where the votes were. By 1940 labour had become the capstone of the Democratic Party's new reform coalition.

LABOUR: ACHIEVEMENTS, LIMITATIONS, AND OPPORTUNITY

Labour had made great strides in a few years towards new powers and a new economic role. The 1938 Fair Labour Standards Act, which established a minimum wage, a 44-hour week and the end of child labour, seemed to put the seal on the years of great advance. Yet severe limitations remained. The AFL's expulsion of the CIO in 1937 and the division between craft and industrial unions, which was to last nearly two decades, came at a time when unity was needed most. This weakness was worsened by political and economic events after 1938. By 1937 New Deal reform legislation had run its course. Industrial production was above 1929 levels, business activity had recovered. Just as the first labour upsurge had occurred during the tentative economic recovery of 1933–34, so permanent gains for labour coincided with the more substantial growth of 1937, when profits, employment, pay and hope all recovered. Preoccupied increasingly with foreign affairs as war loomed, the President took this opportunity to cut Federal spending. The result was a sharp rise in unemployment – and this time people called it 'the Roosevelt recession'.

Shorter but steeper than after 1929, the recession hit the CIO hard. Production declined by 70 per cent in steel, 50 per cent in autos, 40 per cent in rubber and 35 per cent in electrical manufacturing. Unemployment rose to one in five of the working population, not far short of the 1932 level. Hundreds of thousands of newly organized workers were laid off. Those who remained in work saw their union, its collective power gravely weakened, struggle to enforce hard-won seniority and grievance systems. Between 1938 and 1940 organizing work ended abruptly. SWOC dismissed some 250 field representatives, put the rest on short

253

time and concentrated on mills where union members already had bargaining rights. The UAW lost fifty international staff members and abandoned any effort to unionize Ford for the foreseeable future. The CIO sacked sixty-three staff members in 1940 and withdrew organizers from its campaign to establish new unions in aircraft, meatpacking, textile and farm-equipment industries. Lewis might claim the CIO had 4 m. members, but the actually dues-paying figure fell as low as 1.5 m. in the late depression era.

This sharp economic downturn had a decisive influence. Labour became more amenable to management. 'Enlightened union leaders', Hillman wrote in the 1938 CIO handbook, 'believe that the attitude of organized labour must be one of co-operation with the employer in their mutual interest – increased prosperity for all'.[21] Philip Murray supported this view, and reflected the new realism of SWOC following the 'Little Steel' drubbing when he observed: 'The fight for unionization is over in the greater part of the steel industry and we want no lingering spirit of contentiousness to survive. We realise that mutual interests are best served by working with and not against each other.' The emphasis switched from confrontation to Keynesian consensus. Hillman summarized the position thus: 'Greater production, guided by efficient management, means lower cost per unit. Lower costs tend towards lower prices. This enables our people to buy and use more goods. This, in turn, makes possible putting our unemployed back to work. With little or no unemployment, the bargaining power of labour is increased, resulting in higher wages. Higher wages, coupled with lower prices, mean a high standard of living.'[22]

In the late 1930s the United States was facing the problem Britain had lived with since 1921. Even with the economy running in top gear 10 per cent of the total workforce remained jobless. Public spending was no longer a temporary expedient but a key tool in controlling the economy. New Deal spenders such as Lauchlin Currie of the Treasury owed a clear debt to Keynes. For others, such as the President and Harry Hopkins, Keynesianism simply served as a convenient rationalization for what they were doing anyway. As far as Keynes himself was concerned they were not doing enough. In 1940 FDR for the first time discussed his Budget in Keynesian terms. But Keynes himself was unconvinced this was a genuine conversion. 'It seems politically impossible', he wrote in July 1940, 'for a capitalistic democracy to organize expenditure on the scale necessary to make the grand experiment which would prove my case – except in war conditions.'[23] The fall of France brought such conditions into being. Within four months Roosevelt had broken the two-term convention, won re-election and, through lend-lease and generous aid to embattled Britain, placed America's economy on a war footing. Within sixteen months the Japanese attack on Pearl Harbor completed the process. Public spending was now not just acceptable but a patriotic imperative.

This produced a quantum leap. Tax receipts rose ten-fold, though never keeping pace with the cost of war, as the national debt rose from 40.4 billion dollars in 1940 to 258.7 billion dollars in 1941. The real value of the nation's output rose by more than 70 per cent, private product expanded by more than half, while the government's share of output more than trebled and its share of total output rose from just under 10 per cent in 1939 to between a fifth and a quarter in 1944.[24] Still unemployment – which Currie believed was 'greatly understated' as late as 1940 'since [the figures] take no account of the transition from part-time to full-time work' – did not end until 1943.[25]

Yet for organized labour the war was a matchless opportunity. Some leaders like Lewis, isolationist in spirit, were fearful that by co-operating with government they would see temporary war-time gains destroyed by post-war reaction, as after 1918. But Lewis, angered by Roosevelt's apparent ingratitude after all he and the CIO had done for him in 1936, had lost his leadership of the CIO by opposing FDR in 1940, and now was no longer the dominant figure he had been in the mid-1930s. Labour leaders like Hillman and David Dubinsky, Jews whose homeland had been overrun by Hitler's armies, threw their full weight behind the anti-fascist crusade, determined labour would make great long-term gains.

THE INITIAL EFFECTS OF THE SECOND WORLD WAR

The war ended unemployment, which had never fallen below 10 per cent during the 1930s. It made high public spending a permanent part of economic planning. Finally, it established the new labour unions, launched so rapidly and aggressively as a result of the Wagner Act. The war also transformed the role of organized labour within the economy. In May 1940, while France was falling, the President appointed a seven-man National Defense Commission with Sidney Hillman, the CIO garment workers' leader, in charge of employment.[26] Hillman, rather than Lewis or Murray, was now emerging as the most significant member of America's new labour leadership. Now Murray had succeeded Lewis as leader of the CIO he had become bogged down in administration, leaving Hillman to play the creative role. From the spring of 1940 until the spring of 1942 Hillman headed the Labor Division of the National Defense Administration, first in the National Defense Advisory Commission, then in the Office of Production Management, and finally in the War Production Board. When he began government work German divisions were driving towards Paris, and after Dunkirk the British army was almost totally disarmed. If America were to act as the Arsenal of Democracy, then labour's co-operation was clearly crucial. In Hillman's view, what made the Second World War different from any other was that it would be fought and won by the might of labour and industrial production.[27] He quickly established friendly, informal relations with President Roosevelt and the NDC director-general, W. S. Knudsen, boss of GM.

The *New York Times* compared Hillman to the British trade-union leader Ernest Bevin, now Minister of Labour in Churchill's War Cabinet. Though Bevin exercised far more real executive power than any American labour leader, the comparison was a portent. So was the newspaper's reference to 'a young tool and die maker' named Walter Reuther who 'encouraged by the Labor Division of the defense organization ... worked out a plan to utilize the unutilized machine and man power of the automobile industry for mass production of airplanes'. The *Times* article added that Philip Murray was preparing a similar plan for steel, concluding: 'Direct responsibility for such plans by labor in equal partnership with industry ... is a novel departure.'[28] In fact, both the Murray and Reuther plans failed to win adoption revealing the advisory, non-executive roles of labour leaders in the war government. Yet as the military crisis deepened, with Britain's back to the wall, Hillman stimulated both production and propaganda. In an NBC broadcast to the nation on 3 June 1941 he called for 'a new spirit of national unity as bombs fall on London and Liverpool. ... By peak production alone can we guarantee our own national safety and bring about the victory of Democracy. ... We must put modern weapons into the hands of Democracy's front-line defenders – the Army, the Air Force and the people of Britain.'[29]

Within three weeks, when Hitler invaded the Soviet Union on 22 June 1941, the Russian people had joined the British in the front line. Communist unionists, so active in creating the CIO at grass-roots level, had opposed the war since the Nazi-Soviet pact in August 1939. Now overnight they became its most vociferous supporters. Within six months, Pearl Harbor had completed United States conversion to a war economy. On the home front the CIO's struggle in the 'captive mines' – wholly owned by the steel companies – to establish the union shop continued throughout the year. On this issue Lewis, the miners' leader, won a substantial victory which partly offset his humiliating defeat over Roosevelt's third term. But news of the arbitration board's favourable decision on 7 December 1941 was swamped by events in the Pacific. Meanwhile, in the Little Steel dispute the CIO had forced the four smaller steel companies to recognise the steelworkers' industrial union and accept other important principles, notably the 'checkoff' provision, whereby employers deducted union dues and fines from the pay packet before handing it over to the worker. In return for complete co-operation in the war effort the union gained security and power over its members – at least during the term of the contract.

THE WAR ECONOMY

The effect of joining the war was at first not as dramatic as it might have been for – as the Roosevelt papers make clear – American policy makers had believed themselves to be in the war since at least the summer of 1940. By 1942 and 1943, as full employment returned, fears of inflation grew. Yet the war economy bristled with other problems: the need to maximize production, minimize inter-union disputes and strikes, avoid bottlenecks, keep prices stable and avoid profiteering were among the most important. Though the Federal government's control of the economy increased during the war, the paramount belief in free enterprise meant that such control was limited. Moreover, it was clear that none of the production problems could be solved without the full co-operation of organized labour.

Such co-operation was not to be easily secured. Jurisdictional disputes between unions, like those between AFL and CIO shipyard welders, had been a constant source of bad publicity and lost production in vital war industries since mid-1940. The speed up of production was another fertile source of friction. Union leaders argued that productivity had greatly increased, because of worker patriotism, while pay had remained the same. Throughout 1941 strikes, unfair labour practices and union excesses continued to preoccupy businessmen, politicians and public opinion fearful that pay increases would lead to spiralling inflation. Strongly influenced by hostility towards the CIO during the 'captive mines' and 'Little Steel' disputes, the conservative Virginia Democrat Howard Smith saw his anti-labour bill pass the House in July 1941, but then get delayed by the Senate Labor Committee.

Pearl Harbor cut short this clamour for Open Shop and No Strike legislation which the Smith bill expressed. Pro-labour members of the Administration argued that union solidarity in war-time would best be harnessed by giving the whole labour movement a more responsible role in defence arrangements along the lines suggested by Philip Murray and the CIO. Now that the United States had joined the war, labour co-operation became more urgent; and the Smith anti-labour bill was soon voted down, as FDR had hoped. The Senate Labor Committee urged legislative adoption of the Murray plan for joint action by labour, industry and government in the interests of national unity. Based on the social reformist encyclicals of Pope Leo XIII, and NRA tripartite planning experiments, it called for joint administration of defence industries. Like Walter Reuther's plan to build 500 planes a day, the Murray proposal won support from such influential members of the Administration as Leon Henderson, Harry Hopkins and Jerome Frank. While never put fully into effect it promised fundamental reform of industry and a powerful labour presence in the war effort.

Yet even if organized labour were co-operative, the issue of strikes in wartime remained. Presidential advisers examined experience during the First World War in both the United States and Europe. The 1917 munitions strike in Britain, they told FDR, had been led by spontaneous committees of shop stewards. When British strike-leaders had been arrested, others had sprung up in their place. A major cause of trouble had been that strikes had been legally prohibited; and since British labour was in 1917 much further advanced than American labour in 1941, that experience 'may afford a basis for understanding the feelings underlying unrest in America today'. In Sweden, steel makers would not think of operating their mills without having all their employees organized in a union, and the managers of Sweden's steel industry believed labour's status as a full partner in industry must be fully accepted through recognition of the union shop. 'Labor is striving towards permanent economic democracy', the report concluded, 'not power as the reactionary Press claims. America's future strength may depend on recognition of that fact.'[30]

Roosevelt told Hillman that the time had come for Congress to set up machinery for treating labour fairly and equally; that 17 m. man-days lost in the United States through strikes in the first eight months of 1941 indicated 'the lack of co-operation in the past'; and that 'we can't get to first base . . . without your help'.[31] Accordingly, FDR summoned a conference of labour and business leaders just ten days after Pearl Harbor to plan new measures for industrial co-operation. After some weeks discussion, representatives agreed to a three-point programme for industrial peace: no strikes or lockouts for the duration of hostilities; peaceful settlement of all industrial disputes; and the creation of a tripartite board with labour, management and the public each represented by four members to be called the National War Labor Board. Part of the problem facing the new Board was clearly the continuing schism between AFL and CIO; but the President was determined to get a binding No Strike pledge out of both in 1942.

The immediate result of this agreement in January 1942 was a steep decline in work stoppages. Whereas 23 m. man-days had been lost in 1941, the total for 1942 fell to only 4.18 m. But as the pressures and tensions of war mounted, this record could not be sustained. Labour leaders argued that workers' interests were being ignored by government in the powers it now exercised over pay and prices. Green declared that labour had only given the No Strike pledge on the understanding that collective bargaining would be sustained, and that Washington was now following a course wholly inconsistent with its earlier promises. Lewis, as usual, was far more belligerent and soon defied all government authority to protect the interests of the UMW. Strikes rose in 1943 when a total of 13.5 m. man-days were lost and, though they declined after that, climbed again as the war drew to an end in 1945. Fear of the effects of demobilization and reconversion to a peacetime economy caused insecurity and labour unrest. Still, man-days lost to strikes averaged below 2 m. a month until mid-August. After V-J Day, they doubled to 4.3 m. in September; and doubled again in October. In the last four months of 1945 alone, 28.4 m. man-days were lost.

This explosion of strike activity *after* the war, paradoxically, highlights the fact that labour on the whole supported the war effort and that most unions sought to restrain strikes. Man-days lost actually averaged only one-tenth of 1 per cent of total working time in industry, or no more than one day per worker during the war years. Many of the strikes were unauthorized walkouts or wildcats. Workers whose grievances were intensified by the strain of long hours, speed-ups, complicated bonus systems and other hardships resulting from war conditions took matters into their own hands. In frustrated protest they laid down tools or walked out, but having let off steam quickly went back to work. The few more threatening strikes were the exception rather than the rule.

The key to understanding labour's wartime history is the War Labor Board. A first and vital problem it faced was the issue of union security. It met this problem by adopting the principle of maintenance of membership. Though the closed shop or union shop would not be enforced in contract negotiations, union members, or those who subsequently joined unions, would be required to maintain membership for the life of the contract. Should they fail to remain union members in good standing they would be subject to dismissal. Labour members of the Board accepted this solution without qualification; management representatives acquiesced very reluctantly. Once agreed, however, the principle of maintenance of membership was consistently upheld throughout the war. It ultimately applied to some 3 m. workers, or about 20 per cent of those covered by collective-bargaining agreements.

This guarantee of both union security and individual freedom of action made a major contribution to industrial peace and was largely responsible for the low level of strikes during 1942. However, the War Labor Board soon found itself facing even more troublesome problems than union security. Rising prices induced by wartime inflationary pressures led unions to demand wage increases at least in line with the rise in the cost of living. When strikes were threatened to enforce such claims action was needed. The Board first adopted a union-by-union approach. But when the government, gravely concerned about a wage–price spiral, adopted an overall stabilization programme, a more consistent and comprehensive policy was clearly required. Some sort of formula was needed to hold wages in line, yet allow increases clearly justified by the rise in the cost of living which had already occurred.

The War Labor Board worked out and applied such a formula, which became a most influential wartime precedent. In July 1942 workers at the Little Steel companies demanded a wage increase of a dollar a day. Lengthy hearings decided that a rise was justified, but limited to an equivalent of the increased living costs between January 1941 – a time of relative price stability – and May 1942, when the government stabilization programme began. Bureau of Labor Statistics reports showed the cost-of-living index had risen some 15 points during this period, and recommended wage increases be kept to this percentage over existing levels. Accordingly, on 16 July 1942 the War Labor Board awarded Little Steel workers 44 cents rather than the dollar a day they had originally demanded.

The Little Steel formula, as it was known, became the basic yardstick by which all wartime wage disputes were settled. It had been adopted, however, on the assumption that the new stabilization programme had ended what Board chairman William H. Davis called 'the tragic race between wages and prices', and that a 15 per cent pay rise would be fair. This assumption soon proved false. Prices could not be held completely in line. The War Labor Board found itself trying to reconcile the Little Steel formula with price increases which progressively exceeded the figures on which it was based. By the end of 1942 Hillman had left government service to return to the Clothing Workers and no labour leader of equal weight replaced him. What made it harder to secure labour's complete co-operation over the Little Steel formula and No Strike pledge was wartime profiteering. The President had anticipated this problem. As he told business leaders at a secret meeting at the end of 1941:

> If we get like what happened in the [first] world war . . . you almost inevitably get labor trouble. I can hold labor to the present level if I can say to them, 'You [industry] won't profiteer. The cost of living hasn't gone up'. I think we can avoid that most dangerous spiral.[32]

Yet profiteering did occur. Lauchlan Currie, an influential Keynesian official at the Treasury, warned that the impact of war on profits had been spectacular, driving them to an all-time high in 1941 and likely to drive them even higher in 1942.[33] Roosevelt was particularly incensed by the fact that some American firms appeared to be making profits from European subsidiaries now under German control, which were effectively part of the Nazi war effort. His anger and astonishment were increased when the American directors of such firms tried to persuade the government to spare them from Allied bombing. At home the cost of living had increased a further 7 per cent since December 1941, with the greatest increase – around 10 per cent – occurring in food prices, so hitting the poorest hardest. Rising costs were initially controlled by the Office of Price Administration and by mid-1942 FDR's adviser Leon Henderson was able to report: 'For the first time since November 1940 the cost of living hasn't budged since last month. In fact . . . it actually declined by one-tenth of 1 per cent.' Roosevelt commented, 'this is good news indeed', and in April 1943 issued his Hold-the-Line order on prices and wages.[34] But by then inflation had started again in earnest, and by June 1944 the CIO was arguing that the cost of living had actually risen 43 per cent during the war.[35]

Not only did higher prices for food bear most heavily on those least able to pay, but workers directed to war industries frequently faced extra expenditure on keeping two homes, while working mothers had to pay for child care, laundry, meals out and so on. What compounded these problems was the way the October 1942 Economic Stabilization Act was working out. It gave Congressional sanction to the government's programme and expanded the War Labor Board's authority beyond the original disputed Little Steel cases and others. Now the Board was obliged to restrict all pay rises to 15 per cent in straight hourly rates unless flagrantly sub-standard conditions existed. For the rest of the war the War Labor Board had two distinct functions: settlement of pay disputes and supervision of voluntary agreements. In both cases the Little Steel formula was now set in concrete as the official ceiling on all wage rises.

Organized labour felt cheated. They had given the No Strike pledge in 1942 on the understanding that they would have more say in determining pay and conditions. Now the Little Steel formula was being interpreted so narrowly it made nonsense of such promises. Employers sought to evade the formula by offering more, and more generous, fringe benefits – a development full of future significance. In the short term these circumstances encouraged the rising strike wave of 1943. As noted above, many of these strikes were short and did not seriously impede war production. Though both AFL and CIO criticized the government's wage policy, they did everything they could to keep things under control. But a quite different situation developed in the coal industry, where the UMW had left the CIO in October 1942 and was under nobody's control but that of John L. Lewis. Lewis believed the War Labor Board had breached its contract with labour in establishing the Little Steel formula and had no intention of submitting the UMW to its authority.[36]

THE MINERS

Coal miners had suffered more than other groups of workers because greater war production had led to a much higher level of accidents and deaths. With miners growing more restive and rebellious in consequence, Lewis was fearful that he might lose

control of them. Instead, he led them in a series of strikes which
blatantly defied the Federal government and provided the most
dramatic chapter in labour's war at home. Trouble began in April
1943 when the annual contract between the coal operators and the
UMW expired. The union demanded not just a rise of two dollars
a day, but the new concept of portal-to-portal pay, covering the
time it took miners to get from their pithead to the coalface, which
could often be as long as an hour.[37] Lewis, as usual, was ready
to compromise part of this original demand. Yet the War Labor
Board, to which the dispute was referred, treated the UMW case
with disdain. Lewis walked out of the hearings, attacked the Board
as 'prejudiced and malignant' and announced that while he would
not, of course, call a strike in wartime 'the miners were unwilling
to trespass upon the property of the coal operators in the absence
of a contract'.[38]

This somewhat jesuitical distinction was all the encouragement his
members needed. As they began to quit even before the old contract
expired, the nation found itself facing the gravest industrial crisis
of the war. Fearful of the disastrous effects a coal stoppage would
have on production, President Roosevelt gave orders that the coal
mines be seized and on 2 May 1943 in a radio broadcast asked
the miners to go back to work. They did so, not because of the
appeal of the President of the United States but on the orders of
the president of their union. Minutes before the broadcast, Lewis
had announced a fifteen-day truce (later extended to thirty days)
to seek a settlement with Secretary of the Interior Harold L. Ickes,
who was now directing the mines. But Lewis made no promises
about what might happen when the truce expired, or concessions
on his original demands.

Six months of hectic events followed, punctuated by renewed
work stoppages and temporary truces.[39] Throughout this period
Lewis remained in control and intransigent. He insisted the war was
no excuse for the operators to exploit the miners, whose struggle
for higher wages was a matter of simple justice. Union president
and members were in complete agreement. When Lewis ordered
the miners back to work, they went. When he ordered them out,
they quit. Whipped up by an apoplectic press, public opinion
became increasingly angry and alarmed. Though critical of an
apparently powerless Roosevelt the newspapers reserved their
greatest vituperation for Lewis himself, calling him arrogant,
unpatriotic and heedless of national security in time of war.
The embattled warrier treated all this with contempt, pointing

out that miners had sent more than their share of men to war. He also used government figures to try to show that more miners had died in accidents than servicemen in action up to mid-1943 but the UMW had been compensated by being asked to bear the brunt of the wage freeze.

Finally, Ickes and Lewis hammered out a compromise which met most of the union leader's original demands. In return for increased hours, and the inclusion for the first time of the principle of portal-to-portal pay, the miners settled for an increase of 1.50 dollars a day on prevailing rates. By means of such expedients, the coal settlement conformed at least nominally to the Little Steel formula and the War Labor Board reluctantly approved it. Lewis had forced the government's hand. Fearful that other union leaders might be tempted to follow his example, angered by his outrageous tactics and alarmed by the threat of inflation which might be posed by the coal settlement and other work stoppages in the spring of 1943, corporate and Congressional conservatives exploited public alarm to seek new legislation which would curb union power. Such pressure had been building up ever since 1941. The Smith anti-labour bill had been delayed by the Senate, and after Pearl Harbor pro-labour members of the administration argued that union solidarity in wartime would best be harnessed by giving the labour movement a more responsible role. Yet the Senate Labor Committee's proposed industrial councils had come to nothing, and though labour co-operation in wartime was vital, the Little Steel formula seemed to have been breached, and the No Strike pledge to have failed, by 1943. The coal strikes encouraged Representative Howard Smith to revive his 1941 proposals in partnership with Senator Tom Connally of Texas, which led to the passage of the notorious Smith-Connally Act in June 1943.

Initially, this Act merely gave clear statutory power to the War Labor Board but then added a whole series of provisions which were clearly anti-labour. It empowered the President, whenever government mediation in a labour dispute failed, to seize any plant or industry where a halt in production threatened the war effort. As if this were not enough, it further enforced criminal penalties against anyone who instigated or promoted such a strike. However, it did not place a ban on strikes where the government had not felt compelled to intervene. In contrast to the existing No Strike policy, the Smith–Connally bill in such cases proposed a thirty-day cooling off period, during which the NLRB would hold a strike ballot among the workers concerned. For a government solemnly to conduct a strike vote while seeking at the same time to enforce a No Strike policy was crazily inconsistent. The most important of other provisions was the absolute ban on union contributions being used to help fund political campaigns – a Republican blow at the Democrats.

Hostility created by the coal strikes hastened passage of this Bill by decisive majorities in both houses of Congress. Labour was incensed. The Act ignored widespread observance of the No Strike pledge, by applying criminal law, yet at the same time undermined this by allowing strike ballots. Murray called it 'the most vicious and continuous attack on labour's rights in the history of the nation'[40] and the President promptly vetoed it; but Congress overrode the veto to make the War Labor Disputes Act law on 25 June 1943. The *New York Times* described it as 'a hasty, ill-considered and confused measure'.[41] Though never fully invoked, the Act and its criminal provisions remained on the statute book for the rest of the war.

Strikes declined in 1944 but then increased to record levels in 1945 and 1946, despite the new law. Moreover, the most disturbing crisis occurred in an area which fell outside the Smith–Connally Act when a threatened railway stoppage in autumn 1943 imperilled the war effort as seriously as the coal strikes had done and was settled on the railwaymen's terms. In fact the Smith-Connally Act was counter-productive as far as strikes were concerned. Though union leaders had bitterly denounced the Act, they soon learned to take advantage of it. Workers often voted for strikes they had no intention of starting simply to pressure employers during bargaining. In the first three months of the new law, the NLRB held 53 strike votes, of which 47 resulted in a majority for striking; but of these only 15 led to strikes. Yet in the same period at least 500 other strikes occurred. Only 34 of the 1,919 strikes that took place during the last half of 1943 followed strikes ballots. Even in 1945, when unions were more experienced at using ballots tactically, fewer than 5 per cent of stoppages had been authorized by votes. Yet at the same time, the NLRB's small staff had to neglect more important work to conduct them.[42]

RACE RELATIONS AND SHOP-FLOOR CONFLICT

Labour unrest during hostilities was of course closely related to problems of union security, pay, conditions, complicated bonus systems, prices and inflation. Yet other underlying problems were equally important and part of the immense social upheaval which the war had brought about. Since Hitler based his appeal on doctrines of racial superiority, and Americans had long viewed the Japanese with suspicion, it became important throughout the war that the United States appear to treat black, Jewish and other ethnic groups fairly. Much government effort was expended throughout the war on fair employment practices. Though the Commission dealing with this had only been set up in 1941 under the threat of the black march on Washington, attention to racial discrimination heralded a decisive shift in race relations which was to last far into the post-war period. Black workers were becoming more mobile again as the war economy created new jobs. In Los Angeles, a major aircraft manufacturing city, public hearings where black, Jewish, Japanese, Mexican and Latin-American groups were all represented discussed ways of avoiding racial prejudice.[43] Meanwhile FDR's so-called 'black cabinet', comprising Ralph Bunche, Robert Weaver and others, grew more influential.

The problem racial prejudice posed for unions was revealed starkly during the United Auto Workers' wartime organizing drive at Ford in Detroit, the last major motor manufacturer to be unionized. By 1942, in a city vital both to the aircraft industry and the whole war effort, the UAW had replaced Ford in the eyes of blacks as the provider of better opportunities. Yet the union was not always a reliable friend to black workers. Seniority rules, necessary in union eyes to preserve job security, often gave white workers better claim to the semi-skilled and unskilled jobs they already had. Moreover, the UAW leadership was far ahead of its own rank and file in racial attitudes. The Ku Klux Klan infiltrated many UAW Locals, especially at the Packard plant, where nearly half the delegation to the UAW's 1941 convention were Klansmen.

The union's leadership was in a bind. In battling to end discrimination and advance black interests, the UAW constantly risked arousing fears and prejudices in recently won white members and union officers. But if it soft-pedalled on this, it encouraged black contempt and hostility. Though in the long run the UAW played a notable part in accelerating integration and civil rights in the post-war years, in the short run such episodes as the Sojourner Truth Housing Project disorders in 1942 and the full-scale race riot in Detroit in 1943 showed that an important function of unions – even left-wing unions like the UAW – was to reinforce structural weakness within the black community.[44] Just as more than forty years earlier the eminent black scholar and political activist W. E.

B. Du Bois had argued that political machines made it impossible for blacks to develop fully independent and effective institutions of their own, so now white-led unions tended to act in the same way, excluding blacks or placing very low ceilings on their possible advancement. Nevertheless, the number of black union members rose from 150,000 in 1935 to 1.25 m. by the end of the war, more than three times the rate of overall union growth.

The dilemma of race was part of a far wider pattern of demographic change within which the whole course of wartime labour relations must be viewed. Older workers, radicalized and unionized by the great CIO upsurge of the 1930s, were by the 1940s being drafted into the military or promoted to foreman and other supervisory grades to replace those that had. Their places on the shop floor were being filled not only by blacks but by others – women, teenagers, rural Okies and Arkies and mountain people from Appalachia – mostly from low-wage, non-union or agricultural jobs. For them wartime wages were far higher than anything they had ever earned, sometimes by as much as 150 per cent, making unions seem irrelevant. Yet for those still in low-wage industries – textiles, retail and aircraft, for example – labour's initial acceptance of the Little Steel formula kept their pay rises below those in higher-wage work, which seemed no reason to support a union.

So veteran industrial unionists saw wartime newcomers – Okies, blacks, women – as disruptive elements now reaping rewards for which others had sacrificed. Moreover, while widespread promotion to supervisory grades may have improved pay and conditions for millions of workers, it brought new problems too. Inexperienced foremen had to grapple with conflicts and resentments stemming from the demographic upheaval just discussed, while dealing with the chaos of piece-rates and bonuses created by government contracts in the war economy. War production undermined factory discipline and quality standards while stimulating shop-floor militancy, especially when the Little Steel formula became constricting. Thus the old foreman system collapsed forever and the new one proved unable to cope.[45] The problem was exacerbated for management by the union movement which swept through the foremen's ranks after 1941. Both the calibre and status of foremen had fallen sharply as a result of the war. As one big employer put it: 'We recognize that in some of our shops the union committee man exercises greater authority than the foreman.'[46] Labour unions had been sucked in to fill the vacuum. Management accepted that disciplining the workforce had become, in part at least, a union task. This was a development of major long-term significance for American labour. Increasingly in future its role would be not to lead but to contain shop-floor militancy. Despite the rising strike rate through much of the war, unions did manage to put a lid on rank-and-file activism stimulated by all these pressures.

Such control was made easier by the rising real incomes most workers enjoyed. The nation's wage bill more than doubled between 1940 and 1944, while average earnings in manufacturing industry rose by 65 per cent. Allowing for inflation, real income went up at least 26 per cent in steel, 36 per cent in coal, 20 per cent in cars and 27 per cent in all manufacturing. True, much of this rising real income came from overtime, which was really a disguised cut in the workers' standard of living. The work week expanded from 40.6 hours in 1941 to 45.2 hours in 1944. Yet most workers prized their new prosperity and feared it would end with the war. In fact, the wartime union drives not only made labour stronger but also helped raise aggregate demand, so stimulating the conversion to the kind of Keynesian economic management which was to be sustained into the postwar period.

ROOSEVELT'S FOURTH TERM

While economic policy was being transformed, the 1944 Democratic Party nominating convention highlighted the growing political importance of the CIO in the wake of the Smith–Connally Act. Hillman's CIO Political Action Committee backed the the pro-labour incumbent Henry Wallace in the vice-presidential spot, while the AFL backed the more conservative Missouri Senator, Harry S. Truman. Before Truman's selection FDR was said to have warned advisers to 'clear everything with Sidney'. In fact, Roosevelt and his aides cleverly managed the convention and got everything they wanted. So on election day, when the President won a fourth term, London's *The Times* commented: 'Crude attempts to invoke the "communist" bogey – whether in the form of alleged subservience to Marshal Stalin abroad or to Mr Hillman's Political Action Committee at home – seem to have conspicuously missed fire.'[47] Later Roosevelt thanked Hillman and the PAC, adding: 'I was glad to learn that the CIO . . . authorized the continuation of the PAC. I can think of nothing more important in the years to come than the continuing political education . . . of the people.'[48] The President had cause to be thankful, for CIO support provided the winning margin in his narrowest election victory. In fact, with Roosevelt's death and the rapid onset of the Cold War after 1945, what *The Times* had called 'crude attempts to invoke the "communist" bogey' reappeared and destroyed organizations like the PAC.

With victory over Germany in sight, FDR campaigned for re-election in 1944 on a platform which included a strong bid for labour support in the post-war years. His Economic Bill of Rights, proposed in a Chicago campaign speech, was a piece of propaganda couched in Keynesian terms which envisaged huge government investment in industry. Yet such planning was not socialist – indeed, as the President was at pains to point out, its whole purpose was to head-off any possible socialist challenge. 'All the measures proposed in this program', he said at Soldier Field on 28 October 1944, 'are . . . designed to make American capitalism and private enterprise work in the same great manner in peace as in war.' War in fact had revealed how to make capitalism successful in the second half of the century.

> Greater output is not the only benefit from this plant expansion. In fact, it also includes the wages paid to the labor employed in building these plants, in constructing the machinery to be used in these plants and in operating the plants after they are erected. These payments as wages all contribute to the nation's buying power so that as a nation we will have the money to buy the goods produced by these expanded plants. . . . Why, just the job of *building* these plants and the machinery for them would give America five million more jobs a year than we had in this work before the war. And this does not include the workers who would be needed to operate these plants after they are built.[49]

When Roosevelt spoke these prophetic words no one could confidently anticipate the future. For though the Economic Bill of Rights was by no means fulfilled, the speech did anticipate the trend of post-war economic thinking which developed on Keynesian lines. Labour leaders and employers feared that when the war ended chronic mass unemployment, which had characterized the pre-war period, would rapidly return. Acceptance of the idea that the Federal government should regulate and control the economy ensured the opposite outcome. So the war-time partnership which had grown up, however, haphazardly and uneasily, between labour, management and government had important consequences for peace. Fringe benefits, which boosted workers take-home pay without violating strict limitations on hourly rates, were to become increasingly popular post-war. They provided holidays with pay, allowances for travel time and lunch breaks, shift differentials, incentive and bonus payments, premium rates and the like. Insurance, hospital benefits and other welfare provisions also became the topic for collective bargaining. Partly as a result, total union membership rose between 1940 and 1945 from just under 9 to almost 15 m, or from 27 per cent to 36 per cent of the non-agricultural workforce. The CIO had doubled its membership. Labour may have been co-opted into capitalism and given the job of disciplining the workforce. But by bidding up wages, and thus aggregate demand, it had helped solve the riddle of unemployment. Finally, it had become a crucial part of the Democratic Party coalition and built the mass base which would make it a force to be reckoned with in the economic, political and social history of the postwar world. In the 1920s, many believed unions were *en route* to extinction. By 1945, in contrast, the Harvard economist Sumner Slichter wrote that 'the United States is gradually shifting from a capitalistic community to a laboristic one . . . in which employees rather than businessmen are the largest single influence'.[50] Labour had travelled far in fifteen years.

NOTES AND REFERENCES

The author wishes to thank the American Council of Learned Societies for award of a fellowship in 1981–82 when much of the research for this chapter was completed.

1. D. Brody, 'Labor and the Great Depression: the interpretive prospects', *Labor History*, 13, 1972, pp. 231–44, and 'Radical labor history and rank-and-file militancy', *Labor History*, 16, 1975, pp. 117–26 surveys the field and the literature, especially the work of such new-left historians as A. and S. Lynd, S. Aronowitz, L. L. Cary, J. Green, J. Weinstein and others. M. Dubofsky, 'Not so "turbulent years": another look at the American 1930s', *Amerikastudien*, 24, 5–20. For the battle with corporate capitalism, and the union contract or the supreme prize, see S. Fine, *Sit-Down: the General Motors Strike of 1936–37* (Ann Arbor, 1969) 307, 75.

2. George Schuyler, quoted in G. Osofhy, *Harlem: the Making of a Ghetto, New York 1890–1920* (New York, 1966) p. 149.

3. P. K. Edwards, *Strikes in the United States, 1881–1974* (Oxford, 1981), Appendix A, table A.6, p. 260.

4. For a succinct summary of their evidence, see A. M. Schlesinger Jr., *The Crisis of the Old Order* (Boston, 1956), pp. 457–8.

5. Perkins to FDR, President's Secretary File (hereafter PSF) 77, Labor Department, March 1933 (italics in original).

6. Letter in President's Official File (hereafter OF) 407 (1), 19 April 1934. Signatories included Paul F. Brissenden, labour economist and historian of the IWW, Bruce Bliven, John Dewey and Reinhold Niebuhr. A Brookings Institution survey had concluded that the nation's 631,000 richest families had a total income far higher than the total income of the sixteen million poorest families.
7. Quoted in A. M. Schlesinger, Jr., *The Crisis of the Old Order* (Boston, 1956) pp. 185–6. M. Dubofsky & W. Van Tine, *John L. Lewis: A Biography* (New York, 1977) is the definitive study. M. Josephson, *Sidney Hillman: Labor Statesman* (New York, 1948) is a more pedestrian life.
8. A. M. Schlesinger Jr., *The Coming of the New Deal* (Boston, 1958), p. 141.
9. Ibid p. 90.
10. Schlesinger, *Crisis* p. 186.
11. United Textile Workers Press Release, OF 407 (1), 5 June 1935.
12. Quoted in I. Bernstein, *Turbulent Years* (Boston, 1969) pp. 322–3.
13. Quoted in Schlesinger, *Coming* pp. 387–8.
14. Bernstein op. cit. pp. 330–5.
15. J. A. Gross, *The Reshaping of the National Labor Relations Board: National Labor Policy in Transition*, (Albany, 1981) is the latest examination of the NLRB's work.
16. Lee Pressman, 'Reminiscences', *Columbia Oral History Project* (hereafter *COHP*), 1977, p. 55.
17. Bernstein, pp. 432–98 gives an excellent brief account of the SWOC drive in steel. For the historical background, see David Brody, *Steelworkers in America: the Non-Union Era* (New York, 1969).
18. Text in OF 407 (1), 6 September 1936.
19. Perkins, 'Reminiscences' *COHP* p. 253 and Pressman, 'Reminiscences' *COHP* p. 88.
20. Bernstein, pp. 482–3. Republic steel alone spent $50,000 a year in this way.
21. 'Labor's Long-Range Job' condensed from a CIO handbook *Production Problems*, 1, Hillman Correspondence, 1930–46, A-G. at New York Industrial and Labor Relations School Library, Cornell University.
22. Ibid., 2.
23. *New Republic*, 103, 29 July 1940.
24. Robert Lekachman, *The Age of Keynes* (London, 1966) pp. 127–9.
25. Currie to FDR, PSF Box 115, 1 February 1940.
26. OF 4245-E (Labor Division), 28 May 1940.
27. OF 407. Box No. 3, Dept. of Labor, 17 March 1941.
28. *New York Times*, 28 May 1940.
29. Text in OF 4245-E (Labor Division).
30. Leland Olds to FDR, OF 407 (2), 13 November 1941. See also Senate Document No. 114, 65th Congress, 1st Session, vol. II.
31. FDR to Hillman, OF 407 (3), 10 October 1941.
32. Labor Department, PSF, No. 152, Harry Hopkins.
33. Currie to FDR, OF No. 237 and PSF No. 147.
34. Henderson to FDR, OF No. 237, 19 and 23 June 1942 and 8 April 1943.
35. Henderson to FDR, OF No. 237, 24 June 1944.
36. Dubofsky and Van Tine, *John L. Lewis* p. 419.
37. Ibid., p. 423.

38. F. R. Dulles and Melvyn Dubofsky, *Labor in America* (Arlington Heights, 1984) p. 326.
39. For a masterly account of this dispute see Dubofsky and Van Tine, op. cit., pp. 415–40.
40. *New York Times*, 18 June 1943.
41. *New York Times*, 26 June 1943.
42. Joel Seidman, *American Labor from Defense to Reconversion* (Chicago, 1953) p. 190.
43. Mark Ethridge, chairman of the Commission on Fair Employment Practices, to FDR, OF 4245-G, 27 October 1941 and 16 March 1942. The CFEP was established by Executive Order 8802 on 25 June 1941.
44. August Meier and Elliott Rudwick, *Black Detroit and the Rise of the UAW* (New York, 1979) *passim.* esp, pp. 37, 49–51, 61, 104, 108 and 109–10.
45. Nelson Lichtenstein, *Labour's War at Home: the CIO in World War II* (Cambridge, 1982) *passim* esp. pp.110–35 contains a revealing analysis of what he calls 'the ecology of shop-floor conflict'.
46. Quoted in David Brody, *Workers in Industrial America* (Oxford, 1981) p. 181.
47. *The Times*, 8 November 1944 and President's Personal File (PPF) 8172.
48. FDR to Hillman, 25 November 1944, PSF File No. 152, Sidney Hillman.
49. PPF 1017, 28 October 1944 (Italics in original).
50. Cited in Dulles and Dubofsky op. cit. p. 341.

Notes on Contributors

Martin Blinkhorn is Senior Lecturer and Head of the Department of History at the University of Lancaster. He is the author of *Carlism and Crisis in Spain 1931–1939*, and editor of *Spain in Conflict 1931–1939* and a forthcoming volume on *Fascists and Conservatives*. He is currently writing a study of *The Origins of the Spanish Civil War*.

Paul Corner is Professor of Contemporary Italian History at the University of Siena. He is the author of *Fascism in Ferrara 1915–1925*, and numerous articles in British and Italian journals. He is currently working on a history of Italian fascism.

John Coutouvidis is Principal Lecturer in International History at Staffordshire Polytechnic. He is co-author with Jaime Reynolds of *Poland 1939–47*. He has recently co-edited (with Tom Lane) a new edition of *The Dark Side of the Moon*, and is currently working on a biography of *Sir Frank Roberts: A Diplomatic History 1930–68*.

Andrzej Garlicki is Professor of the Modern History of Poland at Warsaw University and Dean of its History Department. His field is the political and social history of the nineteenth and twentieth centuries. Amongst Dr. Garlicki's numerous books is a biography of Joseph Piłsudski. He has been a visiting professor in the USA and Japan.

David Kirby is Reader in History at the School of Slavonic Studies, University of London. He has a special interest in the northern European countries and has published a history of *Finland in the Twentieth Century*. He has also published numerous

273

The working class and politics

articles on aspects of labour history and a study of international socialism during the First World War. At present, he is working on a two-volume history of the Baltic world.

Tim Kirk is Lecturer in History at the University of Warwick. He has recently completed a doctoral thesis on the Austrian working class under national socialist rule, which he is currently preparing for publication. He has also worked on a series of guides to source materials in European political history.

Hiroaki Kuromiya is a Research Fellow at King's College, Cambridge. Dr. Kuromiya is the author of *Stalin's Industrial Revolution: Politics and Workers, 1928–1932,* and a number of articles on the social and political aspects of Stalinism.

Roger Magraw is Lecturer in Modern History at the University of Warwick. He is the author of *France 1815–1914: The Bourgeois Century,* and of articles on popular anti-clericalism and peasant radicalism in nineteenth century France. He is currently writing a book on the social history of the French working class c.1830–c.1940.

Patrick Renshaw is Senior Lecturer in American History at the University of Sheffield. His publications include *The Wobblies: the Story of Syndicalism in the United States,* which was translated into Italian and Japanese, and *The General Strike.* A frequent visitor to the United States, he was awarded a research fellowship by the American Council of Learned Societies in 1981–82. He is currently completing a study of *The American Worker in the Century of the Common Man.*

Jaime Reynolds received a Ph.D. for research in London and Warsaw on the establishment of communist rule in Poland. He is co-author with John Coutouvidis of *Poland 1939–47,* and has published a number of articles on Polish affairs. He is a Principal in the Department of the Environment, London.

Stephen Salter is Lecturer in Modern History at the University of Sheffield. He has published a number of articles on industrial workers in Germany during the Weimar and Nazi periods based on his 1984 doctoral thesis. His current research interests include the political thought of Max Weber.

274

John Stevenson is Reader in the Department of History at the University of Sheffield. Longman has published his study, *Popular Disturbances in England, 1700–1870,* in the *Themes in British Social History* series of which he is General Editor, and also a number of historical reference works which he has written in collaboration with Chris Cook.

Index

276